About this Book

The Zapatista movement and its spokesman Subcomandante Marcos have attracted enormous political and scholarly attention ever since their uprising began in Chiapas, Mexico, in 1994. The movement not only struck a chord inside the country at the very moment when Mexico was linking itself to the USA in the North American Free Trade Agreement (NAFTA) and switching direction to follow the dictates of neoliberal economics, but, as this book shows, rapidly evoked an extraordinary surge of political interest and solidarity in the Americas and worldwide. Thomas Olesen's book is the first to examine the emergence of this global Zapatista solidarity network.

He does this in the context of globalization and, more particularly, the role of the Internet in radically and very speedily connecting physically, socially and culturally distant events and actors in today's world. He explores crucial questions: What is the infrastructure of the global Zapatista solidarity network? What are the activities in which it has engaged? What conditions facilitated its formation? And, most important of all, what are the longer-term implications for new kinds of political action and international solidarity in a globalized world where the dysfunctions of neoliberalism are likely to throw up new movements of resistance in diverse social sectors and many different countries?

This compelling work not only tells the story for the first time of the new kinds of solidarity networks and movements which are likely to play an increasing political role in future years. Its author also skilfully deploys various approaches in social theory to throw light on the new global patterns of interaction characterizing today's civil society actors.

About the author

Dr Thomas Olesen is Assistant Professor in the Department of Political Science at the University of Aarhus in Denmark. In 2000 he was Visiting Scholar in the Department of Government at the New Mexico State University. He has published a number of scholarly articles and chapters in edited volumes on globalization and social movements.

International Zapatismo

The Construction of Solidarity
in the Age of Globalization

Thomas Olesen

ZED BOOKS
London & New York

International Zapatismo was first published in 2005 by
Zed Books Ltd, 7 Cynthia Street, London N1 9JF, UK,
and Room 400, 175 Fifth Avenue, New York, NY 10010, USA

www.zedbooks.co.uk

Designed and typeset in Monotype Bembo by Illuminati, Grosmont
Cover designed by Andrew Corbett
Printed and bound in the EU by Biddles Ltd, www.biddles.co.uk

Distributed in the USA exclusively by Palgrave, a division of
St Martin's Press, LLC, 175 Fifth Avenue, New York, NY 10010

A catalogue record for this book is available from the British Library
Library of Congress Cataloging-in-Publication Data available

ISBN 1 84277 386 0 (Hb)
ISBN 1 84277 387 9 (Pb)

Contents

Acknowledgements

Over the last four years, a great number of people have come into contact with this book in one way or another and deserve mention for their various contributions. At the Department of Political Science I wish to thank Associate Professor Jørgen Dige Pedersen and Professor Georg Sørensen for their critical and useful comments. I am also indebted to Lone Winther for her assistance in weeding out linguistic errors and weaknesses and preparing the manuscript. In general, I wish to thank the staff at the Department of Political Science for always being helpful, especially Inge Rasmussen, Birgit Kanstrup, and Karen Prehn.

In 2000 I stayed four months at the New Mexico State University as a visiting scholar. This stay was the result of a unique effort by Neil Harvey and proved to be greatly rewarding on both a professional and a personal level. I sincerely wish to thank Neil Harvey and his family, Wendy, Alhelí, and Jázmin, for providing me with a 'home away from home'. I am also deeply thankful to all the solidarity activists who have taken the time to do the interviews from which I believe the book has greatly benefited.

Finally, my warmest thanks to Lene for bearing with physical and mental absence during the period of writing, and sharing the ups and downs, and to Alma Cecilia who came along in the middle of it all.

To Alma Cecilia

I

Introduction: The Transnational Zapatista Solidarity Network

The uprising of the Zapatista Army of National Liberation (Ejército Zapatista de Liberación Nacional, or EZLN[1]) on 1 January 1994, in the Mexican state of Chiapas, immediately posed a challenge to students of Mexican politics. The appearance of an armed movement, composed in its majority of indigenous peasants, and representing demands ranging from land and housing to democracy and justice, was a surprise to the Mexican political establishment and scholars alike. The EZLN, at first, seemed almost anachronistic in the post–Cold War setting of the 1990s and following on from the recently proclaimed end of history. It soon became clear, however, that the EZLN was not simply a continuation of Latin America's historical experiences with armed movements. Or, perhaps more accurately, the EZLN quickly realized that the prospects for an armed uprising at this historical juncture were not very promising. After twelve days of armed confrontations between the EZLN and the Mexican army in January 1994, the EZLN thus embarked on a new course in which the role of weapons has become increasingly symbolic, shifting the terrain of its struggle from the battlefield to the level of words and ideas. In doing so, the EZLN became a key actor in the process of democratic social change that Mexico has been going through since the late 1980s.

Yet the impact of the EZLN has not stopped here. One of the most salient aspects of the EZLN, and what in many ways makes this movement sui generis, is its resonance beyond the borders of

Mexico. Since January 1994, an extraordinarily large number of civil society actors from, mainly, Europe and the USA have directed solidarity efforts to events in Chiapas and Mexico, notwithstanding the obvious distance in physical, social and cultural terms. This international Zapatismo has been characterized by flux and reflux over the past eight years, but it has never disappeared. Instead, it has shown a capacity for reinvention and remains vibrant to this day.[2] Despite their geographical dispersal, the actors engaged in solidarity activities around the EZLN and Chiapas are not unrelated units. On the other hand, they do not constitute a unitary or homogeneous actor, but are rather tied together in an informal network with the EZLN as a symbolic centre. This transnational Zapatista solidarity network is the main object of study in this book.[3]

The interest and attraction generated by the EZLN beyond its national borders is matched by no other movement in the post-Cold War period.[4] This fact becomes even more conspicuous when considering that it is a relatively small movement with few resources, made up as it is of impoverished indigenous peasants in an area unknown to most people outside of Mexico prior to the uprising. Or, to put it differently, when the EZLN staged its uprising nobody could have foreseen its subsequent repercussions outside Chiapas and Mexico, and that the uprising would soon pose a challenge not only to students of Mexican politics but also to students of globalization. These apparent paradoxes raise a number of important questions concerning the growing interconnectedness of physically, socially and culturally distant events and actors in today's world. This book, accordingly, has two primary ambitions. On the one hand, it presents an analysis of the specific case of transnational solidarity around the EZLN and Chiapas. On the other hand, and on a more general and theoretical level, it aims to further a research agenda on the increasingly transnational patterns of interaction characterizing today's civil society actors.

Mapping the 'Invisible Continent'

Before we proceed, a brief outline of the development of the transnational Zapatista solidarity network since the EZLN uprising in January 1994 is in order. The following serves as a guide and point of reference for the coming discussion. The development of the network may be divided into six main phases:

Phase 1 (January 1994 to February 1995) The incipient transnational Zapatista solidarity network is formed already in January 1994 when transnational activists converge on Mexico to protest against armed confrontations in the wake of the uprising. The network does not have an independent infrastructure at the time, and activities build on existing networks and movements.

Phase 2 (February 1995 to summer 1996) The transnational Zapatista solidarity network starts to develop an infrastructure of its own. The very intense activities in this phase are mainly aimed at monitoring the human rights situation in Chiapas following the Mexican army's invasion of EZLN territory in February 1995.

Phase 3 (summer 1996 to December 1997) The transnational Zapatista solidarity network becomes more politicized and begins to overlap with other transnational networks. The politicization is largely a result of the EZLN's call for the First Intercontinental Encounter for Humanity and against Neoliberalism (Primer Encuentro Intercontinental por la Humanidad y contra el Neoliberalismo) in Chiapas in 1996.

Phase 4 (December 1997 to mid-1998) Following the Acteal massacre in Chiapas in December 1997, the transnational Zapatista solidarity network experiences probably its most intense period of activities. The major concern once again becomes the human rights violations in Chiapas and the militarization of Chiapas.

Phase 5 (mid-1998 to April 2001) This period has been fairly quiet, partly because of the silence maintained by the EZLN leadership during most of the period. EZLN initiatives have mainly targeted Mexican issues. Transnational Zapatista solidarity network activities have protested against the Mexican government's refusal to accept the San Andrés Accords on indigenous rights. This was reflected in the participation of network activists in the March for Indigenous Dignity (Marcha por la Dignidad Indígena) in February/March 2001.

Phase 6 (April 2001 to February 2004) Following the march the EZLN falls silent after disagreements with the government over the issue of indigenous rights. As a consequence transnational activities begin to wane. In November 2002 the EZLN breaks its silence with an initiative regarding the conflict between the Spanish government and the Basque separatist group ETA (Euzkadi Ta Askatasuna) and initiates a period of renewed transnational activity. This intensifies in late 2003 as the tenth anniversary of the EZLN uprising approaches (on 1 January 2004). However, the level of attention and activity appears unable to match that of previous periods. The book mainly addresses the first five phases (see the Conclusion for a discussion of this latest phase).

The transnational aspect of the EZLN uprising sketched above has by no means gone unnoticed. On the contrary, researchers working on social movements and issues of globalization often make reference *en passant* to the EZLN as an example of a local/national movement that has taken on a transnational dimension.[5] Yet, even if we add to this a handful of studies addressing the transnational issue more specifically, this interest has not to date resulted in any independent systematic research. In other words, the transnational Zapatista solidarity network largely remains the invisible continent that Galtung (1980: 326) pointed to already in 1980 when speaking of transnational social action. This is unfortunate for at least two reasons.

First, the lack of systematic attention to the transnational aspect of the EZLN stands in stark contrast to the large amount of well-researched literature on the EZLN as a local/national phenomenon. What we need, then, is a better understanding of the interaction between local, national and transnational social spheres in the case of the EZLN. Focusing on the transnational aspect of EZLN solidarity does not imply a denigration of the importance of the large number of Mexican EZLN and Chiapas solidarity activists. On the contrary, it is impossible to separate this level from the transnational level, as there is a high degree of cooperation between Mexican and non-Mexican solidarity activists.

Second, the transnational Zapatista solidarity network offers a useful opportunity to study the increasingly transnational and networked character of civil society and the left in the post-Cold War period. The network is particularly interesting in this regard, as it has a relatively long history and has been an important predecessor to the transnational justice and solidarity network, which made its first important mark at the so-called Battle in Seattle of November

1999 (Bob 2001).[6] Since 1995/1996, the transnational Zapatista solidarity network has thus acquired a life of its own and a high degree of politicization in the sense that its *raison d'être* is no longer exclusively tied to events in Chiapas and Mexico, but overlaps with other transnational networks.

In order to address these issues and advance the study of the transnational Zapatista solidarity network, the book asks the following questions:

1. What is the infrastructure of the transnational Zapatista solidarity network?
2. What are its activities?
3. What actions and conditions have facilitated its formation?
4. What is the present state and what will be the future of the network?
5. How can study of the network help us understand the future direction of the left?

As mentioned earlier, the questions primarily relate to the first five of the six phases outlined above; that is, to the period between 1994 and 2001. The first question primarily considers why it is useful to think of transnational EZLN solidarity in terms of a network. It is argued, mainly in Chapter 3, that this aspect is particularly evident in the informational infrastructure.

The second question explores the wide range of activities that transnational Zapatista solidarity network actors take part in. The discussion focuses on the fact that activities take place in civil society as well as on an institutional level. This dual involvement, it is argued, expresses itself in a transnational counterpublic, which constitutes the social space of the network. This is considered in Chapter 4.

The third and central question of the book focuses on the actions (primarily of the EZLN) and the conditions that have facilitated the formation of the transnational Zapatista solidarity network. The formation of the network is seen as a process of social construction involving both subjective and objective factors. These issues are examined mainly in chapters 5 to 8.

The fourth question concerns the present condition of the network and advances a range of suggestions regarding its future development. This entails, *inter alia*, discussion of the common ground shared by the Zapatista solidarity and the transnational justice and solidarity networks, visible especially since the 1999 Battle in Seattle.

The fifth question continues the discussions by considering how the transnational Zapatista solidarity network may provide useful insights into the future direction of an increasingly transnational left. The network, that is, is seen as a significant expression of the changes the left has undergone since the end of the Cold War. This wider assessment is the concern of the concluding chapter of the book.

By asking questions that touch on the nature of social phenomena located in civil society, the book positions itself within a sociological tradition. In sociology, however, society has traditionally been equated with the nation-state (Urry 2000), and, until recently, theory and analysis of civil society actors has located them mainly within this context. Developments in recent decades have challenged this notion of the nation-state as the primary 'container' of social action, a factor which a growing number of scholars are recognizing. Nevertheless, social movement theory, though developed primarily to suit a context defined by the nation-state, is still considered useful for the study of transnational phenomena such as the Zapatista solidarity network. Social movement theory thus serves as the theoretical axis of the book, albeit supplemented and developed by insights from globalization literature. The exercise in theoretical integration is in itself a significant objective, finding expression in the concept of transnational framing.

Thus it is important to distinguish between three levels of empirical analysis. At the micro-level is the EZLN, at the meso-level the transnational Zapatista solidarity network. The generic and theoretical equivalents of these empirical concepts are: social movement organization;[7] informal transnational network;[8] and transnational field of synergy. Further, it is argued that study of the transnational Zapatista solidarity network should entail a constant mediation between the micro- and macro-levels. The network can, accordingly, only be properly understood if we view it from the perspective of the EZLN and the justice and solidarity network. The Zapatista solidarity network may in turn shed new light on these phenomena. That is to say, research on transnational civil society must be attentive to the fact that the globalization process makes it increasingly untenable to conduct research on a single level. Instead, research must move on

Figure I.I Analytical levels in the study of the transnational Zapatista solidarity network

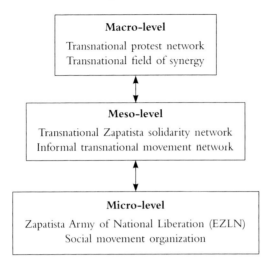

several levels of analysis simultaneously, in order to draw out the relationships between them.

Informal transnational networks may encompass a very wide variety of civil society actors. As Tarrow (2002) insists, however, scholars need to be more precise about how actors are transnational, in regard to their strategies, to their demands and objectives, and to their structure. This, in turn, has implications for the conceptualization of globalization, as the different forms of transnational action involve different relationships between the local, the national and the transnational. There are at least three categories of transnational civil society actors involving the imbrication of local, national and transnational levels: those active within a national territory but dependent on extra-national support due to repressive or otherwise difficult national conditions; those who are nationally located but whose actions are directed mainly to events and situations beyond their national territory; those without a country-specific affiliation but with national branches. We are dealing mainly with the first two categories: the EZLN fits into the first category; the solidarity activists fit into the second. In our case, we are concerned with single organizations or groups, and occasionally individuals. It is when these actors interact across physical, social and cultural distances that informal transnational movement networks take shape.

Searching for Answers

The central concern of the book, then, is to examine the actions and conditions underlying the formation of the transnational Zapatista solidarity network. The remainder of this chapter is devoted to the development of a suitable theoretical framework for this work. I begin by reviewing the existing literature, including EZLN documents and interviews. Despite the dearth of independent and systematic research on the Zapatista network, the existing literature does provide a number of useful entry points. This literature may be divided into three explanatory currents: subjective, systemic and technological.

Broadening the struggle

Acknowledging its indigenous roots, the EZLN referred to itself in its first public statement as the product of five hundred years of struggle (EZLN 1994b). Yet it soon expanded its vision beyond the indigenous people of Mexico. The EZLN was quick to realize that its struggle had struck a chord both within Mexican society and beyond, albeit in an unforeseen way. In an interview with Le Bot (1997: 241), Subcomandante Marcos notes that the EZLN expected their uprising either to be met with indifference or to ignite a general uprising in the Mexican population. Neither scenario materialized. Instead, the EZLN was taken by surprise when national and transnational civil society demanded that they enter into negotiations with the Mexican government. Following twelve days of armed confrontation between the EZLN and the Mexican army in January 1994, negotiations duly began. Subcomandante Marcos has referred to this moment as the emergence of a *zapatismo civil* (Le Bot 1997: 306), thereby recognizing the role of civil society in halting military operations (EZLN 1994e).

The resonance of the uprising within Mexican society and abroad, and the public emphasis on a peaceful solution to the conflict, persuaded the EZLN to rethink its initial strategy of advancing 'towards the capital of the country, defeating the federal Mexican Army, protecting the civil population in its liberating advance, and permitting the liberated people to freely and democratically elect their own administrative authorities' (EZLN 1994b).[9] While the concepts of civil society and democracy occupied a less prominent position in the martial rhetoric of the first public statement, they soon started to play the leading part in the EZLN vocabulary of social change (e.g. EZLN 1994e). As indicated, by late January 1994 the EZLN already seemed to have its new and democratic vision of social change flushed out. Speaking of revolution in Mexico, Subcomandante Marcos (EZLN 1994g: 97) stated that:

> it will be a revolution resulting from struggles on various social fronts. … And the result will be not that of a triumphant party, organization or alliance of organizations … but a kind of democratic space for the resolution of confrontation between different political proposals.

Even though the EZLN is a movement concerned primarily with the rights of the indigenous people of Chiapas and Mexico, it has succeeded in turning this particular struggle into a symbol for other struggles, thereby universalizing its appeal. This is largely the result of the open-ended and inclusive nature of the EZLN's political vision (Harvey 1998b).[10] The EZLN invokes a kind of global consciousness enabling people to recognize their own situations in settings far removed in terms of physical, cultural and social distance.

The EZLN's view of social change rejects a vanguard role. Civil society is to be the driving force of change, and the role of the EZLN restricted to 'opening spaces and summoning actors' (Bellinghausen 1999). On several occasions since 1994, the EZLN has invited civil society actors in Mexico and from the rest of the world to participate in dialogue. The best-known of such events are the encounters 'for humanity and against neoliberalism' staged in Chiapas in 1996. The process of transformation early on prompted Mexican author Carlos Fuentes (1994) to label the EZLN the first post-Communist rebellion in Latin America. Others have described the EZLN as armed reformists (Castañeda 1995) and armed democrats (Touraine

1996). In a 1999 interview with Durán de Huerta, Subcomandante Marcos outlines the anti-vanguardist and democratic self-perception of the EZLN:

> It is not only that we do not set ourselves the task of taking power, but we propose that the very relationship of power with society must itself change. It must invert itself, or turn itself around in some form. This new relationship with power we have synthesized in the phrase, *mandando obediciendo* (to rule by obeying). (1999: 270)

Thus, despite the fact that the EZLN emerged as, and remains, an armed movement, its challenge to power is eminently more political, with the military aspect playing an increasingly symbolic role (Kampwirth 1996). The EZLN represents a way of thinking about social change that is a far cry from the armed uprisings of previous decades, while at the same time retaining the powerful imagery of such insurrections, so seductive to activists and the media alike. This transformation of the EZLN has been successful in attracting more sympathizers to the movement than would have been possible had the EZLN maintained its initial ideas and goals.

Subcomandante Marcos, who authors most EZLN communiqués, has played a central role in making the EZLN accessible to a non-Mexican audience (Bob 2001).[11] This horse-riding warrior poet, who quotes Shakespeare and Cervantes, has become a symbol of resistance in the post-Cold War era. He is to the post-Cold War era what Che Guevara was, for decades, prior to the collapse of the Soviet Union (Berger 2001). Subcomandante Marcos is one of the few non-indigenous people in the EZLN, but his words, according to Higgins (2000: 360), have become 'bridges between the Indian world of the southeast and the ever-more-pervasive world of global politics'. This definition is consistent with Marcos's perception of himself as a window between the indigenous communities and the world around them (Le Bot 1997: 155). With a well-developed sense of public relations (Knudson 1998), he is a mediator who translates the EZLN indigenous struggle into a language comprehensible to a non-Mexican audience (Leyva Solano 1999). This translation involves the invocation of a global consciousness allowing the EZLN and Subcomandante Marcos to project the particularity of the EZLN struggle onto a universal level.[12]

The left after the Cold War

McMichael (2001: 16) has noted that the 'power of the Zapatista movement lies ... in its ability to situate its political intervention world-historically.' The coincidence between the EZLN uprising and the coming into force of the North American Free Trade Agreement (NAFTA) on 1 January 1994 was thus charged with symbolism, and at the same time connected with centuries-old issues of colonization and resistance. By conjuring up the revolutionary icon of Emiliano Zapata and the marginalized *México Profundo* (Bonfil Batalla 1994) of the indigenous population, the EZLN caused the notion of Mexico as a country on its way to the First World to evaporate into thin air.[13] For those celebrating the end of history and the victory of liberal democracy and free markets, the EZLN uprising with its impoverished indigenous army seemed almost surreal, an ill-timed joke. For others, however, the emergence of the EZLN served as a morale boost (Ayres 2003) re-enchanting the world (Löwy 1998) and carrying the promise that history had not ended after all.

The EZLN is often credited with helping to redefine the common enemy (Cleaver 1998c) at a time when the left finds itself in an identity crisis. For people on the left, the EZLN represented the hope that social struggle was still possible, and it helped reactivate dormant networks of resistance and solidarity (Leyva Solano 1999). The EZLN struggle quickly started to reach into a wide variety of related struggles (Cleaver 1998c), which recognized some of the problems facing Mexico. The theme of recognition is echoed by a number of observers on the left (e.g. Holloway and Peláez 1998; Esteva 1999; Chomsky 1999) and is often emphasized in attempts to explain why the EZLN has generated so much attention outside Mexico. That the EZLN struggle is so widely recognizable is clearly a consequence of its dialogical and anti-vanguardist self-perception described in the preceding section. On the other hand, it is also a result of a globalization process reflected in the creation of political and economic conditions shared by people all over the globe and 'a spreading uniformity of policies and international agreements among governments to implement world-wide sets of rules' (Cleaver 1999: 12). The EZLN uprising was therefore tied at an early point to a criticism of NAFTA (Morton 2000) and the neoliberal development model that became prevalent during the 1980s.

While there is no doubt that the EZLN represents a reaction to these neoliberal aspects of the globalization process, the challenge is portrayed by sympathetic observers on the left as being offensive rather than defensive (Paulson 2000: 275):

> Liberal common sense today has the insurgency pegged as the inevitable, reactionary response of an ignorant but justifiably angry indigenous peasantry to the new global economy.... But ... many peasant and campesino movements ... have demonstrated an increasingly effective ability to frame the terms of the debate such that they, too, are in favour of moving into a 'globalized' world – albeit of a different kind. The Zapatista struggle in particular advances the very notions of autonomy, collective action, and dignity that are denied under neoliberalism, and in doing so it demonstrates that its movement 'against the tide' is in fact progressive rather than merely one of putting on the brakes.

The EZLN's call for 'a world in which many worlds fit' (*un mundo donde quepan muchos mundos*) thus 'simultaneously asserts identity and transcends it' (Holloway and Peláez 1998: 4). Only by turning the particular into something universal, and envisioning an alternative form of globalization rather than rejecting it altogether, has the EZLN succeeded in opening the movement to different currents on the left. Transnational support for the EZLN would have been less conspicuous had it opted for a defensive and particularistic answer to the challenge of neoliberalism (Holloway 1998). This is not to suggest that the EZLN has moved away from the themes that sparked the movement. On the contrary, the EZLN's chief concern remains the question of indigenous rights and the critique of neoliberalism in Mexico. This critique is, at the same time, rooted in a rather nationalistic terminology (Johnston and Laxer 2003). What the EZLN calls for, then, is not a global coalition of resistance dissolving national and cultural differences. The EZLN instead emphasizes the value of local and national differences. At the same time, however, it defines a number of global trends that are threatening these values. Such threats, as discussed above, are often condensed in the concept of neoliberalism (EZLN 1996b, 1996e).

Neoliberalism is considered to be anti-democratic due to its marginalizing and excluding effects (EZLN 1996b, 1996f). This also implies a critique of the liberal or electoral democratic model that characterizes most of the world today (EZLN 2000).Yet this critique itself is also formulated in democratic terms. The EZLN does not reject liberal democracy, but proposes its radicalization (Nash 1997; Yúdice 1998). By formulating its critique in democratic terms, the EZLN has demonstrated an awareness of the changed global political situation following the end of the Cold War, which, inter alia, means that social critiques not formulated in a democratic language lack resonance and legitimacy.

The media and the Internet

Following the attempted army crackdown on the EZLN leadership in February 1995, there was a surge of interest in the role of the Internet and information in the EZLN uprising. This interest was closely related to the fact that transnational solidarity activists were becoming increasingly visible in relation to the conflict. This emergent aspect caught the attention not only of academics and activists but also of the media (e.g. Doyle 1995; Robberson 1995; Watson et al. 1995).[14] Some of these accounts (e.g. Robberson 1995) characterized the EZLN as a high-tech movement, with Subcomandante Marcos carrying his own laptop and uploading communiqués directly to the Internet via a cellphone. This type of account seems unfounded. Rather, the EZLN uses intermediaries to distribute its communiqués around the world (Cleaver 1998a: 628). The Mexican newspaper *La Jornada* has been a particularly useful medium in this regard: on-line since 1995, it has made EZLN communiqués readily available to anyone with an Internet connection. Some of the most vital sources of information on the EZLN have been listservs such as Chiapas95 and Chiapas-L, and the Ya Basta! website, established in March 1994.

It is often claimed that activities on and through the Internet helped put pressure on the Mexican government to resolve the conflict peacefully (Ribeiro 1998; Chomsky 1999; Stephen 2000). However, the causal chain between transnational solidarity activities and the Mexican government's decision to halt military operations in January 1994 and February 1995 is not self-evident. That said, there is no doubt that the wide and almost instant availability of EZLN communiqués and on-site participation served to prevent disinformation by the Mexican government (Halleck 1994), which was trying to downplay incidents in Chiapas and portray them as a local problem. This soon turned out to be an impossible strategy, not least because of information diffused on the Internet. In a widely circulated statement from April 1995, Mexican Foreign Minister José Angel Gurria thus referred to the conflict as 'a war of ink, of written word, a war on the Internet' (quoted from Montes 1995).

In a 1993 paper, 'Cyberwar is Coming!', RAND researchers Ronfeldt and Arquilla anticipated the use of the Internet in social conflicts. This paper of course predated the EZLN uprising, but the authors soon started applying their framework to the EZLN. In 1998, this work resulted in an entire book dedicated to what the authors termed *The Zapatista Social Netwar in Mexico* (Ronfeldt and Arquilla 1998). Social netwar, according to Ronfeldt and Arquilla (1998: 21–2):

> is mainly over 'information' – who knows what, when, where, and why. Social netwar aims to affect what an opponent knows, or thinks it knows, not only about a challenger but also about itself and the world around it. More broadly, social netwar aims to shape beliefs and attitudes in the surrounding social milieu. A social netwar is likely to involve battles for public opinion and for media access and coverage, at local through global levels.

This definition echoes Foreign Minister Gurria's reference to the Chiapas conflict as a war of words and the Internet. When Ronfeldt and Arquilla speak of social netwar, they make it clear that this cannot be reduced to a function of the Internet (Ronfeldt and Arquilla 1998: 11). The social netwar concept rather tries to convey an image of social actors as increasingly organized in networks rather than in hierarchical forms (like more traditional guerrilla movements). Yet the lingering impression from Ronfeldt and Arquilla's work is that the Internet greatly facilitates network forms of organization, and that the transnationalization of events in Chiapas and Mexico cannot be properly understood if the role of the Internet is not taken into account. This view is shared by Castells (1997: 80) when he notes that:

> Extensive use of the Internet allowed the Zapatistas to diffuse information and their call throughout the world instantly, and to create a

network of support groups which helped to produce an international public opinion movement that made it literally impossible for the Mexican government to use repression on a large scale.

This interpretation has inspired Castells (1997) to label the EZLN the first informational guerrilla movement. There is, however, one problem with Castells's statement when he says that the Internet allowed the EZLN to create a network of support groups. It is a common misunderstanding that the EZLN consciously used the Internet to draw attention to its struggle and to generate support from actors in and outside of Mexico. In line with the points above regarding the distribution of EZLN communiqués through *La Jornada* and the Ya Basta! website, Cleaver (1998a: 628) notes that the EZLN has a mediated relationship to the Internet – that is, a relationship maintained primarily through the activities of transnational Zapatista solidarity network activists. These Internet-based activities have led to the formation of what Cleaver (1998b) refers to as a new electronic fabric of struggle around the EZLN.[15]

Weaving the Threads Together

The main argument of the book is that the formation of the trans-national Zapatista solidarity network should be explained and analysed through a combination of the explanatory dimensions outlined above. Put differently, we may contend that the network would not have developed, at least not in its present form, had any one of the factors been absent. The major weakness of studies hitherto is that the three dimensions are not integrated in a coherent analytical and theoretical framework. It is the aim of this section to outline the foundations of a theoretical framework that incorporates all three factors.

Special attention is given to the subjective dimension. The systemic and technological factors are objective in the sense that they provide a set of external opportunities available to all social actors in a more or less similar way. The formation of the solidarity network and the considerable degree of transnational interest generated by the EZLN can thus not be explained with reference only to these opportunities. Opportunities are in many ways dead or dormant until they are oper-ationalized and brought to life through the actions and innovations

of particular social actors. Explaining the formation of informal transnational networks should be founded in an attentiveness to present
objective factors or opportunities (systemic and technological in our
case), but these should be theoretically subordinated to subjective
factors. Only by analysing how the EZLN has operationalized and
interpreted the opportunities will we be able to understand the
formation of the transnational Zapatista solidarity network.

Globalization: a multidimensional framework

The major contribution of globalization theory is its preoccupation
with the increasing difficulty of analysing social change as taking
place within or between states. The growth in the number and
influence of non-state or civil society actors since at least the 1960s
is compelling evidence in support of this argument. This development
serves as the pivot of our discussion of globalization in this section
and throughout the book. Globalization thus primarily refers here
to the increasing number of these actors engaged in transnational
interactions; to the growing influence of civil society actors on states
and intergovernmental organizations; and to the growing degree of
networked cooperation between such actors beyond their immediate local and national settings. In more general terms, globalization
represents an increasing number and intensity of interactions across
physical, social and cultural distances, and a situation where the social
cannot be mapped or analysed solely in terms of geographical space
(Held et al. 1999; Scholte 2000).

The concept of globalization provides us with a descriptive rather
than an explanatory framework for analysing social change. Too often,
analyses use the concept to denote a force that causes events and
developments (e.g. Castells 1996, 1997; Bauman 1998). This approach
often springs from a view that equates globalization with the phase
of neoliberal restructuring since the 1970s. Applying the concept in
this monocausal manner, however, reifies it and turns it into a force
with its own life beyond the reach of social actors, hovering above
localities and subordinating them to its logic. There are at least three
problems associated with this understanding.

First, the monocausal approach blinds itself to the fact that globalization is not only about economic phenomena (Giddens 1994a: 4),

but a process with political, cultural and technological dimensions. It is not feasible to single out any one of these dimensions as the primary driving force of globalization. We must content ourselves with the conclusion that globalization is multidimensional (Held 1998: 13), and that all of the above aspects are profoundly interlinked and part of the overall dynamic.

While globalization has been under way at least since the sixteenth century, it was not until the latter half of the twentieth century that globalization had matured to the extent that it made sense to speak of a broadly shared global consciousness. As argued by Shaw (2000), this development has to some extent been a result of the experiences of World War II and its devastating consequences for large parts of humanity. The end of the Cold War in the late 1980s and early 1990s marked the beginning of a new phase. The disappearance of bipolar conflict and the East–West division of the world has greatly accelerated the globalization process (Shaw 1997) and opened up for a new stage in the development of a global consciousness. The notion of a global consciousness constitutes the basis of our approach to globalization. Global consciousness refers to a conception of the world as a single place or society (e.g. Albrow 1990; Robertson 1992). It is closely related to the availability of communications media which enable people to receive images and knowledge of events and experiences in distant places. Communications media make possible a situation where symbolic exchanges become increasingly important and influential (Waters 1995: 9), and where the geographical localization of a problem or situation may be of secondary importance compared with its symbolic impact on the global system (Melucci 1994: 111). The Internet constitutes the latest stage in this development and denotes a qualitative change in the potential for constructing a global consciousness through communications media (Giddens 1994b: 96).

A second problem with the monocausal approach to globalization is that it overlooks how reactions to some aspects of globalization actually reinforce the process and how much civil society action is itself a globalizing force. Globalization is not something that occurs outside civil society action and vice versa (Pieterse 2001: 24), because resistance is expressed in an increasingly global manner and through a global consciousness. The view advanced here contends that resistance to some of the forces inherent in the globalization process is, in fact, part of this process rather than mere reaction to it. This globalization from below (Falk 1999) is often advanced in opposition to what is seen by critics as a hegemonic neoliberal ideology, dominant since the early 1970s on an increasingly global scale. From a left-wing perspective, the opposition to neoliberalism is mainly formulated in a radical democratic terminology drawing on the almost global spread of liberal democratic ideas since the end of the Cold War, while at the same time engaging in a struggle over the definition of democracy. To its critics, neoliberalism is considered undemocratic for two main reasons: first, the social inequalities created by neoliberal policies are incompatible with democracy (Jelin 1997); second, neoliberal globalization has created a democratic deficit as decisions are increasingly made by unelected technocrats in international institutions away from those affected by their decisions (Ayres 2001a).

A third problem with the monocausal perspective is that it views globalization as a process that reduces 'old' spatial spheres, such as the local, the regional, and the national, to a function of globalization. Globalization is, rather, woven into a complex relationship with these spheres (Held et al. 1999; Scholte 2000). In other words, it only makes sense to speak of globalization as a process taking place through local and national levels. Globalization denotes a situation where these spheres of interaction are increasingly imbricated (Slater 1998; Seidman 2000) rather than increasingly separated. In fact, we should be aware that contemporary transnational social action and resistance are often rooted in the local and the national, or, perhaps more accurately, at the intersections of the local, the national and the transnational (Escobar 2001). Robertson (1995) has referred to this situation as 'glocalization'. The term suggests that events at the local level may also shape the course of globalization, and that globalization should not be viewed as a process that necessarily leads to homogeneity and universality.

This point also indicates that there is no obvious direction to globalization (Giddens 1994b: 96; Rosenau 1997: 97). In geographical terms, there seems to be a common assumption that globalization originated in the USA and Europe, gradually subsuming the rest of the world and in the process developing a world culture based on

Western ideas and values (Boli and Thomas 1999). While this was undoubtedly the case in the imperialist phases of history, the picture is more complicated today (Giddens 1994b: 96). Social actors and events in the non-Western parts of the world may, accordingly, also influence the direction of globalization. In other words, globalization is not a force that simply subsumes and erases the local and particular or leads to cultural homogenization in a Western image. Therefore the allure of the claim that globalization weakens the local and the national should not be readily accepted; it may in fact also strengthen the local and the national by providing social actors with new arenas of contest and sources of support. The historically high number of intergovernmental organizations and other international institutions in the present situation has created an additional level of influence apart from the local and national levels (Brysk 2000; Guidry et al. 2000). Moreover, the increasing interdependence of states has made it possible for social actors to exert influence on their national state via other states, a situation termed by Keck and Sikkink (1998) a boomerang pattern. Our focus on the increasing interactions between civil society actors across borders, in other words, is not intended to suggest that institutional actors such as states have lost relevance. Instead, the globalization process is reflected in the opening of sites of authority to the influence of civil society actors (e.g. Tarrow 2001; Rosenau 1997; Smith et al. 1997; Keck and Sikkink 1998).

We now have four mainstays in our understanding of contemporary globalization: the development of a global consciousness since the end of World War II; the process of neoliberal restructuring since the 1970s; the spread of democracy since the 1980s and the end of the Cold War; the proliferation of the Internet since the 1990s. These mainstays largely correspond to the subjective, systemic, and technological explanatory factors discussed earlier in the chapter. We now return to this discussion and extend it to theoretical concepts derived from the literature on social movements. This, in turn, forms the basis of the theoretical framework of transnational framing.

Social constructionism and social movement theory

It was argued above that special attention should be paid to the subjective aspect in the formation of the transnational Zapatista

Figure 1.2   The three explanatory threads and globalization

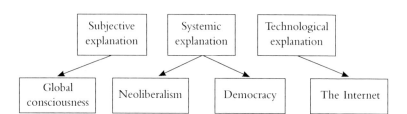

solidarity network. It was also indicated that this is fundamentally a social constructionist process, albeit one that takes place in a context of certain external (systemic and technological) conditions. Social constructionism as applied in social movement theory is concerned with the construction of common understandings considered to underlie the formation of social movements. In our case, it is thus argued that a certain common understanding must be present between the variety of actors involved before it is plausible to speak of a network. At the heart of the concept of transnational framing, then, is the question of how such an understanding is constructed despite the existence of physical, social and cultural barriers.

Due to the dominant position of the resource mobilization approach to social movements in much contemporary literature, the role played by common understandings has been inadequately theorized in the debate on transnational social action. In an early formulation of this approach, McCarthy and Zald (1977) claimed that social movement organizations are the result of deliberate and rational attempts by movement entrepreneurs to bring people together and mobilize resources around certain issues. This process, moreover, takes place on the basis of previous organizational experiences or mobilizing structures (McCarthy 1996). The most important insight, arguably, is that resource mobilization places the emphasis on actors rather than structures in explaining the formation of social movements. Nevertheless, this perspective remains limited in at least three respects. First, resource mobilization places insufficient emphasis on grievances as an explanatory factor in the formation of social movements. Second, it does not take explicit account of the historical and external conditions under which such movements take shape. Third, the approach pays insufficient attention to the construction of common understandings.

During the 1970s, the resource mobilization approach and its US-based scholars led the development of social movement theory. From the 1980s, however, it came increasingly under pressure from approaches directing specific attention to questions of identity formation and grievance interpretation. This challenge was mounted on two fronts: the (mainly European based) new social movements approach, and social constructionism (Buechler 2000). It is the latter that concerns us here, as it is the main theoretical tool used in this study. The social constructionist perspective shares with resource mobilization a rejection of structural determinism and an emphasis on creativity and subjectivity in the formation of social movements (Diani 1996: 1055). However, it departs from it in its contention that the formation of social movements is inextricably linked to the construction of common understandings. It is the question of how these are created which lies at the heart of the social constructionist perspective. The concept of framing (Snow et al. 1986; Snow and Benford 1988) has become widely used to denote this process of creating common understandings. It is thus particularly useful in explaining the dynamics of social movement formation. Nevertheless, certain qualifications are needed when considering our interest in transnational and networked forms of social action.

First, the framing concept is understood here in a less strategic sense than is often the case in the framing literature. It is applied not only to denote the processes through which social movements attract resources and members but also to point to the construction of common understandings as a central element in the formation of social movements.

Second, while the framing concept is used in the literature mainly to analyse how social movements attract members and support in a micro-mobilization process, here we shift the analysis to the level of meso-mobilization (Gerhards and Rucht 1992). This obviously reflects our interest in networks as opposed to more structured and organizational forms. Meso-mobilization thus refers to the processes whereby different groups, through the activities of specific actors, come to act together in networks.

Third, our use of the framing concept is extended, as it also draws on concepts developed in the resource mobilization and political opportunities approaches. These are, on the other hand, subordinated to the framing concept in the sense that we consider how the conditions they refer to may facilitate framing processes.

Fourth, the framing concept has been applied (as has most social movement theory until recently) primarily in a national context. Below we address this limitation by coupling the concept with insights from the globalization literature. In order to move beyond this limitation, the concept of transnational framing is proposed as the theoretical pivot for analysing the formation of the transnational Zapatista solidarity network. This allows us to advance a theoretical framework that is open to the dynamic, subjective and contingent character of the social without losing sight of the historical and external conditions within which social action always takes place.

Towards a theory of transnational framing

Transnational framing refers to the processes through which physically, socially and culturally dispersed social actors develop a degree of common understanding, enabling us to speak about the existence of informal transnational networks. The theory of transnational framing does not lend itself to strictly causal analysis. Rather, it is a framework for analysing the processes underlying and facilitating the formation of informal transnational networks. As such, it favours inquiries into the 'how' in preference to the 'why'.

On the one hand, the theory of transnational framing presented here has been developed in close association with our empirical case study, the transnational Zapatista solidarity network. As illustrated in Figure 1.3, this is evident in the fact that the theory is in many ways an expansion of the explanatory threads in the literature on the transnational dimension of the EZLN. The rather close relationship between the theory and the case study derives from the grounded theory approach to theoretical development used in this book.[16] On the other hand, however, the theory of transnational framing also aspires to be of relevance in analyses of informal transnational networks other than that of the EZLN. This claim rests on the objective factors incorporated into the framework, illustrated in Figures 1.2 and 1.3.

As noted, transnational framing processes are seen as leading to the construction of common understandings. This process often revolves around a node of special influence (Gerlach 1987: 115): that is, one or more actors whose innovative actions and interpretations serve as a point of reference and source of inspiration (as opposed to an organizational or directive centre) for the actors involved in the network. In the case of the Zapatista solidarity network, the EZLN is the node of special influence. In other words, the framing process underlying the formation of the Zapatista network involves a sender–recipient relationship where the EZLN is the primary sender and the recipients are the transnational actors engaged in EZLN solidarity activities. Analysing the process in this case should, accordingly, consider primarily how the EZLN has formulated and transmitted its ideas and interpretations, and how these have been received by those involved or potentially involved in related solidarity activities. To systematize this analytical endeavour further, we need to define the conditions that facilitate transnational framing processes. Four conditions structure this theoretical framework.

First, a frame is likely to be more successful if it resonates with the social and cultural beliefs of recipients (Snow and Benford 1988; Tarrow 1992). This aspect is, of course, particularly problematic in regard to transnational framing. It is argued, however, that the development of a global consciousness (especially after the end of World War II) makes it increasingly possible to achieve such resonance beyond physical, social and cultural borders. Drawing on the resource mobilization approach, I suggest that reservoirs of global consciousness are present in previous and contemporary organizations or mobilizing structures (McCarthy 1996).

Second, a frame must define a problem and propose its solution (Snow and Benford 1988; Gamson 1995). This process is also referred to as the adoption of an injustice frame (Gamson et al. 1982: 123). The framing perspective was developed partly in reaction to the lack of attention given to grievances in the more entrepreneurial versions of resource mobilization, and as such denotes an attempt to bring grievances back in (Buechler 2000: 197–8). The process of neoliberal restructuring since the 1970s and 1980s is argued here to have af-

Figure 1.3   A model of transnational framing

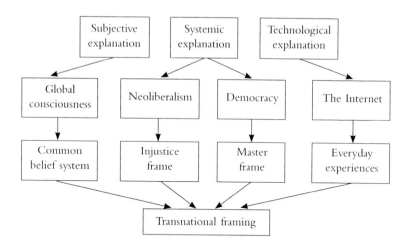

fected large parts of the world's population in a more or less similar way. This condition enhances the potential for constructing injustice frames that resonate beyond physical, social and cultural borders.

Third, frames are likely to be more successful when they are derived from a master frame – that is, an interpretive medium through which collective actors within a cycle of contention (Tarrow 1998) assign blame for their problems (Snow and Benford 1992). It is contended that the proliferation of democratic ideas since the end of the Cold War provides a (latent) master frame for the construction of transnational frames. Since the critique of neoliberalism is often formulated in radical democratic terms, there is a close relationship between injustice frames and master frames. Using the terminology of the political opportunities approach, we may propose that this democratic master frame is closely associated with the political opportunities created by the end of the Cold War. Political opportunities primarily refer to changes in political power structures facilitating social movement formation (e.g. McAdam 1996; Tarrow 1998).

Fourth, a successful frame must establish a degree of resonance between the everyday experiences of senders and recipients in the framing process. In other words, a frame must have empirical credibility (a fit between the frame and actual events) and experiential commensurability (resonance with the experiences of potential target groups) (Snow and Benford 1988). It is suggested that the Internet makes it easier for physically, socially and culturally distant actors to share everyday experiences. Borrowing from the resource mobilization approach, we may consider communication technologies as vital resources (Freeman 1979) in transnational framing processes.

Figure 1.3 illustrates the main features of our theoretical framework of transnational framing.

Structure of the Book

In this chapter we have introduced the main object of analysis, the transnational Zapatista solidarity network, and posed five questions. We have considered the actions and conditions underlying the formation of the network. The theoretical framework of the book has been outlined, centred on the concept of transnational framing.

Chapter 2 is a theoretical chapter, taking as its point of departure social movement theory and globalization theory. It further develops the concept of transnational framing and discusses the conditions of its facilitation. Chapter 3 considers the informational infrastructure that holds together the Zapatista solidarity network. Chapter 4 focuses on the network's activities, on the level of both civil society politics and that of institutional politics. Chapter 5, the first of four analytical chapters, demonstrates how the ability of the EZLN to invoke a global consciousness and a common belief system has been instrumental in the formation of the network. Chapter 6 considers how the almost global spread of neoliberal policies has been constructed by the EZLN as a common injustice frame vital to its appeal. Chapter 7 shows how democratic and human rights ideas have constituted a master frame following the end of the Cold War, and how the EZLN has drawn on this in the formation of the solidarity network. Chapter 8 demonstrates how the availability of new information technologies like the Internet, through their potential for mediating and exchanging everyday experiences, have played a vital role. Chapter 9, in conclusion, assesses the present state and the possible future of the transnational Zapatista solidarity network, and the hopes of the left.

Notes

1. The EZLN is often referred to as 'the Zapatistas'. This term and the adjective 'Zapatista' are used in cases where this is considered more fitting. The term 'Zapatismo' refers broadly to the EZLN's political ideas. The term 'EZLN' used throughout the book includes both armed and civil elements of the movement. The armed element primarily comprises the military leadership of the movement, the Clandestine Revolutionary Indigenous Committee–General Command of the Zapatista Army of National Liberation (Comité Clandestino Revolucionario Indígena-Comandancia General del Ejército Zapatista de Liberacíon Nacional, or CCRI–CG del EZLN), which authors most EZLN documents. The civil element comprises the indigenous communities of Chiapas that form the social base of the movement.

2. A survey in March 2002 found forty-two organizations in Europe and the USA currently active on Chiapas- and EZLN-related issues (see Appendix). These organizations all devote large parts or all of their time to the cause. The survey thus excludes the large number of organizations that participate on an occasional basis. Moreover, as the survey was carried out partly by following the hyperlinks of central Chiapas- and EZLN-related websites, it excludes organizations without an Internet presence.

3. Contrary to what the term 'International Zapatismo' may seem to indicate, it is important to stress that not all of the actors engaged in the Zapatista solidarity network are direct supporters of the EZLN. Many solidarity activists dissociate themselves from the armed element of the movement, while they sympathize with the EZLN's social and political demands. Transnational Zapatista solidarity network actors may thus be defined as those who have an interest in the impact of the EZLN uprising, share some of the EZLN's political views, and engage in information distribution, material aid delivery, human rights observation, and lobbying efforts in relation to the EZLN and Chiapas.

4. A webpage count (Google, 9 March 2002) gives a rough measure of the comparable 'popularity' of the EZLN. Coupled with the search word 'solidarity', these Latin American movements turned up the following number of webpages: EZLN, 5,620; FARC (Fuerzas Armadas Revolucionarios de Colombia/Revolutionary Armed Forces of Colombia), 3,760; MST (Movimento dos Trabalhadores Rurais Sem Terra/Landless Workers' Movement) of Brazil, 3,540; MRTA (Movimiento Revolucionario Tupac Amaru/Tupac Amaru Revolutionary Movement) of Peru, 2,320; EPR (Ejército Popular Revolucionario/Popular Revolutionary Army) of Mexico, 720.

5. It is preferable to speak about a transnational rather than a global dimension of the EZLN. As indicated, the large majority of Zapatista solidarity network actors are concentrated in the USA and Europe. Whereas the adjective 'global' gives the impression of a phenomenon evenly distributed on a global scale, the adjective 'transnational' is less ambitious, referring simply to interactions across national borders. To avoid confusion, it should be stated that the adjectives 'transnational' and 'global' are not interchangeable, but indicate different analytical levels. 'Globalization' is thus an overall descriptive framework for understanding and analysing contemporary social

change, while 'transnational' interactions are one of the dynamics that constitute this process.

6. The notion of a transnational justice and solidarity network is preferred here to other designations describing the wave of protest since Seattle 1999 – for example, the anti-globalization movement. The latter concept is problematic as it conveys the impression of a defensive political project, and depicts protests as a movement when in reality they consist of a diverse range of actors. Actors in the transnational justice and protest network are seen here as concerned primarily with a radical democratic critique of capitalism/neoliberalism. This point is further discussed in Chapters 6 and 7.

7. Apart from the concept of social movement organization, we also, and more frequently, make use of the concept social movement. The two are related but not interchangeable. The former is used more narrowly to describe organized forms of collective civil society action, while the latter is applied as a broader description of different types of collective civil society action, as well as of the field of study in general.

8. The informal transnational movement network concept encompasses not only transnational solidarity networks, but also transnational networks engaged in a critique of neoliberalism/capitalism from a leftist and radical democratic point of view. Consequently, it differs from the transnational advocacy network concept employed by Keck and Sikkink (1998). See also Chapters 2 and 5 for discussion of this concept.

9. Unless otherwise indicated, translations from Spanish texts are mine.

10. These characteristics, among others, have led some observers to label the EZLN as postmodern (e.g. Burbach 1994). See Nugent 1995 for a critique of this perspective. For analyses of the EZLN from a more traditional left-wing and Marxist perspective, see for example Veltmeyer 2000 and De Angelis 2000.

11. The prolific writings of Subcomandante Marcos have been collected and commented upon in several books over the last decade (e.g. Ponce de León 2001).

12. For more critical approaches to the role of Subcomandante Marcos, see for example Paz 1994; Oppenheimer 1996; Castañeda 1997; de la Grange and Rico 1998.

13. Emiliano Zapata was a peasant leader during the Mexican Revolution (1910–19), whose demands for land reform were echoed in the creation of the so-called *ejido* system in subsequent decades.

14. The February 1995 offensive was part of an attempt to break the influence of the EZLN, which had increasingly become a thorn in the flesh of the ruling PRI (Partido Revolucionario Institucional/Institutional Revolutionary Party), and to restore faith in the Mexican economy and leadership after the financial crisis of December 1994.

15. Where Cleaver seems to be generally optimistic and positive about the possibilities of the Internet in broadening and deepening social struggle, Hellman (1999) has launched a significant criticism of the use of the Internet in transnational solidarity work related to Chiapas and the EZLN. In Hellman's view, the Internet creates a discrepancy between a virtual and a real Chiapas. This debate is taken up in more detail in Chapter 8.

16. The research method in the book mainly builds on qualitative research. It reflects a concern with the development of new theoretical tools for studying phenomena such as the transnational Zapatista solidarity network. Qualitative research is therefore a question not only of generating empirical material but also of developing an appropriate theoretical framework. This research method is referred to as grounded theory (e.g. Strauss 1987) and is especially useful in areas characterized by a lack of theorizing. Grounded theory is thus developed in an intimate relationship with the generation of qualitative data – 'grounded' refers to the fact that the theory is grounded in data. Data collection and theory generation take place in a reciprocal process where new data further sharpen the theory, while this in turn enables the researcher to ask better and more precise questions. The strength of theory is obviously best tested through its application to comparable cases. This book, however, is a single case study; there are therefore limited possibilities for testing the strength of the theory developed.

2

Theorizing Transnational Framing

Framing and the Construction of Common Understandings

The main focus of social constructionism is the process whereby the collective identities that form the basis of social movements are created. This process is considered both the precondition of such movements and a necessary feature of their trajectories. The development of social constructionist theory has taken two directions, with differing perspectives: the collective identity approach and framing. This book concentrates on the framing approach, with its focus on the creation of common understandings rather than collective identities.

Framing has its theoretical roots in a critique of the resource mobilization perspective. In an early formulation, McCarthy and Zald (1977: 1215–16) noted how grievances and discontent may be 'defined, created, and manipulated by issue entrepreneurs and organizations'. In this entrepreneurial (Buechler 2000) version of the resource mobilization approach, it is the availability of resources and the use to which they are put by rational actors which lead to the formation of social movements, rather than discontent or grievances (Klandermans 1989: 8; Jenkins 1983: 528). Discontent and grievances are considered to be permanent features of society and do not hold any explanatory power in regard to social movement formation. In an original formulation of the framing perspective, Snow and Benford (1988: 198) thus criticize the traditional resource mobilization approach for treating 'meanings or ideas as given, as if there is an isomorphic relationship between the nature of any particular set of conditions or events and the meanings attached to them'. What is overlooked, in other words, are the processes of grievance interpretation and social construction of problems that must precede and form the basis of social movement formation (Snow et al. 1986: 465). The framing approach, consequently, is an attempt at bringing the question of grievances back into study of social movement after its relegation to obscurity by the rational versions of the resource mobilization approach (Buechler 2000: 195ff.).

Snow et al. (1986: 467ff.) distinguish four types of framing process. *Frame bridging* is the attempt by a social movement to mobilize elements of the public who share some of its concerns and grievances, but who do not have the organizational base for expressing this discontent. *Frame amplification* is the process through which the social movement emphasizes certain ideas and values that have hitherto been dormant in its self-presentation, but are considered to have resonance with potential constituents. *Frame extension* is the attempt by social movements to encompass new ideas and values that so far have not been part of the social movement's ideational baggage, but are considered to have resonance with potential constituents. *Frame transformation* is the fundamental replacement by a social movement of its ideational foundation.

What are the conditions underlying a successful framing process? A successful frame facilitates a relatively large degree of resonance and common understanding between sender and recipient in the framing process, thus ensuring a stable flow of material and symbolic resources between the actors involved. Accordingly, framing processes always involve a sender–recipient relationship (see Chapter 1). Building mainly on Snow and Benford (1988: 199ff.), but changing their structure somewhat, we may identify four elements considered central to a successful frame.

First, Snow and Benford note that a framing process is more successful if it resonates with the overall social belief systems of the recipients in the framing process, or, as argued by Tarrow (1992), with the social mentalities and political culture of society.

Second, Snow and Benford argue that a successful frame presupposes an element of grievance interpretation. They distinguish three tasks related to grievance interpretation: recognizing a problem and defining it as being in need of alteration; proposing a solution to the problem; and making it clear that social movement action could lead to the desired changes. This argument is akin to that of Gamson et al. (1982: 123), who point to the adoption of an injustice frame as a precondition for social movement action. An injustice frame, in contrast to a legitimating frame, is 'an interpretation of what is happening that supports the conclusion that an authority system is violating the shared moral principles of the participants. An alternative to the legitimating frame, it provides a reason for non-compliance.'

Third, Snow and Benford emphasize that frames are likely to be more successful if they correspond to a master frame. Specific action frames are derived from master frames, providing an interpretive medium used by collective actors within a cycle of protest to assign blame (Snow and Benford 1992: 139). The development of new master frames is thus often associated with cycles of contention, which, according to Tarrow (1998: 142), are phases

> of heightened conflict across the social system: with a rapid diffusion of collective action from more mobilized to less mobilized sectors; a rapid pace of innovation in the forms of contention; the creation of new or transformed collective action frames; a combination of organized and unorganized participation; and sequences of intensified information flow and interaction between challengers and authorities.

Thus cycles of contention are most likely to occur in the context of a new and innovative master frame. Master frames can often be retraced to the actions and interpretations of one or more social movements that have emerged early in a cycle of contention. Recalling the discussion in Chapter 1, these actors may also be referred to as nodes of special influence (Gerlach 1987: 115). As noted by Snow and Benford (1992: 143–4), the absence of mobilization in a situation with otherwise ripe conditions may to some degree be explained by the absence of an active master frame.

Fourth, Snow and Benford stress how successful frames must strike a chord in the everyday experiences of the targets of mobilization. In other words, a frame must have what they term empirical credibility and experiential commensurability. Empirical credibility refers to 'the fit between the framing and events in the world' (Snow and Benford 1988: 208) – that is, to the verifiability and testability of the messages and interpretations of the senders in the framing process. Experiential commensurability refers to whether there is a fit between the way the sender in the framing process presents its messages and interpretations and the way the issues in question have been, and are, experienced by the recipients in the framing process.

In summary, then, frames are considered to be more successful if they display the following features: resonance between the societal belief systems of sender and recipient; development of an injustice frame; resonance with a master frame; resonance between the everyday experiences of sender and recipient.

These points do not represent a natural sequence through which frames evolve, but rather a selective number of elements forming the basis of most successful frames. This is not to say that successful frames necessarily contain all four elements. It should also be said that the term 'resonance' does not imply complete agreement or homogeneity, but rather insight and understanding between sender and recipient in the framing process. Later in this chapter, these points are applied in a discussion of globalization, leading us to outline a range of conditions considered to facilitate the development of transnational frames.

Points of Convergence between Framing and Resource Mobilization

As noted, framing is based on a critique of the resource mobilization approach. This, however, should not lead us to discard altogether the insights of this approach into the conditions surrounding social movement formation and development. Indeed, there are a number of points of convergence between the approaches that may strengthen the analytical precision of the framing concept. Resource mobilization is used here as a common denominator for three perspectives, dealing with questions of resources, mobilizing structures and organization, and political opportunities.

Resources

In framing processes, social movements 'assign meaning to and interpret, relevant events and conditions in ways that are intended to mobilize potential adherents and constituents' (Snow and Benford 1988: 198). Thus formulated, the framing process has features in common with the resource mobilization approach. The goal of framing processes, in other words, is to create 'effective' frames that can attract resources to the movement. McCarthy and Zald (1977: 1220) posit four types of resource relevant to social movement formation: money, facilities, labour and legitimacy. Freeman (1979) distinguishes between tangible and intangible resources. Money and facilities, as well as means of communication, are tangible resources; intangible resources are, *inter alia*, the personal skills of social movement participants.

Resources often come to social movements via the participation of 'conscience constituents'. McCarthy and Zald (1977: 1222) have defined conscience constituents as supporters of social movements who do not benefit in any direct way from goal accomplishment, but who have a psychological and material surplus allowing them to support cases with little or no direct bearing on their personal lives. They are attracted to an actual or potential social movement through its ideational and interpretive frame, and consequently there is an intimate relationship between resources and framing processes. Communication resources deserve special mention. Considering that any framing process is a highly extrovert endeavour attempting to reach a large audience beyond the immediate social movement, it will often take place, to a significant extent, through particular media. It should be expected, therefore, that framing processes have a better chance of succeeding if the social movement has access to communication resources. This notion is taken up in more detail later in the chapter, where particular emphasis is put on the role of the Internet in framing.

Mobilizing structures and organization

Central in the resource mobilization approach is a focus on organizations. The generation of resources is thus intimately linked to the creation and maintenance of social movement organizations. Only by channelling protest through an organization can social movements hope to make a sustained effort at changing things (Oberschall 1973: 119; Gamson 1975: 90). Related to this perspective is the argument that social movements do not arise ex nihilo; the greater the level of prior organization in a given population, the greater the probability that new organizations may emerge (McAdam 1982: 44). We may also refer to this factor as 'mobilizing structures'. Mobilizing structures are those 'collective vehicles, informal as well as formal, through which people mobilize and engage in collective action' (McAdam et al. 1996: 3). One of the better-known conceptualizations of organization in social movement formation has been developed by Tilly (1978: 62–3), who distinguishes between categories ('catness') of people who share a characteristic or identity, and networks ('netness') of people who are linked through interpersonal bonds. Tilly argues that in a setting with a high degree of both catness and netness there exists what he calls a 'catnet'. Thus, we are more likely to see the formation of organizations and social movements in situations with strong catnets.

If we take seriously the claim that framing and the construction of common understandings and meanings are preconditions for social movements, we must view framing processes in the light of already existing common understandings. When dealing with organizational experiences as a facilitating factor for social movement formation, it is often overlooked how these experiences may also contain certain active or dormant common understandings. Organizational experiences, therefore, provide potential social movements not only with certain resources but also with more or less well-defined common understandings that may be (re)activated and shaped by new social actors. Framing and the construction of common understandings thus do not take place in a void. They build on previous or already existing common understandings, which are in turn intimately linked to previous organizational experiences. This point will be addressed in greater detail later.

Political opportunities

In an early argument for the relevance of political opportunities in explaining social movement formation and behaviour, Eisinger (1973: 12) states that there is 'interaction, or linkage, between the environment, understood in terms of the notion of a structure of political opportunities, and political behavior'. With the political opportunities approach, attention becomes directed to the state and the political system as a structure providing social movements with a combination of opportunities and constraints. The approach builds on the rationalist assumption that social movement action 'costs' something, and that the opportunities and constraints in the social movement's external environment raises or lowers the 'price' of social movement action (Tilly 1978). Traditionally, the concept of political opportunities has been employed in a national context. In recent years, however, theorists have become increasingly attentive to the need to project the concept onto the transnational level. In this perspective, supranational institutions, such as the UN, may provide social movements with political opportunities that are not confined by specific states.[1]

The concept of political opportunities is used mainly as an explanatory variable in regard to dependent variables such as the timing and outcome of social movements (McAdam 1996: 29). While there is little disagreement that political opportunities constitute an important variable, there is less clarity as to exactly what should be included in the concept. McAdam (1996) argues for a definition that is sufficiently narrow to make it open to falsification. By integrating differing interpretations in a number of works, McAdam (1996: 27) points to the following aspects as central variables in the political opportunities approach: the openness or closure of the institutional political system; the stability or instability of the elite alignments that the polity rests on; the presence or absence of elite allies; the state's capacity for and propensity to repression.

This focus on political and institutional variables is the most common approach to political opportunities, and it is acknowledged here as analytically useful. However, I contend that it is necessary to move beyond the purely institutional definition in McAdam's exposition. Gamson and Meyer (1996) thus argue for the inclusion of what they refer to as the cultural dimension of political opportunities. The cultural dimension refers to those belief systems and world-views that permeate society. These in turn set certain limits for what can be discussed in public discourse. When they begin to change, social movements are provided with the opportunity to put new issues on the agenda that had previously been excluded from public discourse. Such cultural and ideational shifts may be linked, for example, to the cessation of elite conflict or to the opportunities created by the crisis of dominant cleavages (Diani 1996). The issue of the cessation of conflict is absent, or only implicit, in most definitions of the political opportunities concept. Referring back to the framing concept, we can suggest that cultural and ideational shifts may give rise to, and be reflected in, the emergence of new master frames. By 'elevating' the political opportunities concept to this somewhat structural and ideational level, we also extend the limited time framework of the political opportunities concept in its more institutional and political formulations.

Gamson and Meyer (1996: 276) make an additional observation that places them at variance with most accounts of political opportunities. They draw our attention to the fact that social movements relate not only mechanically to certain given constraints and opportunities in their external environment; they also shape and create political opportunities through their actions. This observation extends the political opportunities concept beyond the objective and institutional factors in McAdam's (1996) definition and into the subjective area of meaning and interpretation. Social movements thus do not automatically flow from the presence of political opportunities (McAdam 1982: 48). These are facilitating factors for social movement formation, and are without explanatory power on their own. In other words, an opportunity unrecognized is no opportunity at all (Gamson and Meyer 1996: 283). Political opportunities, then, are not only objective factors; they are also subjective and perceived (Tarrow 1988: 430; Gamson and Meyer 1996). It is the framing process that breathes life into otherwise dead opportunities.

Facilitating Transnational Framing

The framing concept in its original formulation was developed with reference mainly to the national context. Framing processes and the construction of common understandings are always fraught with contingency and characterized by political, social and cultural obstacles. But transnational framing processes are likely to face even more significant limitations and hindrances due to the conspicuous physical, social and cultural distances between the actors involved (McCarthy 1997: 245; Khagram et al. 2002: 12).

In the original literature, the framing concept was applied mainly to analyse how social movement organizations attract new members and support in what we may refer to as a micromobilization process. Here we move the analysis to the level of meso-mobilization (Gerhards and Rucht 1992), whereby social movement organizations and individuals, through transnational framing processes and the development of common understandings, become parts of informal transnational movement networks.

Solidarity and global consciousness

It takes a global consciousness to view social dynamics as part of a globalization process. Global consciousness is the ability to think about the world and humankind as a single entity. Globalization, then, is not just a matter of objective factors. It also has a significant subjective and cultural dimension (Robertson 1992: 183). Put differently, the three dimensions of globalization presented in Chapter 1 – neoliberalism, democracy, Internet – would have a much smaller effect on transnational social action if they were not viewed through a global consciousness.[2] On the other hand, this global consciousness is not something that exists as a given. Rather, it is constantly produced and reproduced in the transnational framing process.

The concept of globalization did not enter general vocabulary until the 1980s and gained wide currency only in the 1990s. This does not mean, of course, that there was no global consciousness before that time. The notions of a global consciousness and a common humanity have deep historical roots and build on Enlightenment visions, on Christian cosmology, and on socialist traditions (Passy 2001: 8). Furthermore, as Seidman (2000: 344) notes, activists have appealed to an international community since at least the middle of the nineteenth century.[3] The plethora of interstate and intrastate wars in the last five centuries, however, has contradicted any notion of a common humanity. In many ways, though, the last major war seemed to spark a revival of this idea: World War II, in contrast to World War I, was a genuine worldwide conflict (Shaw 2000: 121), involving not only Europe but also Asia, Australia and parts of Africa. The severity of human suffering during the war, and the fact that an extraordinarily large number of those affected were civilians, called for a codified expression of future protection of human rights (Clark 1997: 113). The adoption of the Universal Declaration of

Human Rights in December 1948 was the first attempt in human history to extend the same set of rights to all people, and thus to construct them as formally equal. These developments were important precursors to the concerns in subsequent decades with the extension of solidarity beyond national boundaries and the construing of the world as an imagined community (Anderson 1983).[4] In recent times, the disappearance of the bipolar conflict between the East and West has opened up for a new stage in the development of a global consciousness.

As described by Baglioni (2001), the idea of solidarity born as a result of wartime experiences is reflected, for example, in the creation of the Red Cross in the latter part of the nineteenth century. The Red Cross has traditionally been linked to states and is largely dependent on state approval before it can intervene in conflicts. In the Vietnam and the Biafran wars in the 1960s and 1970s, this stance suffered a loss of legitimacy and gave rise to a new model of solidarity 'without borders' (Baglioni 2001: 225). This change came to involve a concern with the developing countries that in turn also denoted a growing global consciousness. In the politicized climate of the 1960s and 1970s, and in the light of the entrenchment of the Cold War, solidarity work gradually moved from altruistic and charity-oriented concerns towards a more political and reciprocal content. In some ways, this situation was a result of the disillusion with traditional politics that also characterized the 1960s and 1970s and the so-called new social movements (Dalton et al. 1990). Solidarity work, in other words, provided a new outlet for political activism (Baglioni 2001: 225).

In the contemporary situation we witness similar trends towards a politicization of solidarity. We may even suggest that the currents set in motion in the 1960s and 1970s are coming to fruition in the development of what we refer to here as informal transnational movement networks. Transnational solidarity today, however, generally builds on a greater degree of reciprocity than previous solidarity movements motivated by altruism or narrow political concerns (Waterman 1998: 237; Eterovic and Smith 2001: 201). This way of understanding transnational solidarity reflects a global consciousness that is making it increasingly difficult to view the 'other' as inert (Giddens 1994b: 97) or as a helpless object of aid. As such, it represents a growing departure from traditional working-class solidarity, often tied to the state (Drainville 1998), as well as from one-way distant issue movements (Rucht 2000), where a 'we' is helping a 'them'.

By locating the origins of present solidarity work in the 1960s and 1970s, and referring back to the earlier discussion, we may note important points of convergence between the framing and the resource mobilization approaches. As indicated, a central tenet of resource mobilization theory is its concern with mobilizing structures (McCarthy 1996). Mobilizing structures provide potential social movements with resources such as organizational experience, materials, legitimacy, and so on. What seems to escape attention here is that mobilizing structures also contain active or dormant common understandings that may form the basis of new forms of social action. In other words, contemporary informal transnational movement networks build on identities and understandings rooted in already existing organizations and previous solidarity activism. This argument may also be linked to what Rosenau (1997: 58ff.) has referred to as the skill revolution. The skill revolution consists, among other things, in an increased ability to analyse events in a larger global context. It does not imply the convergence of values on a global scale, but a greater ability to articulate particular values so as to make them conceivable for others. If we return to the question of mobilizing structures, we may suggest that, to a large extent, these skills are developed and preserved in the context of mobilizing structures and previous organizational experiences.

In conclusion, a few words need to be said about the nature of solidarity from a more philosophical point of view. As shown above, solidarity rests on a notion of universality and a common humanity – that is, on a degree of global consciousness. This is not the place to try to resolve the philosophical debate between proponents of a basic human nature and proponents of contingency and social construction. Nevertheless, it is useful to point to Rorty's (1989) work on solidarity because it contrasts with the notion of universality in significant ways. The main issue for Rorty is that there is no basic human essence. He does not dismiss the existence of a human solidarity or a global consciousness as empirical fact or normative ideal, but contends that they cannot be grounded in any notion of universality. Feelings of solidarity, in other words, are 'easier' when the potential recipients of solidarity share some identity characteristics with us (Rorty 1989: 189ff.). What is stressed, then, is the socially constructed nature of solidarity. Giugni (2001: 243) makes a similar point when he argues that:

> We do not behave altruistically because we are fundamentally 'good,' nor because in our society we are taught to do something for others…. Yet, if we are to understand why we act altruistically in certain situations and egoistically in others, we had better abandon both a totally voluntaristic and a completely deterministic view to embrace a perspective acknowledging that (what at least appears as) altruistic behaviour is the product of situations and circumstances, that is, of social relations.

It is accepted that solidarity is indeed a social construction depending on social circumstances, and that we find it easier to relate to those who are to some extent 'like us'. This claim, on the other hand, makes it difficult to imagine the extension of solidarity beyond the local or national setting. If a transnational solidarity is to be constructed it thus requires a 'diminishing' of the differences between those in need of solidarity and the potential solidarity activists. This process takes place, *inter alia*, through transnational framing. Globalization is fundamentally understood as a process involving an extension of the 'we' to more and more people, thereby increasing the likelihood that transnational framing processes can build on, and refer to, a common belief system. But it is worth stressing that what we are witnessing is not a teleological march towards a global consciousness and common humanity. First, local, national and regional differences remain important and will continue to do so. Second, it is a process fraught with contingency and may be reversed. The world today is full of examples pointing in the opposite direction. As mentioned earlier, however, it is the aim of this chapter to point to some of the conditions and resources that can be said to facilitate transnational framing processes and the construction of transnational solidarities and understandings.

The neoliberal injustice frame

Informal transnational movement networks would hardly be conceivable if there was not a common social critique tying together physically, socially and culturally distant actors. This section argues that a common point of reference is found in some of the economic (neoliberalism) and political (elite democracy) aspects of globalization. It is contended that these developments provide a background for transnational grievance perceptions and for the construction of injustice frames.

It was argued in Chapter 1 that an important element in the globalization process has been capitalist restructuring since the 1970s, a process often referred to as neoliberalism. Neoliberalism is significant in an objective sense. In spite of obvious differences from country to country and from region to region, it is fair to say that never in the course of human history have a larger number of people been affected by the same complex of political and economic ideas. On the other hand, this development would hardly have a bearing on transnational social movement activism were it not for the fact that it is increasingly viewed through the lenses of a global consciousness. This global consciousness allows people to perceive neoliberalism as a global condition with more or less similar, and predominantly negative, effects in geographically distant locales.

Neoliberalism is not a neutral concept. In fact, it is often employed to denote a certain political vision related to a specific liberal and elitist view of democracy. This connection has been brought to the fore especially by scholars working within a critical international political economy tradition. The process of capitalist restructuring can be traced to the worldwide economic recession of the early 1970s (Cox 1996). These changes took place in the background to the political and economical order that had prevailed since the end of World War II under the aegis of a Pax Americana (Cox 1987). This order was characterized by a Keynesian political economy and welfare state orientation. The pressure of the economic crisis on this order led to the breaking of the social contract that had underpinned this order since the 1940s and 1950s. Governments increasingly allied with capital in order to create conditions favourable to the revival of investment (Cox 1987: 281), thus encouraging the adoption of similar forms of state-capitalist development geared to an offensive strategy in world markets (Cox 1987: 299). This disciplinary neo-liberalism (Gill 1995) has given rise to a political and economic order institutionalized in constitutional arrangements such as NAFTA and the EU, and enacted through international financial institutions such as the IMF and the World Bank. From this perspective, globalization is considered to be highly ideological in the sense that it is tied to a process of capitalist restructuring and expresses the political visions of certain dominant social groups and countries.[5]

As a result of their weak and dependent economies, the developing countries are especially subject to the rules and standards defined by this elite. This dependency was exacerbated with the debt crisis of the developing countries, beginning with Mexico's moratorium on its international debt in 1982. In the wake of the debt crisis, the IMF and the World Bank started taking on a much more active and political role. This new role was mainly embodied in the so-called structural adjustment programmes. With this change in the status of the developing countries, the agenda of inequality that had been prevalent throughout the 1960s and 1970s was replaced by one of poverty. Poverty came to be seen as a result of 'wrong' policy choices by states rather than as a consequence of structural barriers, and international efforts became increasingly directed towards poverty alleviation (Woods 1999: 15) and good governance.

While the process of neoliberal restructuring can be traced back to the economic recession of the 1970s and the debt crisis of the 1980s, it is important to stress that this process was significantly hastened by the end of the Cold War (Gill 1995: 406). Accordingly, it is possible to distinguish three phases of neoliberal restructuring since the early 1970s. In the second and third of these, from the early 1980s to the end of the Cold War, and then from the end of the Cold War to the present, the process of neoliberal restructuring has been intimately linked to a specific version of democracy – liberal democracy. While some observers have tended to view this process in a more or less teleological light (e.g. Fukuyama 1989), others have emphasized the underlying ideological concerns (e.g. Gills and Rocamora 1992). In the developing countries, the dependency on the IMF and the World Bank following the debt crisis thus opened the door for an 'export' of liberal democracy. During the 1980s, this process was obviously intended to expand the ideological sphere of influence of the USA and the West, and correspondingly to weaken Soviet influence in the developing countries. This influence had peaked throughout the 1960s and 1970s and was evident in the large number of socialist-inspired governments and opposition movements in the developing countries.

After the end of the Cold War, the spread of liberal democracy to all corners of the world has been both easier and more profound, and in the developing countries 'democracy' largely replaced 'development' to become the buzzword for the 1990s (Gills and Rocamora 1992). The result has been a historically unprecedented number of countries with formal democratic institutions. Yet in the developing countries, these are often low-intensity democracies (Gills and Rocamora 1992). In this sense, they are also elite democracies, embraced only by a leading portion of the population, and responsible more to the exigencies of an elite of international financial institutions and foreign governments than to their respective constituencies. While this low intensity interpretation of democracy has had particular salience in the context of the developing countries, it is beginning to be applied also to the more stable Western democracies. In other words, there seems to be a growing understanding (witnessed, for example, in recent protests against the IMF and the G8) of democracy as increasingly subsumed to a transnational capitalist class (Sklair 1995) and corporate agenda (Brecher and Costello 1994).

What follows from the above is a view of globalization as characterized, *inter alia*, by the spread of liberal democracy and free markets to almost every corner of the globe. This is an empirical fact. As noted earlier, however, the great significance of this development for the present study lies in the fact that people are increasingly conscious that this is the case. This perceived aspect of globalization is especially pertinent in regard to the discussion of transnational framing. The transnational framing process thus presupposes a degree of global consciousness of the consequences and nature of neoliberalism and elite democracy; on the other hand, this consciousness is also produced and constructed through the process.

Closely tied to the grievances experienced as a result of the proliferation of neoliberalism and elite democracy is the development of ideas of radical democracy. The injustice frames lying at the basis of transnational framing processes are often rooted in an interpretation of radical democracy as standing in opposition to neoliberalism and elite democracy. Put differently, notions of radical democracy often make up the content of the grievance interpretations constituting

a fundamental element of transnational frames. This also means that
there is a particularly close relationship between, on the one hand,
the issue of neoliberal injustice frames, and, on the other hand, the
question of democracy as a master frame for contemporary social
action that will be taken up below.

The democratic master frame

Even if the notion of radical democracy challenges the dominant
liberal view of democracy, it rests on a range of assumptions shared
with liberal democracy. The main point to be made here is that
the complex of democratic and human rights ideas that have taken
hold since the late 1980s on a more or less global scale provides a
master frame in transnational framing processes. At the same time,
however, these processes often draw on this general master frame
in a way that involves a struggle over the definition of democracy.
This is what we seek to capture by speaking of radical democracy
as a social critique standing in opposition to dominant liberal interpretations of democracy, as well as to the neoliberal development
model discussed earlier.

For the master frame concept to be useful in our context, we
need to elaborate somewhat on the original formulations and make
a distinction between latent master frames and action master frames.
A latent master frame is understood as a reservoir of ideas and interpretations providing social actors with a kind of ideational toolbox.
In the present context, the ideational complex of democracy and
human rights is considered to be the dominant dimension in the
latent master frame. An action master frame, in turn, is built on a
latent master frame but is elaborated more concretely by particular
social movements so as to be directly applicable in the construction
of specific movement frames. We will first take up the issue of the
latent master frame and then go on to discuss this in relation to
the concept of action master frames.

The proliferation of democratic and human rights ideas to almost
every corner of the globe cannot be considered in separation from
the end of the Cold War (Kriesberg 1997; Held et al. 1999). It is
important to note that the spread of democratic and human rights
ideas after the end of the Cold War did not come out of the blue.

Dividing the Cold War world into three sectors, the West, the Soviet bloc, and the developing countries, Shaw (2000: 134ff.) observes different trends in the struggle for democracy during the Cold War period. In the Soviet bloc, demands for democracy surfaced for example in the well-known cases of Hungary in 1956 and Czechoslovakia in 1968; but, as we know, these experiments with limited democracy were short-lived and suppressed by the Soviet Union. In the developing countries, the quest for democracy was mainly expressed through movements against Western colonialism coming to power in a number of countries. The majority of these new regimes, however, degenerated into oligarchic rule.

Yet protest informed by democratic ideas flourished also in the Western countries where liberal democratic ideas and institutions were well established. The demands for democracy in the Soviet bloc and the developing countries were limited to the basics of liberal democracy (popular rule and access to political decision-making). In contrast, the so-called new social movements that embodied the democratic movement in the West during the 1970s and 1980s challenged what they considered to be some of the limitations in Western democracies. In many ways, their social critique was formulated in radical democratic terms and concerned with an extension of democracy to forms of grassroots or direct democracy (Scott 1990: 27). Inherent in the new social movements' critique was also a protest against the Cold War system itself (Shaw 2000: 136). These challenges entailed a focus on civil society as a terrain of struggle (Cohen and Arato 1992) and as the foundation for a more people-centred approach to democracy.

The Cold War era was thus not without trends towards democracy. During the Cold War, though, demands for democracy and human rights were constrained by the bipolar rivalry that also extended to the developing countries. The end of the Cold War, in other words, may be considered a political opportunity in regard to social movements. The end of the Cold War, which involved significant changes in the nature of latent master frames available to (potential) social movements, can be seen in a broader time frame, along the lines of Gamson and Meyer's (1996) definition of the political opportunities concept discussed earlier in the chapter. From this angle, the end of the Cold War constitutes a conjuncture-time (Braudel 1980) change and a cultural and ideological shift affecting the opportunities for social movement action in a more profound manner than political change within the shorter term.

While it is reasonable to say that there is only one latent master frame today, it may have been plausible to speak of two competing latent master frames during the Cold War. These were largely defined by the ideological fault line characterizing the Cold War period, a situation reflected not least in the developing countries, where most protest movements derived their ideological foundation from one of these frames. This circumstance seriously limited the potential for building social protest within a genuinely democratic frame. Put differently, the bipolar rivalry implied an obstacle to the globalization of the latent master frame of democratic and human rights. In the developing countries, aspirations towards democracy were often viewed by Western powers through a Cold War logic as manifestations of communism (Shaw 2000: 135). The end of the Cold War to some extent loosened the straitjacket imposed by the bipolar rivalry on the global potential of democratic and human rights ideas as it eliminated, for example, the USA's rationale for supporting repressive regimes (Donnelly 1993: 133). The global character of what Shaw (2000: 167) refers to as the contemporary democratic revolution is therefore

> rooted in the extent to which … democracy and human rights have become universal values to which individuals and groups can appeal, if need be over and against national state institutions. During the Cold War, when the 'democratic' West tolerated authoritarian state entities in its ranks and encouraged anti-Communist repression worldwide, such universal norms were widely limited in practical significance. In the worldwide democratic revolution of our times, however, they have a new role. Oppressed groups widely appeal, not only to the founding documents of universal human rights, but to the international institutions of a Western-led world order as guarantors of those rights.

The primary consequence of the end of the Cold War has thus been the globalization of democratic and human rights ideas. This trend is apparent with regard to opposition movements as well as with regard to political regimes that now, almost without exception, profess to be democratic (Held 1995). What we witness today is in large part a contest over the definition of democracy (Alvarez et al.

1998). Political struggle no longer seems to be a struggle between two fundamentally opposed political complexes. Rather, it increasingly appears to be a struggle over the appropriation of democracy; hence our previous discussion of radical democracy as an opposition to dominant liberal notions of democracy coming from within the same latent master frame. Returning to our distinction between latent master frames and action master frames, we may suggest that radical democracy constitutes an action master frame derived from the latent master frame of democracy. In contrast to the latent master frame of democracy, the action master frame of radical democracy offers a number of concrete social critiques that make it more applicable in, for example, transnational framing processes.

Another area in which we may identify a distinction between latent and action master frames is the proliferation of transnational advocacy networks working on issues of human rights (e.g. Keck and Sikkink 1998; Risse and Sikkink 1999).[6] These transnational advocacy networks are made up of physically, socially and culturally distant actors addressing human rights violations all over the world in a more unconstrained way than would have been possible during the Cold War. They do this mainly by putting norm-violating states on the agenda and by empowering domestic opposition groups (Risse and Sikkink 1999: 5). Transnational advocacy networks, in other words, are examples of social actors that operationalize latent master frames into more specific action master frames.

The Internet: mediating everyday experiences

All human relations are based on communication. Any technology that alters the way we communicate therefore entails a social invention. This is a particularly salient feature of social movement activism. When we are concerned with networked and transnational forms of human interaction, the issue of information and communications technology is especially pertinent. The transnational framing process is highly dependent on the availability of means of communication as it is an essentially communicative process that takes place across considerable physical, social and cultural distance.

The Internet holds great potential for establishing a resonance between the everyday experiences of sender and recipient in the transnational framing process.[7] Through its ramifications for other social processes, the Internet has transformed the conditions and effects of social movement activities in a qualitative way. The approach taken here thus takes issue with the argument made by Hill and Hughes (1998: 43) that the Internet is used mainly as an extension of 'older, more common ... media', and instead concurs with definitions of the Internet as a social space (e.g. Poster 1997: 205; Harasim 1993).[8]

In Chapter 1, the proliferation of the Internet since the early 1990s was held to be a vital part of the globalization process. It would be wrong to elevate technology to a position where it is perceived to be the primary force of globalization; on the other hand, globalization would not be conceivable without innovations in communication and transportation (Rosenau 1997: 47; Talalay 2000: 208). In the absence of a degree of global consciousness, however, the Internet would only be used in a limited manner to cross physical, social and cultural boundaries. Global consciousness, in other words, is what moulds the Internet into a social construct embodying globalization. This is a dialectical process. Global consciousness is not only a precondition for the globalizing use of the Internet; it is also produced and constructed when social activists make use of the Internet in a way that involves communication across physical, social and cultural borders.

With reference to Freeman's (1979) argument earlier in the chapter, the relatively cheap access to the Internet may be considered in a resource mobilization perspective as a vital resource for social movement formation.[9] Yet the Internet is more than a resource and a tool. It is a social construct embedded in a wider social context shaping its use (Slevin 2000: 7). To pursue the role of the Internet in regard to transnational framing, it may be useful to register some of the main differences between the Internet and more traditional means of communication. Gitlin's (1980: 3) work on the relationship between the New Left and the media in the 1970s provides an interesting point of reference for a comparison along these lines:

In the late twentieth century, political movements feel called upon to rely on large scale communications in order to matter, to say who they are and what they intend to publics they want to sway; but in the process they become 'newsworthy' only by submitting to the implicit rules of newsmaking.... The processed image then tends to become 'the movement' for wider publics and institutions who have few alternative sources of information, or none at all, about it.

This rather negative view is informed by a notion of the media as being public and mediated (Diani 2001).[10] With the above quotation in mind, let us now consider in a little more detail exactly how the Internet differs from other forms of mediated communication and how it is put to use by social movements and activists. A central defining aspect of traditional mass media (especially television and newspapers) is the one-way character of communication. There is, in other words, a clear distinction between the producers and recipients of information. In this relationship, moreover, the recipient has no direct influence on what kind of information is received, how it is received, and when it is received. It is this situation that is referred to when Gitlin, in the latter part of the quotation, notes that audiences have few alternative sources outside the mass media to learn about social movements.

The Internet, argues Slevin (2000: 74), blurs this relationship, as Internet users may be both producers and recipients of information. Everyone with a computer and modem connection can distribute information accessible to people all over the globe with the same facilities at their disposal. This can be done with relative ease, at low cost and at high speed, and it leads to a situation where people and groups with a message are much less dependent on living up to mass-media standards of what is newsworthy and what is not. These latter requirements, argues Gitlin (1980), are exactly what distort and deform social movement messages. The potential for social movements to reach an audience in a more direct and undistorted fashion is thus increased with the availability of the Internet (Slevin 2000). A variant of this perspective is the difficulty of suppressing and censoring information distributed on the Internet, an aspect with relevance for social movements operating under authoritarian or semi-authoritarian conditions.

Compared to traditional mass media communication, the Internet significantly reduces the time lag between events and the reception of information about these events. It is therefore often stated that the Internet differs from other mediated forms of communication in that it allows for almost instantaneous communication. However, communication via telephone, for example, is also instantaneous. In fact, the major difference between the Internet and other forms of communication is that the Internet enables many-to-many (Kollock and Smith 1999: 3; Slevin 2000: 79) communications with the potential for a high degree of continuity and co-presence (Harasim 1993; Slevin 2000).

Excluding person-to-person communication, there are three ways of sending and receiving information via the Internet. The most unstructured and private form is email forwarding (Myers 1994). This takes place through a network of people and groups connected through weak ties. Consequently, an activist may start by sending a message to a handful of other social activists with whom he or she is more or less formally connected. These recipients in turn may forward the message to other groups and people who are not related to the original sender of the message. In principle, this process can go on indefinitely, exemplifying the argument that weak ties are in fact strong ties (Granovetter 1973). But the process still takes place in closed and semi-private circuits. The second type of Internet communication is semi-public in nature and takes place through listservs and news groups to which recipients subscribe. Listservs are devoted to a specific topic and may be moderated or unmoderated. In many cases, messages posted to listservs are archived and accessible, for example to researchers. A third type of public Internet communication is websites, where individuals and groups can post information on a variety of topics. Information posted on websites is public as it is directly accessible to everyone with a computer and modem connection. Websites often provide hyperlinks to other websites, thus creating information collages (Slevin 2000: 65) allowing for fast and easy navigation between sources of information.

Since framing is a highly extrovert process, communication is obviously vital. Accordingly, any invention in communications technology surpassing former means of communication should be expected to have consequences for framing processes.[11] In the case of transnational framing, the importance of communications technology is even more conspicuous considering the physical, social and cultural distance often involved. In general, we may say that the Internet should be expected to facilitate transnational framing processes due to the following features: the blurring of the producer–recipient dichotomy;

the potential of many-to-many communication; the relatively low cost of communication via the Internet; the relative ease with which people can use technically sophisticated equipment; the reduction of the time lag between sending and receiving information; the difficulty of suppressing/censoring information distributed on the Internet.

While these aspects of the Internet should be expected to facilitate transnational framing processes at all levels, a few points call for special attention. It was stressed earlier that successful frames resonate with the social mentalities and belief systems, and strike a chord in the everyday experiences, of the recipients in the framing process. These are problematic points in regard to transnational framing since a movement and the target of its framing efforts cannot be expected to share the same experiences or social and cultural backgrounds. It is argued, however, that this problem becomes less conspicuous with the advent of the Internet. The Internet enables direct communication between people in distant places in a way that facilitates the exchange of everyday experiences, thus creating improved conditions for the diffusion of ideas and understandings. These 'small' stories are the kind that rarely make it through the traditional mass media, concerned as they are mainly with 'large' issues. Recalling Tilly's (1978) concept of catnets, we may suggest that the Internet is making shared place less demanding as a precondition for social movement formation (Diani 2001), though by no means obliterating the importance of it.

Notes

1. For a discussion of the political opportunities concept in relation to the transnational level, see for example McCarthy 1997; Smith et al. 1997; della Porta and Kriesi 1999; Passy 1999; Maney 2002.

2. The argument here for the existence of a global consciousness does not entail (normatively or empirically) an argument for a movement towards a homogeneous world culture. In other words, there is no contradiction between the existence of a global consciousness and the contingency and plurality of national and transnational social phenomena.

3. See Keck and Sikkink 1998 and 2000 for an account of historical precursors to transnational activism.

4. Anderson's (1983) concept of imagined communities was used mainly in relation to questions of nationalism and nation building, but may have relevance also on the global or transnational level.

5. Scholars working within the world-system tradition (e.g. Wallerstein 1979) also emphasize capitalism as a driving force of globalization, even though they do not use the term 'globalization' explicitly. The world-system approach thus in many ways predates the more recent globalization debate.

6. Transnational advocacy networks should not be equated with informal transnational movement networks. In contrast to transnational advocacy networks, informal transnational movement networks are more politicized and often involved in a more fundamental social critique.

7. Here, and in the remainder of the book, the term 'Internet' is used to denote communication on the World Wide Web (for example via websites) as well as communication via email. In conjunction, these forms of communication are also referred to in the book as computer-mediated communication.

8. Making a distinction between the Internet and other communications media does not imply that the latter are seen as irrelevant for the arguments advanced here. In fact, it is becoming difficult to separate the Internet clearly from other media as these are increasingly present on the Internet. This is perhaps most evident in the growing number of newspapers available in an online version.

9. Many authors, however, have emphasized the unequal opportunities for access to the Internet between the rich countries and the developing world (e.g. Hamelink 1997; Choucri 2000).

10. In the article, Diani discusses media through the conceptual pairs public–private and direct–mediated.

11. While there have been some attempts at linking framing processes and media, these have focused on 'old' media such as television and newspapers (e.g. Gamson and Modigliani 1989; Gamson 1995).

3

Network Infrastructure

This chapter presents a largely internal view of the transnational Zapatista solidarity network. Chapter 4 will then provide a more externally oriented account. Here we take a closer look at the infrastructure of the network. The term 'infrastructure' may seem somewhat misplaced, considering that the network was defined in Chapter 1 as loose and informal rather than a consciously formed structure. In fact the network has an infrastructure in the weak sense that it is possible to discern centres and regular ties. The very use of the term 'network' in this book rests on this understanding. Thus, applied to the case of transnational Zapatista solidarity, the terms 'infrastructure' and 'network' presuppose more or less stable patterns of ties mainly involving the distribution and exchange of information.

The Network Information Circuit

Networks are relations among actors. Whether or not actors in a network share the same physical location, the relations among them are primarily circuits for the exchange of information. Information, in other words, is the 'glue' holding networks together. This is also the case with the transnational Zapatista solidarity network. Actors become tied to the network because they need and value the information made available through the circuits of it, and they stay connected to it because they become dependent on its information flows for their respective activities. Emphasis in the section is laid on computer-mediated forms of information circulation (i.e. the Internet), even though other mediated forms of communication such as telephone and fax obviously also play a role. It will be demonstrated how the informational infrastructure has changed since the EZLN uprising in 1994. This will bring to the fore one of the basic arguments of the book: that the transnational Zapatista solidarity network reflects a growing imbrication of local, national and transnational levels of interaction rather than their increasing disconnection. It will be demonstrated how the informational infrastructure of the network rests on an intimate and inseparable relationship between actors at the local and national levels in Chiapas and Mexico, and actors at the transnational level.

Organizations and groups

We begin at the local and national levels by considering some of the Mexican groups and organizations that feed information into the circuits of the Zapatista solidarity network. Most notable among these is probably the Zapatista Front of National Liberation (Frente Zapatista de Liberación Nacional, or FZLN). The organization was formed in 1996 following the 1995 National Consultation for Peace and Democracy (Consulta Nacional por la Paz y la Democracia), in which the EZLN (1995b) asked the Mexican population to express its views on the future direction of the EZLN. The consultation was subsequently extended to a number of other countries and included a consultation aimed specifically at young people. The consultation received 1.3 million votes, and indicated clearly that the voters opted for the creation of a non-military organization related to the EZLN (EZLN 1995e). This eventually resulted in the formation of the FZLN, which defines itself as 'a space in which the Zapatistas of civil society can meet the Zapatistas of the EZLN' (FZLN 2001a).[1] The emphasis of its work is in the search for civil-society-based initiatives towards peaceful and democratic social change in Mexico. One important function in regard to the Zapatista solidarity network is the distribution of daily email messages, primarily containing excerpts from Mexican newspapers relevant to Chiapas and the

EZLN, as well as links to the full story. The FZLN also distributes action alert messages calling for national and transnational solidarity activities when events in Chiapas and Mexico demand it. Moreover, the organization maintains pages in English, French and Portuguese on its website and generally pays close attention to EZLN-related activities. This work has been reflected in a range of publications on 'Zapatismo in the world' (*zapatismo en el mundo*), notably throughout 1998 and 1999.[2]

Other Mexican organizations providing vital information for the circuits of the network include Enlace Civil, CIEPAC, and Melel Xojobal, all of which are located in San Cristóbal de las Casas, Chiapas. Enlace Civil is an organization that seeks to provide a connection between the indigenous communities of Chiapas and the world around them. It also provides an email-mediated information list, with over two hundred subscribers in more than forty countries (Enlace Civil 2001). The messages distributed on the Enlace Civil list are mainly denouncements of human rights violations perpetrated against the indigenous communities of Chiapas. In this way, Enlace Civil creates a direct link between the indigenous communities and network activists outside Mexico (see Chapter 8 for further discussion).

CIEPAC (Centro de Investigaciones Económicas y Políticas de Acción Comunitaria/Centre for Economic and Political Investigations of Community Action), founded in 1998, is a centre for analysis of the political situation in Chiapas; it maintains a more neutral position in relation to the EZLN than, for example, the FZLN and Enlace Civil (Castro 2001).[3] Its main contribution to the Zapatista solidarity network is the distribution of a weekly bulletin, *Chiapas al Día*, which is published in Spanish and English and goes out to recipients in more than forty countries. According to information on its website, CIEPAC maintains relationships with a number of non-Mexican organizations, including Global Exchange and the Mexico Solidarity Network (CIEPAC 2001).

Melel Xojobal is an organization founded by Dominican monks in 1997. Its aim is to provide the indigenous communities of Chiapas (not only those related to the EZLN) with educational and informational resources allowing them to further communication among themselves as well as with their external environment. With regard to the Zapatista solidarity network, this takes the form of distribution of a daily news summary based on publications in local and national newspapers and magazines. This is distributed via email to recipients outside Mexico but also, by way of personal delivery, to the indigenous communities of Chiapas – where only few indigenous people have access to computers and modems. In addition, Melel Xojobal produces a fortnightly publication, targeted mainly at the indigenous communities (Jiménez 2001; Melel Xojobal 2001).

As demonstrated by the above examples, information about the situation in Chiapas and Mexico is provided mainly by organizations with a physical presence in these areas. We now turn our attention to some of the major non-Mexican organizations serving as information providers in the transnational Zapatista solidarity network. These organizations have different ways of obtaining information. In some cases, they will send people to work as observers or as peace camp volunteers in Chiapas, and these will in turn report back to their home organizations. In other cases, non-Mexican organizations rely on Mexican organizations and newspapers for information (see above). Non-Mexican organizations will typically use the information to produce newsletters and updates, mainly distributed via email.

Global Exchange, a San Francisco-based organization founded in 1988, working on issues of human rights and democracy around the globe, mainly bases its Chiapas and Mexico activities on the physical presence of volunteers in the area. According to Ted Lewis (2000), director of the Global Exchange Mexico programme until 2002, the organization has had a presence in San Cristóbal de las Casas since 1995 in the form of an office with permanent staff. In addition to the permanent staff, Global Exchange sends a number of short-term volunteers to stay as observers in the civilian peace camps in the indigenous communities of Chiapas.[4] This volunteer work is channelled through the Chiapas office but takes place in close cooperation with the Fray Bartolomé de las Casas Human Rights Centre (Centro de Derechos Humanos Fray Bartolomé de Las Casas) in San Cristóbal de las Casas. These people on the ground, explains Ted Lewis (2000), are the main source of information for Global Exchange.[5] The information gathered is distributed in a variety of ways. The most important outlet for the Global Exchange Mexico programme is the organization website and email list of some 2,500 recipients. These recipients, in turn, will forward the messages to other people not on the list, thereby reaching an even larger audience and one that lies outside the immediate Zapatista solidarity network (Lewis 2000).

A range of other non-Mexican organizations also distribute newsletters on events in Chiapas and Mexico via email and through their websites. Among these are the Mexico Solidarity Network and SIPAZ (Servicio Internacional para la Paz/International Service for Peace). The Mexico Solidarity Network comprises some 85 organizations with central offices in Chicago and Washington. Like Global Exchange, the mandate of the Mexico Solidarity Network is broader than Chiapas and the EZLN, though the uprising inspired much of its early work – it was created in 1998 as a response to the Acteal massacre in Chiapas in December 1997.[6] The Mexico Solidarity Network is also involved in labour issues, human rights questions and fair trade in Mexico (Hansen 2000). It produces a weekly newsletter distributed via email and through its website.

SIPAZ, based in Santa Cruz, California, is a coalition of North American, Latin American and European organizations. It was formed in 1995 in direct response to the situation in Chiapas. With its religious perspective, SIPAZ maintains a more neutral approach to the conflict in Chiapas, and consequently does not directly support the EZLN. It attempts instead to contribute to a peaceful solution to the conflict in Chiapas by working with all parties. The organization's volunteers in Chiapas prepare updates on the peace process in Chiapas (SIPAZ 2001a), and produce a quarterly report, as well as action alerts when events require transnational action. This information is mainly disseminated via email and website.

Returning to the work of Global Exchange, Ted Lewis (2000) notes that the information distributed by *Global Exchange* will sometimes juxtapose information from mainstream media, such as the *New York Times*, with that provided by people on the ground in Chiapas or by Mexican human rights organizations with which they maintain close contacts (e.g. Centro de Derechos Humanos Miguel Agustín Pro/Miguel Agustín Pro Human Rights Centre). Thus the transnational Zapatista solidarity network as a circuit of information rests on the idea that the information obtained through the network is more reliable and has a greater truth content than that provided by mainstream media – often considered to be dependent on certain financial or political interests. This vision is reflected in the creation of, for example, Indymedia–Chiapas (Centro de Medios Independientes de Chiapas). Indymedia–Chiapas is a node in the global network of Independent Media Centers that have sprung up since the Seattle protests against the WTO in November 1999. During and after the protests, the original Independent Media Center was widely recognized for its coverage of the events in Seattle, which was considered both to be more accurate than that provided by mainstream media, and to take up issues they overlooked. On its website, Indymedia–Chiapas (2001), located in San Cristóbal de las Casas, presents the following statement of purpose:

> With its commitment to freedom of expression, Indymedia–Chiapas offers the opportunity to present visions and perspectives different from those found in the mainstream media. Our goal is to break the monopoly of the corporate-controlled press, and guarantee a space for those voices not heard in the mainstream media.

In the words of a representative of Indymedia–Chiapas (2001), the centre thus tries to

> open a space where the indigenous people, social and civil groups, solidarity groups, may have access to publish and present information on their struggle, and on how they are affected by the conflict created by the government and the paramilitaries. In the sense that we do not censor information, and open doors to Zapatista support bases, as well as many other social organizations, in order to create autonomous media, directed and maintained by the people themselves, we have similar objectives to the Zapatistas.

The aim of Indymedia–Chiapas is therefore to provide a link between the local level (Chiapas) and the national and transnational levels. This demonstrates, again, how a watertight distinction between different spatial levels is untenable in regard to the transnational Zapatista solidarity network. The ability to cross these spatial boundaries is to a large extent a product of the development of new information technologies such as the Internet. As discussed in Chapter 2, one of the main advantages of the Internet in regard to transnational activism lies in the blurring of the producer–recipient dichotomy present in most traditional forms of mass media communication.

The Internet, in other words, allows for more unmediated communication between those who require information about certain events and those who are directly involved in, or at least close to, them. As mentioned above, information of this type is what has the highest status and value within the circuits of the Zapatista solidarity network. It is access to this type of information, and the ambition to facilitate the distribution of it, that induces people and organizations to engage in networked forms of interaction with other individuals and organizations.

While Indymedia–Chiapas was formed specifically to establish an independent and direct source of information about Chiapas and the EZLN, other organizations that existed prior to the uprising have included Chiapas and the EZLN in their work. One organization dating back to before January 1994 that quickly started taking up related issues is *ZNet/Zmagazine*, based in Woods Hole, Massachusetts. In the words of one of the its volunteers (Podur 2000),

> The organization was founded to publish alternative perspectives that were not going to get into the mainstream, perspectives that support activist efforts against racism, sexism, classism, imperialism.... It was immediately apparent that the struggle of the Zapatistas was the kind of thing that is important to Z. It was a movement on the part of the oppressed, it was a movement against colonization, expropriation, economic exploitation, against sexism and racism, and against US imperialism, all things Z is very concerned with and had been from the beginning.

The willingness and motivation of already existing organizations to serve as distributors of information on Chiapas and the EZLN was especially important in the first months following the uprising, when the Zapatista solidarity network lacked an informational infrastructure of its own. Referring back to the theoretical discussions in Chapter 2, we may speak of these organizations and groups as mobilizing structures for the formation of the network.

Email, websites and listservs

In addition to formal organizations and groups, individuals also played a prominent part in the early distribution of information on the EZLN and Chiapas. Molly Molloy (2000), a librarian at New

Mexico State University, became involved in these efforts at a very early stage:

> I can't even remember why I started getting the information in the first place, it must have come through some list of issues related to Mexico, and someone in early January 1994 began posting messages saying that there was an uprising in Chiapas, these folks were in San Cristobal and somehow they had access to email which was kind of rare in Mexico at the time, but there were still lots of researchers and foreigners in San Cristobal, so this email started circulating out there on the web and different people began posting different things, and so what I did, somehow I would forward them ... and somehow other people knew about that I was circulating this mail, so they would send me a message, can I get on your list, and I just made an email list inside my email account.

The account by Molloy shows, again, the importance of people on the ground in Chiapas. Molloy also recounts how the messages she distributed were destined, *inter alia*, for the Mexican Rural Development discussion group (MRD) under the Applied Anthropology Computer Network operated from Oakland, California.[7] Gerardo Otero, a social scientist involved in the discussion group, explains how it has been working since January 1992, partly inspired by the initiative of then Mexican president Carlos Salinas de Gortari (1988–94) to modify Article 27 of the Mexican Constitution in late 1991 and early 1992 (Otero 2001).[8] The first messages relating to Chiapas and the EZLN distributed to the discussion group appeared on 4 January 1994, and were soon a steady flow. James Dow, an anthropologist involved in the discussion group at the time of the uprising, recalls how the first messages came from graduate students in San Cristóbal de las Casas (Dow 2001). The majority of the messages posted to the list were articles and excerpts from newspapers, television and news agencies, but they were also accounts by people in the discussion group with personal and professional experiences in Chiapas.

The importance of such personal accounts is reflected in the interview with Molloy, who also notes how Chiapas, since at least the 1930s, has been home to large numbers of foreigners, especially artists and scientists. During the 1930s, Mexico under Lázaro Cárdenas had become a safe haven for people fleeing the European conflicts in Spain and Germany (Bangerter 2001). As is evident in the case of the

Mexican Rural Development discussion group, it was to an important extent people with personal or professional experiences in Chiapas who were instrumental in providing a nascent infrastructure for the transnational Zapatista solidarity network. The discussion group was mainly active during the first years of the uprising. Subsequently, the Zapatista solidarity network developed a significant infrastructure of its own in the form of information distributors focused exclusively or mainly on the EZLN and Chiapas (Dow 2001).

The Mexican Rural Development discussion group was obviously not the only source of information on Chiapas and the EZLN in the first months of the uprising. Information was spread on countless listservs and news conferences in operation at the time, including through lists dealing with opposition to NAFTA (Cleaver 1994), and through the PeaceNet news conference reg.mexico. The latter is interesting because of its relation to one of the world's first computer-mediated networks of civil society actors, the Institute for Global Communications (IGC), formed in the late 1980s. The mission of the IGC (2001), as stated on its website, is to 'advance the work of progressive organizations and individuals for peace, justice, economic opportunity, human rights, democracy, and environmental sustainability through strategic use of online technologies'. In 1990, the IGC, together with a number of other computer-mediated networks, formed the Association for Progressive Communications in order to 'co-ordinate the operation and development of this emergent global network of networks' (Association for Progressive Communications 2001).

The World Wide Web was not fully developed at the time of the uprising, and dissemination of information took place mainly through email and the forwarding of email. Email-based information distribution may take place in a private circuit (among acquaintances) or through email lists, which are semi-public in nature. Email lists have subscribers and it is therefore relatively easy to trace the spread of emails to this immediate audience. Yet from the moment an email is sent to a list of subscribers, it assumes a life of its own, one which is almost impossible to trace. The forwarding of emails often takes place through weak ties (Granovetter 1973), that is, informal and indirect ties. Just as in the case of physical networks where information may end up with persons who are socially and physically distant, emails spread through the forwarding mechanism will end up in places far from the original sender. In the case of electronic networks, this distant place may in fact be the neighbour of the original sender. In electronic networks, distance is thus measured not only in physical terms but also in social terms. Kerry Appel (2000), a Denver-based importer of coffee from the Zapatista co-operative Mut Vitz, describes how computer-mediated information takes on a life of its own beyond the immediate Zapatista network through the process of forwarding and posting to different lists:

> I have started my own human rights campaign, so here is one guy in Denver who has started a human rights campaign as a protest against this campaign of violence against the co-operative Mut Vitz, so I wrote this information and put in on the Chiapas list [Chiapas-L], and I sent it to a couple of other places as well.… We have some allies in Germany, an anarchist solidarity group, and they began distributing Mut Vitz coffee in Germany, Switzerland, Italy, Spain, France, and they translated it into German … so this has all started from writing one thing and putting it on one list, and then traveling around, now it is in four languages. I have seen some writings that I had written in 1996, I have found them on Eastern European websites, Norwegian websites and Sufi websites, it is the whole life of its own the Internet has, it strikes a chord with some groups somewhere, resonates some-how with something they are doing.

Yet, in the case of the EZLN, does this mean that anyone who receives messages concerning Chiapas and the EZLN is part of the transnational Zapatista solidarity network? This obviously depends on what people do with the information. If they delete it, no con-nection to the network is made. If, on the other hand, they decide to forward the message or to participate in a demonstration called for in the email message, they become nodes in the network, albeit only temporarily. However, it is also possible that the received email may inspire a more direct and stable participation in the transnational Zapatista solidarity network. A recipient may, for example, decide to join a listserv dedicated to the EZLN and Mexico or get involved in local organizing efforts on part of the EZLN and Chiapas. Email forwarding in electronic circuits, and indirect personal ties in physi-cal settings, may thus have the effect of drawing new actors into the network. Put differently, the larger the number of people and organizations becoming involved in the network, the larger its surface of contact with individuals and organizations outside the immediate network, and the better the possibilities for recruiting new activists to the network. In computer-mediated circuits of information, the potential for reaching new audiences is almost unlimited but it is also very easy for an individual to disconnect from the network if she or he has only an electronically mediated position in the network. In other words, the Zapatista solidarity network is not a stable structure but is in constant flux, especially when it comes to its computer-mediated form.

As mentioned above, email-based information distribution may take place in a private circuit or through semi-public email lists. In regard to Chiapas and the EZLN, the Chiapas95 listserv created in late 1994 has played an especially important role.[9] Today, Chiapas95 is a series of listservs with a range of services to subscribers (for example, reduced flows of messages; messages in either English or Spanish). Chiapas95 is strictly concerned with the passing on of information, and the messages posted are mainly culled from other listservs or news conferences on the Internet or contain articles from magazines and journals. In discussing the role of email forwarding, Harry Cleaver (2000b), an economist at the University of Texas at Austin and a moving spirit in the creation of Chiapas95, notes that a large number of subscribers also function as gateways who forward messages on to other lists and to personal acquaintances. In contrast, the other major extant listserv on Chiapas and the EZLN, Chiapas-L, is also a discussion list where subscribers can engage in debates about issues relating to Chiapas, Mexico and the EZLN.[10] Today the Chiapas95 listserv is run by a collective of moderators scattered around the globe (Chiapas95 2001); according to Harry Cleaver (2000), it has about 750 subscribers, a number that has remained fairly constant over the years.

The World Wide Web was in an early phase of development when the EZLN launched its uprising, but it was soon playing an important role in the Zapatista network informational infrastructure. One of the first attempts to make use of the Web-distributed information was the Ya Basta! website. In March 1994, Justin Paulson, then a student at the University of Pennsylvania, decided to establish the Ya Basta! website having experienced difficulties obtaining reliable information about the EZLN in the first months following the uprising (Paulson 2001). In an interview conducted by de la Guardia (1999) for the Mexican journal *Comunicación Educativa*, Paulson explains the objective of the Ya Basta! website in the following manner:

> I decided to make available to the Web any information that I would find, in the form of an archive, and in a way that would present Zapatismo as it is, without distorting its nature and without appropriating it for the use of some organization. By the end of 1994 the number of visits to the website started growing rapidly. The objective of the website is to promote Zapatismo and distribute reliable information about Chiapas and the EZLN, most importantly through an extensive archive of communiqués and documents written by the EZLN itself. News is only published if it is verified or comes from reliable sources.

Paulson (2001) recalls the early phases in the creation of the website and the special role played by the Mexican daily *La Jornada* in this regard:

> As it turned out, it became the earliest (as far as I know) use of the web in support of an insurgency anywhere in the world.... It started slowly, but in November of 1994, I was asked by *La Jornada* to help them develop a website (at the time, no Mexican newspapers were online), and in return I would not only have access to their paper before it even hit the newsstands in Mexico (I had to get up early each morning to set it up and put it online), but I also had permission to reprint news articles and graphics. Since *La Jornada* was also the first place EZLN communiqués were printed, this vastly increased the amount of information I had at my fingertips, and I was able to much more quickly and thoroughly add news and communiqués to the webpage as soon as they became available. This became especially important when the government offensive began in February 1995; at the time, the Mexican government had no significant presence on the Internet, and the Ya Basta site contributed, along with several other websites, email lists, etc., to successfully counter the misinformation being spread by the Mexican government. The offensive ended unsuccessfully a short time later, and although I question to what extent this was due to Internet activities, I'm sure they played some role.

As evidenced by the quotation above, *La Jornada* has played an especially important role as a distributor of EZLN communiqués and documents. In a transnational perspective, this role has obviously been most salient after *La Jornada* went online in early 1995. Already on 2 January 1994, *La Jornada* was running extensive reports on events in Chiapas; it also published the Declaration of the Lacandon Forest (EZLN 1994b), the first public statement by the EZLN. At the time of writing, the Ya Basta! website maintains a central position in the transnational Zapatista solidarity network and is frequently mentioned by activists when asked about their main sources of information about the EZLN and Chiapas.

The discussion so far has made it clear that the informational infrastructure of the transnational Zapatista solidarity network is mediated by solidarity activists around the world. Put differently, the EZLN itself does not play a direct role in this infrastructure (see Chapter 8). There is, however, one notable exception. In advance of the EZLN March for Indigenous Dignity (Marcha por la Dignidad Indígena) to Mexico City in February/March 2001, a new Internet-based communication medium was founded.[11] The Zapatista Information Center (Centro de Información Zapatista, or CIZ) was not run by the EZLN itself, but it provided a more direct outlet for EZLN messages, and came close to being an actual EZLN presence on the Internet. The EZLN (2001a) announced the initiative on 3 January 2001, with the following remarks regarding to its use and objectives:

> Through the Zapatista Information Center, national and international civil society can inform themselves of the initiatives of the EZLN.... Also, one may be informed about aspects related to the logistics of the mobilization: possible accommodation ... possible transportation ... etcetera. Only through the Zapatista Information Center will the EZLN receive the national and international correspondence from the various persons and organizations that want to get in contact with the delegation that is going to the Federal District [Mexico City].... Through the Zapatista Information Center, the EZLN will get to know about the different initiatives that civil society, in Mexico and the world, is realizing in order to ... accompany the Zapatista delegation to D.F. [Distrito Federal; i.e. Mexico City], whether in the form of physical presence, or through public acts in their localities. The Zapatista Information Center will NOT be a press office of the EZLN, it will only be a bridge for us to communicate with national and international civil society.

It should be stressed that the EZLN's use of the centre was mainly connected to the march. Today, the centre serves as an archive of documents and information with regard to the march and the San Andrés Accords. As indicated by the quotation, the main difference between the Zapatista Information Center and other EZLN- and Chiapas-related websites lies in its role as a gatherer of information on activities connected to the March for Indigenous Dignity, and as an outlet for practical information to interested individuals and organizations. The website thus has a very extensive archive of messages of solidarity and support sent to the EZLN from people and organizations all over the world (Zapatista Information Center 2001a). The most conspicuous feature of the website in regard to the discussion of direct EZLN presence on the Internet, however, is the list of frequently asked questions responded to by Subcomandante Marcos (Zapatista Information Center 2001b). This is the only example to date of direct EZLN correspondence through the Internet.

Definition and illustration of the network infrastructure

The above discussion demonstrates that the network argument in relation to transnational Zapatista solidarity primarily takes its point of departure in the computer-mediated information circuits linking solidarity activists together. It should be stressed, however, that these connections are often more indirect than direct. Figure 3.1 illustrates three ways of conceptualizing networks using the direct–indirect distinction (inspired by Diani 1992: 117).

In the clique network, all actors are connected directly through intense and reciprocal ties (e.g. Burt 1978; Diani 1992); in the circle network, each actor is connected to only two other actors; in the star network, all actors except one are connected to only one other actor (the centre of the network). The circle and star types of network build mainly on indirect ties, while the clique network is based only on direct ties. Indirect ties are present when, for example, there is a direct tie between actors A and B and between actors B and C. Here, we may speak of an indirect tie between actors A and C, who are connected via actor B (Wellman and Berkowitz 1988: 42). This is the case, for example, in the circle network. As observed by Granovetter (1973), indirect ties of this kind are not necessarily weak ties. On the contrary, weak ties are strong ties in the sense that they connect and traverse a large portion of a given social field. Another

Figure 3.1 Network types

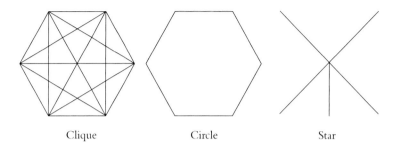

Clique   Circle   Star

variant of an indirect tie is when two actors access and act on the same source of information and resources without having direct ties. This is the case, for example, in the star network. As is shown below, the transnational Zapatista solidarity network infrastructure mainly has elements of the clique and star network types.

We have identified above a number of different levels in the information circuit of the transnational Zapatista solidarity network. At the ground level, we have the range of Mexico- and Chiapas-based organizations. The majority are Mexican, although non-Mexican organizations, such as Global Exchange, also have a presence. These form the second level in the Zapatista solidarity network information circuit, the first level being the indigenous communities of Chiapas that provide these organizations with first-hand information on what is going on in the area.[12] The second-level organizations thus function mainly as information gatherers and condensers. Those working in the organizations are often well-educated and experienced people who possess the necessary social tools to help overcome some of the cultural and language barriers between the indigenous communities and non-indigenous publics within and outside Mexico.

The information processed by the second-level organizations is often passed on to actors beyond the borders of Chiapas and Mexico. This, as we have seen, sometimes involves translation into other languages. In some cases, the work is carried out by Mexicans but translation is also performed by bilingual non-Mexicans who do not necessarily have a physical presence in Chiapas and Mexico.

The information distributed then reaches what we may refer to as third-level organizations or nodes in the information circuit. These are primarily some of the larger non-Mexican organizations in the Zapatista solidarity network, such as the Mexico Solidarity Network, Global Exchange and SIPAZ. As indicated, these organizations have centrality because they produce newsletters and bulletins that are widely distributed within the network and beyond. However, these communications are written primarily on the basis of information received from second-level organizations, but also to some extent reflect media such as *La Jornada*. Another type of third-level information hub is websites and listservs such as Ya Basta!, Chiapas95, and Chiapas-L. The listservs Chiapas95 and Chiapas-L also receive information from the second-level organizations, as well as from papers and magazines, but this is mostly passed on to the list in its raw form. The second and third levels in the information circuit of the network may also be perceived as its core. Core actors, then, are those who have regular ties with a large number of other network actors. They devote a significant part of their time and resources to EZLN and Chiapas issues, and they have centrality as information hubs or brokers (Caniglia 2002: 159) within the network. Core actors are typically connected in a manner similar to that of the clique network.

Recipients of information from second- and third-level information providers constitute what we may refer to as the fourth level in the computer-mediated information circuit. These actors may be said to belong to the periphery of the transnational Zapatista solidarity network. Periphery actors, then, are those who have regular ties to a small number of core actors, devote a significant part of their time and resources to these issues, but are dependent on other actors for information. We therefore often find in the periphery smaller groups and organizations with fewer resources and individuals. Periphery actors are typically organized in a manner similar to the star network, as they often receive information from only a few core actors. That is, such actors have fewer ties to other actors than do, for example, core actors, and may rely on a single core actor for much of their information input.

Finally, it is also possible to speak of a fifth level, constituted by actors who belong to the transitory level of the information circuit.

Figure 3.2 The informational infrastructure of the network

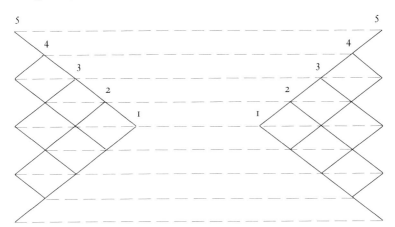

Transitory actors are those who have irregular and ad hoc ties to periphery or core actors in the network, devote little time to the issue of Chiapas and the EZLN, and are dependent on other actors for information. These include politicians and representatives of official bodies. At the transitory level, we thus find individuals and organizations that devote only a small portion of their time, on a temporary basis, to the primary issues of the transnational Zapatista solidarity network. This points to a considerable degree of overlap between the Zapatista solidarity network and other informal transnational movement networks. Organizations and individuals may consequently participate in several networks at the same time. When fifth-level transitory actors connect to the Zapatista solidarity network they do so in a manner resembling the star network, relying mainly on one source of information.

The distinctions between between the five levels is illustrated in figure 3.2. For reasons of clarity, the figure is highly stylized and limited in the number of nodes. The figure gives a visual representation of how information travels within the primarily computer-mediated information circuit. At the third level, the middle node receives information from two second-level nodes. This, in turn, implies that both outer nodes at the third level share information with the middle node. This is an illustration of the fact that in the empirical transnational Zapatista solidarity network, nodes in the network often receive their information from more than one other node, but also, at the same time, rely on some of the same sources of information. The dotted lines are intended to show that information does not necessarily travel in a step-by-step manner from first- to second-level actors, and so on, but may in some cases divert levels going directly, for example, from second-level to fourth-level actors in the information circuit. Moreover, the dotted lines between the two halves of the figure are intended to illustrate that actors at the same level may also exchange information.

The stylized illustration of the informational infrastructure in Figure 3.2 clearly resembles the star network. Put differently, the transnational Zapatista solidarity network is composed of a number of sub-networks of the star type that all revolve around one or more information hubs. What characterizes the star network, as opposed to, say, the clique network, is the fact that not all nodes are directly related. In some cases, nodes in the network may be connected to only one other network actor. On the other hand, the majority of actors are indirectly related because they rely on the same sources of information.

Face-to-Face Encounters

We have up to now focused almost exclusively on the infrastructure of the transnational Zapatista solidarity network as a computer-mediated information circuit. This circuit is at the same time, of course, intimately connected to concrete physical actors and events on the ground. That is, emphasis on the computer-mediated aspects of the network should not lead us to overlook the fact that the nodes that make it up have very real material relations.

The first major phase of transnational activity in regard to the EZLN obviously happened in the wake of the uprising – that is, in the first months of 1994. The activities in this period took place to a large degree through the incipient computer-mediated circuits of information. On the other hand, these information circuits were widely used to disseminate calls for physical action. As early as 8 and 10 January 1994 there were reports of protests in front of Mexican consulates in Los Angeles and Sacramento of between 100 and 200 people (Wilkinson and Darling 1994).[13] As indicated, this incipient physical manifestation of the network was to a large extent facilitated through email distribution of messages onto already existing lists, but also through interpersonal ties in the local setting of the activists. These physical encounters also brought together people who had never met before. This often led to the exchange of email addresses and suggestions about how to obtain more information about events in Chiapas at a time when the accessibility of information was much more limited than today.

Thus, the relationship between the computer-mediated information circuit and the physical aspect of the network is reciprocal. Computer-mediated information may facilitate and convene physical encounters (Slevin 2000: 79). These, in turn, may result in new awareness, knowledge and inspiration, perhaps leading to the establishment of new electronic relationships once the physical meeting is over. The large number of demonstrations and protests in the first years of the EZLN uprising and the rising number of people travelling to Chiapas thus kept bringing new nodes into the transnational Zapatista solidarity network through a combination of electronic and physical encounters. Since 1994 there has, moreover, been a wide range of other occasions where people have met physically in Chiapas or elsewhere through participation in peace-camp work, delegations, caravans, and specific projects in Chiapas. These initiatives have provided ample opportunity for the establishment of interpersonal and inter-organizational contacts.

The early protests, mentioned above, as well as other local activities, have mostly been based in local networks. In the incipient period (1994–95) of the network, these were already existing networks of activists. Today, specialized local networks of activists are not un-common, especially in the larger cities where there is a wider range of groups and organizations. These constitute a kind of sub-network within the larger network and provide a prominent example of the physical aspects of the transnational Zapatista solidarity network. The Chiapas Coalition in Denver, started in 1995, is such a network of a number of local groups that have an interest in the EZLN and

Chiapas. In the words of one of its prime activists, Kerry Appel (2000), the Chiapas Coalition, however, is not a formal organization:

> [W]e started it as a horizontally organized coalition of people who are mostly involved in other organizations ... and we come together occasionally to have an assembly as they do in the communities in Chiapas and then decide by consensus ... what is the situation, what is the need, and how can we best address that need at the time, so we come up with this plan and the people from the different organizations help develop that plan and then we all have our own separate mailing lists and memberships of these other groups, so there isn't any formal rules or charter ... we don't have any newsletters or other ways of formally formulating our policy ... everybody is autonomous and have their own main focus and get together occasionally and depending on the people and the needs at the time try to make a policy or action.

On the national level in the USA, the Mexico Solidarity Network (MSN) is another example of a network within the network. The MSN has held physical conferences on two occasions, including its founding conference in April 1998. Europe has seen a greater number of actual meetings between network activists and groups than has the USA, where the Mexico Solidarity Network is the only nationwide attempt at establishing a formalized relationship between transnational Zapatista solidarity network groups and organizations. The European meetings are not a formalized institution, although meetings have taken place with a certain degree of regularity, especially in the period 1995–97.[14]

Over the years, there have also been a number of formalized gatherings in Chiapas called by the EZLN. The first event that deserves mention was the National Democratic Convention (Convención Nacional Democrática, or CND) convened by the EZLN in its Second Declaration of the Lacandon Forest (EZLN 1994e). The meeting, which took place in August 1994, drew about 6,000 people from a large number and variety of organizations. The great majority of participants were Mexican, but a fair number of non-Mexicans were also present (Stephen 1995). One visible outcome of the meeting was the formation of the US-based National Commission for Democracy in Mexico (Callahan 2000). During the years immediately after the EZLN uprising this organization played a central role as distributor of information, especially in the USA.[15] In later years, however, it has come to play a less conspicuous role in the Zapatista solidarity network.

The idea of convening people from Mexico and the rest of the world in Chiapas, the heartland of the EZLN uprising, was also realized in two encounters during 1996. The first was the Continental American Encounter for Humanity and against Neoliberalism (Encuentro Continental Americano por la Humanidad y contra el Neoliberalismo). The encounter took place in Chiapas in April 1996 and drew about 300 participants from all over the American continent to discuss the effects of the neoliberal development model and to begin a debate about alternatives. This was in many ways a preparatory meeting for the more ambitious First Intercontinental Encounter for Humanity and against Neoliberalism (Primer Encuentro Intercontinental por la Humanidad y Contra el Neoliberalismo) convened by the EZLN in its First Declaration of La Realidad (EZLN 1996b). The meeting attracted more than 3,000 people from all over the world to the Lacandon Forest. During the week-long stay in Chiapas, new personal and organizational ties were established that would later lead to an exchange of information and experience via the computer-mediated information circuit. Of course, the large turnout would hardly have been possible without the use of the Internet (Cleaver 1998a).

Notes

1. The formation of the FZLN was announced by the EZLN in the Fourth Declaration of the Lacandon Forest (EZLN 1996a). So far, the EZLN has published five declarations 'of the Lacandon Forest' and two declarations 'of La Realidad.' The EZLN has mainly used the declarations to present major new initiatives and political standpoints.
2. See, for example, FZLN 1998, 1999.
3. The neutral approach taken by CIEPAC and other organizations in Mexico and Chiapas may reflect a concern with accessibility of funds or be the result of security concerns.
4. Ted Lewis (2000) is keen to stress that Global Exchange does not support the EZLN directly, but that its mandate extends to monitoring the general human rights situation in Chiapas. Moreover, Global Exchange is also involved in human rights work in a number of other Mexican states with large indigenous populations, mainly Oaxaca and Guerrero.
5. At the time of the interview (December 2000), Global Exchange had a

permanent staff of six people in Mexico. Of these, three were located in San Cristóbal de las Casas, Chiapas (Lewis 2000).

6. The Acteal massacre, in which forty-five indigenous men, women and children belonging to the independent organization Las Abejas (The Bees) were murdered, was perpetrated by a paramilitary group believed to have close ties with local financial and political elites. Documents published in the Mexican magazine *Proceso* (Marín 1998) later revealed that the creation of paramilitary groups may have been part of the Mexican army's counterinsurgency strategy and an attempt to establish a basis for 'plausible deniability' when it comes to placing the responsibility for violence against the indigenous communities of Chiapas (*NACLA* 1998: 6).

7. The archive of the MRD, or the Anthap1, which is the technical name for MRD, is available at http://anthap.oakland.edu/anthap1/Chiapas_News_Archive.

8. Article 27 of the Mexican Constitution concerns the so-called *ejido* system. The *ejido* system rests on a degree of shared ownership of land and was established in the wake of the social demands made during and after the Mexican Revolution (1910–19). The reform had the objective of opening up the *ejido* sector to private ownership and investment, and was seen as an important aspect of the neoliberal restructuring that Mexico had been undergoing since the debt crisis of 1982 (see Chapter 6 for a further discussion of neoliberal reform in Mexico). Mayor Moisés of the EZLN later claimed that the adoption of the reforms to Article 27 was a major factor in the decision to launch an armed uprising (Le Bot 1997: 221).

9. Chiapas95 has an extensive archive of all postings to the list. The archive can be accessed at www.eco.utexas.edu/~hmcleave/chiapas95.html.

10. Chiapas-L is run by the BURN collective at the University of California at San Diego. The archive is accessible at http://burn.ucsd.edu/archives/chiapas-l.

11. The March for Indigenous Dignity was an attempt to revitalize support for the EZLN and to put back on the agenda the question of indigenous rights and autonomy. The march ended in Mexico City with speeches delivered by the EZLN in the Mexican Congress. The initiative came after the coming to presidential power of Vicente Fox in December 2000. Fox represents the PAN (Partido de Acción Nacional/National Action Party); his electoral victory in July 2000 ended seventy-one years of uninterrupted rule by the PRI (Partido Revolucionario Institucional/Institutional Revolutionary Party). The PRI government and the EZLN originally commenced negotiations following the ceasefire of January 1994. These resulted in the San Andrés Accords in 1996. The accords aimed to reform the relationship between the state and the indigenous population in the direction of greater autonomy. However, by the turn of the year 1996/7, the government refused to ratify the proposal formulated by COCOPA (Comisión de Concordia y Pacificación/Commission of Concordance and Pacification; COCOPA is a parliamentary contact forum between the EZLN and the government) on the basis of the San Andrés Accords. In 2001, the Fox administration presented a new proposal for constitutional reform on the question of indigenous rights. This proposal was rejected by the EZLN (2001d).

12. The first level, the indigenous communities of Chiapas, is not included in

the distinction between core, periphery and transitory actors below. This is because they are not recipients of information, at least in regard to the transnational Zapatista solidarity network.

13. In Mexico on 7 January there was an even larger gathering of up to 10,000 people, in the Zócalo (main square) of Mexico City (Gil Olmos 1994).

14. For example in Barcelona in June 1995, in Paris in January 1996, in Berlin in May–June 1996, and in Zurich in December 1996. These gatherings, in most cases, were held in order to prepare and organize for the first and second intercontinental encounters 'for humanity and against neoliberalism'.

15. The National Commission for Democracy in Mexico became known especially through the work of Cecilia Rodriguez, who eventually was named official representative of the EZLN in the USA. Following the army offensive in Chiapas in February 1995, Rodriguez became known for a hunger strike intended to draw attention to the situation in Chiapas and Mexico. Later, in October 1995, Rodriguez was raped in Mexico, an incident clearly connected to her activities with the EZLN and Chiapas. The incident gave rise to much activity on the various Chiapas lists.

4

Network Activities

This chapter takes a closer look at the external activities of the transnational Zapatista solidarity network by considering the way it relates to outside actors. The primary objective is to advance an understanding of the intimate relationship between institutional and civil society politics in the activities of the network. To talk about network activities is perhaps somewhat misplaced. It has been stressed at various points that we are dealing not with a unitary actor but with a loose and heterogeneous network of actors. Consequently, when we speak of network activities we refer primarily to the activities of single organizations and groups and not to the Zapatista solidarity network as a whole. On the other hand, these activities that may at first sight seem more or less independent are to a significant extent dependent on the informational infrastructure described in the previous chapter and thus the expression of a networked relationship.

Civil Society Politics:
Direct Solidarity and Information

The phrase 'civil society politics' is used here to encompass two types of activity. The first is carried out by network actors and is directed to the local level in Chiapas in the form of specific projects, material aid, peace observation, and so on. The second type, in contrast, is carried out by network actors in their local or national setting and seeks to inform and educate the public about the EZLN and the situation in Chiapas and Mexico. This is primarily an analytical distinction. Direct solidarity with Chiapas and the EZLN thus has a strong informational and educational dimension for those participating in it. Similarly, informational activities in the local and national arenas of network actors regularly take place with the aim of mobilizing people and resources to engage in direct solidarity activities.

Solidarity work on the ground

Numerous people and organizations are engaged in direct solidarity activities. Here we will look at four quite different examples: the Schools for Chiapas project; the Pastors for Peace aid caravans to Chiapas; the civilian peace camp and human rights observation work by non-Mexican volunteers; and fair-trade activities carried out by non-Mexican organizations.

Schools for Chiapas, based in San Diego, is a project of the non-profit organization Grassroots Events, which has worked on Mexican issues since the late 1970s. The project was presented in 1996 to Zapatista communities that had earlier expressed a need for better school facilities in Chiapas. When the Mexican government renounced the original San Andrés Accords on indigenous rights in late 1996/early 1997, the EZLN nevertheless decided to continue with the implementation of some of the themes in the Accords. This step involved, among other things, the acceptance of the first Schools for Chiapas project, initiated on 6 January 1997: the construction of a secondary school in the community of Oventic. The school was opened in April 2000. Construction of a second secondary school is presently under way in the community of Francisco Gómez. The building of schools is carried out by the indigenous communities themselves; the Schools for Chiapas project is mainly the provider of materials and labour; labour and activists for the school construction come from all over the world. Peter Brown (Brown and Sáenz Ackermann 2000), founder and organizer of the project, explains the procedure:

> People come from all over the world and meet in Mexico City, and then in Mexico City we get on buses, half of the bus seats are for

Mexican nationals, organized by the Frente Zapatista [de Liberación Nacional; FZLN], and the other half of the seats are taken by internationals, and depending on where the internationals come from we pay quite differently ... the buses drive to Chiapas ... and we stay there for two weeks ... some stay longer if they can afford to, but it is designed for working people, you fly on the beginning of a weekend and you leave on a Sunday.

The volunteers who participate in the Schools for Chiapas project are mainly recruited through the Internet. This illustrates a central argument of the book: that there is a close relation between the physical and the computer-mediated aspects of the network. Yet going to Chiapas to build schools is not just a question of providing labour and materials for the indigenous communities. It is also a way of educating people and giving them an opportunity to learn about the situation in Chiapas and Mexico in a way that would not have been possible in the local or the national setting of the project participants or via the Internet (Brown and Sáenz Ackermann 2000).

Pastors for Peace is a branch of the Interreligious Foundation for Community Organizing (IFCO). Pastors for Peace was founded in 1988 and is based in Chicago. In contrast to the Schools for Chiapas project, Pastors for Peace is thus not an organization formed specifically with the EZLN and Chiapas in mind. Dave McConnell (2000/2001), a representative of the organization, relates the circumstances around the formation of Pastors for Peace:

> In the summer of 1988, the Rev. Lucius Walker, Executive Director (since its founding) of IFCO, was in Nicaragua with a small delegation studying how the Sandinistas had organized in the countryside there, to see what IFCO could learn from their efforts. While on a boat on the Rio Escondido, Contra forces fired on the boat, killing two and wounding six, including Lucius. As he tells the story, he was awaiting treatment in a hospital, when it came to him that his tax dollars had helped pay for the bullets that rained down on the boat that day. Casting about for a way to demonstrate to the Nicaraguan people that many in the USA did not approve of official US foreign policy, funding the Contras in this case, he developed the idea of a 'people to people' foreign policy, that spelled itself out in the first Pastors for Peace caravan to Nicaragua in the winter of 1988.

Pastors for Peace began its programme in Chiapas in January 1995. As the quotation shows, there is a visible link to previous solidarity work in the Central American area. Dave McConnell explains that the determining factor for the first-aid caravan to Chiapas was the Mexican army offensive in Chiapas in February 1995. However, he is also eager to stress that Pastors for Peace does not support the EZLN in any direct manner but extends its work to the indigenous people of Chiapas as a whole. As the name of the organization indicates, Pastors for Peace has a Christian foundation; the organization has cooperated, for example, with the diocese of San Cristóbal de las Casas and its bishop Samuel Ruiz (McConnell 2000/2001). Samuel Ruiz has supported the EZLN's demands for justice but has also criticized its use of arms (as do Pastors for Peace).[1] Criticism of the armed aspect of the EZLN is expressed especially by organizations with a religious foundation.

The aid caravans administered by Pastors for Peace run from the USA to Chiapas, picking up food, clothes, medicine and school supplies as they pass through major cities in the USA. The following excerpts from a website-published report on the Spring 2000 Caravan for Peace and Reconciliation to Chiapas and Mexico describes the work carried out by Pastors for Peace (2001):

> Fifteen of us met at the Texas/Mexico border to make the necessary arrangements to transport 15 tons of medicine, medical supplies, school supplies, food and tools through Mexico. We spent two days sorting materials, making certain that they were properly labeled, and becoming familiar with each other and our mission…. We arrived in San Cristóbal de las Casas as scheduled on April 3, where three more persons joined us. We were faced with the fact that we had received very restrictive visas for this caravan, so we had to cut the programme shorter than we would have liked. Thanks to the hard work of Caritas and Enlace Civil (two of the many non-governmental agencies working in Chiapas), we were able to have a very successful programme. We visited nine communities, met with representatives of more than ten organizations in San Cristóbal, delivered the 15 tons of materials mentioned above, purchased and delivered nearly 15 tons of corn and beans to four communities in dire need of food.

Interestingly, Pastors for Peace explicitly mentions cooperation with two Chiapas-based organizations (one of which, Enlace Civil, was discussed in Chapter 3). This again underlines the close relationship between Mexican and non-Mexican organizations in the Zapatista solidarity network, and the intimate link between local, national and transnational levels. While the delivery of materials and aid to the communities in Chiapas is the main priority of the Pastors for Peace caravans, there is also an important element of awareness-raising involved, both for the communities that the caravans pass through on their way through the USA, and for the participating individuals. Pastors for Peace is also involved in human rights delegations to Chiapas and Mexico and in the facilitation of civilian peace-camp work.

This leads us to the third example of direct solidarity work in Chiapas by network activists: *civilian peace camp work and human rights observation*. The need for the presence of foreign observers in Chiapas increased with the February 1995 offensive of the Mexican army. Since that time, numerous foreigners and Mexican nationals have stayed in indigenous communities in Chiapas for varying lengths of time. Civilian peace-camp volunteers are active in Zapatista as well as in non-Zapatista communities. Peace-camp work by non-Mexicans is facilitated by a number of organizations, primarily in Europe and the USA; it is generally required that volunteers visit Chiapas as representatives of an organization. The coordination of activities in Chiapas, however, is the responsibility of Chiapas-based organizations such as Enlace Civil and the Fray Bartolomé de las Casas Human Rights Centre (Centro de Derechos Humanos Fray Bartolomé de Las Casas). In the words of Juan Carlos Paez (2001), a representative of the Fray Bartolomé Human Rights Centre, the work of the civilian peace observers has the following objectives:

> Accompaniment of the communities affected by the violence in the state, always under the strict principle of non-involvement. To be witnesses of the situation in the regions and to document it. To enssure the flow of information between the communities and the Fray Bartolomé de las Casas Human Rights Centre. Accompaniment in special situations such as the return of internally displaced people. Diffusion of information in the places of origin of the volunteers.

According to information on the website of one Europe's largest and most active solidarity organizations, the Barcelona-based Collective of Solidarity with the Zapatista Rebellion (Colectivo de Solidaridad con la Rebelión Zapatista 2001a), the main contribution of civilian peace-camp volunteers is to provide a link between the indigenous communities of Chiapas and the world around them in a situation characterized by a heavy military and paramilitary presence. This argument echoes the quotation above and also refers back to the discussions in Chapter 3 on the importance of information in the infrastructure of the network. Recalling our distinction in Chapter 3 between five different levels in the network information circuit, we may refer to the peace-camp volunteers and observers in Chiapas as second-level actors in the information circuit.

Foreigners have not only been active in Chiapas as peace-camp volunteers but also as human rights observers in delegations. Their significant presence in Chiapas and Mexico has been a major nuisance for the Mexican government. In 1998, following the massacre in Acteal in December 1997, foreign presence in Chiapas and Mexico was particularly high. In March 1998, 210 people from eleven countries visited Chiapas as part of the newly formed International Civil Commission for Human Rights Observation (Comisión Civil Internacional de Observación por los Derechos Humanos). The com-mission has to date made two additional visits to Chiapas (November 1999 and February/March 2002). These have resulted in extensive reports that have been distributed, for example, to the European Parliament and to the UN High Commissioner for Human Rights (Colectivo de Solidaridad con la Rebelión Zapatista 2001b).

During the early months of 1998, the Mexican government embarked on a strategy involving the expulsion of foreigners active on issues related to Chiapas and the EZLN on the grounds that they were interfering with internal Mexican affairs. This kind of activity is prohibited in the Mexican Constitution. The expulsion of foreigners engaged in activities described by Mexican president Ernesto Zedillo as revolutionary tourism (Urrutia 1998) had been part of the Mexican government's stance towards the situation in Chiapas since 1994, but was stepped up significantly in the tense period following the Acteal massacre. This had a somewhat adverse effect for the Mexican government as the expulsions attracted even more attention to the situation in Chiapas. The earliest and most widely published expulsions were those of US citizens Tom

Hansen (former director of Pastors for Peace and later to become the director of the Mexican Solidarity Network), Robert Schweitzer and Maria Darlington in February 1998. They were, however, only 3 out of 144 people from all over the world expelled from Mexico during 1998.

The Portuguese writer and Nobel prizewinner José Saramago is among the best-known foreigners to have visited Chiapas. He went to Chiapas in 1998, the same year he received the Nobel Prize for his literary achievements. Saramago's presence attracted considerable attention, as he visited the village of Acteal and adopted a very critical stance towards the Mexican government's handling of the conflict in Chiapas (Bellinghausen 1998). Saramago later revealed that Mexican president Ernesto Zedillo had considered expelling him from Mexico in early 1998. He had received this information from former Portuguese president Mario Soares, who had discussed the issue with Zedillo. Apparently, Zedillo decided not to go ahead with the expulsion after Soares had warned him about the potential media scandal and possible intervention from the European Union (La Jornada 2001). The latter prospect may have been particularly worrying for Zedillo as Mexico and the European Union were negotiating a trade agreement at the time (see below).

The fourth and last example of direct solidarity with Chiapas and the EZLN is that carried out by people and organizations involved in *fair trade* with indigenous communities in Chiapas. Fair trade in a sense straddles the border between civil society and market activities. However, since fair trade is frequently seen as a form of information activity in the relationship with consumers, it may be viewed also as a particular variety of civil society politics. Kerry Appel (2000) runs the Denver-based Human Bean Company, which imports coffee from the Zapatista indigenous community of Mut Vitz at prices above market value. The idea for the company came after a visit to Chiapas in late 1995 and a meeting with Comandante David of the EZLN. Asked about the best way to show solidarity with the EZLN, Comandante David referred to the importance of developing the infrastructure of the indigenous communities. Historically, the Mexican government has been very passive in this regard, and the economic exploitation of the indigenous communities by coyotes, or middlemen, who buy crops such as coffee at a price far below the world market price, has kept the communities in permanent poverty. A solution to this problem, suggested Comandante David, was to find direct markets in the USA and Europe. The Human Bean Company is a for-profit company based on the idea that business and human values are not incompatible. The Human Bean Company has a website with general information on Chiapas and the EZLN as well as a library of books and documentaries in the company shop (Appel 2000).

Raising awareness and practising Zapatismo at home

The issue of awareness-raising and information in the local community of activists may be approached from different angles. For the purpose of the coming discussions, it is useful to distinguish between, on the one hand, more traditional forms of information campaigns and, on the other, information activities seeking to implement and practise aspects of Zapatismo in the local community of activists.

When asked about their main activities, the large majority of network activists and organizations refer to informational and educational activities. These encompass a plethora of different activities such as writing articles, giving talks, arranging workshops, staging demonstrations, distributing leaflets and flyers. The following account by the Madrid-based Zapatista Support Network (Red de Apoyo Zapatista 2001) describes a range of typical informational activities:

> Our principal activities have been informative; we distribute small publications called the RAZ Notebooks with communiqués and work on different themes related to the Zapatistas. Every Sunday we have an informational booth where we sell materials and T-shirts; we arrange workshops for people who are going to the civilian peace camps. [M]oreover, we organized the consultation on the indigenous law in Madrid, as well as talks, concerts, and manifestations.[2]

Information work in the community of network activists primarily carried out by organization members who have been to Chiapas or have otherwise acquired some knowledge about the situation. In other cases, informational work takes place in close cooperation with people from Chiapas and Mexico who travel around the world in order to disseminate information. Some such envoys have been well known to the public such as the former bishop of San Cristóbal de las Casas, Samuel Ruiz, and Mexican actress Ofelia Medina, but others have been ordinary people from Chiapas – for example, women weavers and representatives from indigenous communities. Again we see the link between local, national and transnational levels in the network. Here it is clear that the transnational level involves both non-Mexicans directing activities towards Mexico and Mexicans, in cooperation with solidarity organizations, disseminating information worldwide.

Such activities are primarily attempts to reach the public directly. Other activities are mainly geared to reaching the public via certain media; these include, most typically, demonstrations and other forms of collective manifestation. Outside of Mexico, manifestations have taken many forms but have been directed primarily at symbols of the Mexican government such as consulates and embassies (Bellinghausen 1997). In addition, representatives of the Mexican government have become targets for network activists whenever they travel abroad. Even the presence of the Mexican football team participating in the World Cup in France in 1998 was seen by activists as a chance for attracting media attention to Chiapas and the EZLN (Ocampo 1998). When the Mexican president Ernesto Zedillo toured Europe in 1998 to meet with heads of states to discuss the EU–Mexico trade agreement, he was met in city after city by activists carrying placards and shouting slogans in support of the EZLN and against the military and paramilitary violence in Chiapas (Hernández Navarro 2001). This type of activity has generally been related to specific events in Chiapas and Mexico, such as the Mexican army offensive in February 1995, the government's refusal to implement the San Andrés Accords in their original form in late 1996/early 1997, and the Acteal massacre in December 1997.

Collective manifestations and demonstrations have not only taken place in physical space but also through the Internet. Internet-based manifestations have become known under different names such as 'electronic civil disobedience', 'net strikes', and 'mail bombs'. The idea of these computer-mediated actions is to go beyond the sending of emails to figures such as politicians. The purpose, instead, is disruptive:

for example, to flood mailboxes and overwork websites to the extent that they break down or become defunct for periods of time (Wray 1998a; Domínguez 2001). In a message circulated on the Internet, the New York Zapatistas (1998) offered the following definitions and suggestions in regard to electronic civil disobedience:

> By Electronic Civil Disobedience we mean applying the principles and tactics of traditional civil disobedience – like trespass and blockade – to the electronic systems of communication upon which Mexican government officials and their supporters depend…. We therefore urge that the following tactics be used against governmental, financial, and corporate sites responsible for the ongoing genocide in Chiapas. 1) Phone Zaps: Repeated calling to disrupt normal operations. 2) Fax Jams: Repeated faxing to overload fax machines. 3) Email Jams: Massive emailing to overload email inboxes and servers. 4) Virtual Sit-Ins: Trespassing and blockading of web sites.

Some of the initiatives described in the quotation originated with Italian activists in 1996, but they seem to have found mass expression in the months following the Acteal massacre. The major aim of these electronic actions was Mexican financial institutions as well as representatives of the government. Although the net strikes and electronic civil disobedience received a great deal of media and public attention due to their novelty, the concrete effect was apparently very small (Wray 1998b). Since 1998 computer-mediated forms of collective action have played an insignificant role in the activities of the transnational Zapatista solidarity network.

In terms of physical manifestations of protest, one of the early incidents that brought people out onto the streets in Mexico, Europe, and the USA was the offensive of the Mexican army on 9 February 1995. This incident soon became related to the disclosure of a memo written by Riordan Roett for the Chase Manhattan Bank, in which he called for the elimination of the EZLN in order to restore stability and investor confidence in Mexico in the wake of the so-called peso crisis of December 1994.[3] The Chase Manhattan Bank memo was apparently passed to *Counterpunch* journalists Ken Silverstein and Alexander Cockburn by a bank insider. The content of the memo was made public in *Counterpunch* on 1 February 1995 (Silverstein and Cockburn 1995a). As noted by Silverstein and Cockburn (1995b) in their follow-up on the story, the disclosure of the Chase Manhattan Bank memo caused an uproar and numerous protests on the part of solidarity groups and organizations, while at the same time receiving a great deal of attention from the media:

> For days, COUNTERPUNCH phones rang non-stop, with activists and journalists requesting urgent fax transmittal of our story and the Chase memo which contained the bank's suggestion. Organizers brandished the memorandum at demonstrations in Los Angeles, San Francisco, Seattle, New York, and other cities. The story was covered by everyone from FINAL CALL, which is published by the Nation of Islam, to THE WASHINGTON POST. On Capitol Hill, Rep. Marcy Kaptur (D-Ohio) held a press conference to denounce the bank…. Similar uproar took place in Mexico after PROCESO, a major news weekly, carried a Feb.13 story about COUNTERPUNCH's disclosures…. Zapatista officials in the U.S. say that publication of the Chase memo was 'a turning point' in that it was the first hard evidence which directly linked Wall Street to Mexico's economic and political crisis.

Network activists were quick to establish a link between the memo and the Mexican army's attempt to capture the EZLN leadership in early February 1995. The story thus proved to be a significant opportunity for activists to interest the media and reach a wider audience in their informational and educational activities. The period following the army offensive and the Chase memo in February 1995 was the most intense to that point in terms of network activities, and was a defining moment in the formation of the Zapatista solidarity network. The degree of attention drawn to the Chase incident led the bank to dissociate itself from the memo and eventually to fire Roett (Silverstein and Cockburn 1995b).

This outcome, together with the eventual decision by the Mexican government to suspend army actions in Chiapas, was seen by network activists as an important victory and a result of the pressure by activists within and outside Mexico. The widespread perception within the network is that the constant physical and electronic presence of transnational activists has helped keep the EZLN alive. This view is echoed by the EZLN itself, which often refers to the transnational presence as a protection or shield for the EZLN and the indigenous communities (Le Bot 1997: 260). However, we should be cautious not to establish a direct link between network activities and, for example, changes in the actions of the Mexican government. It is true that in January 1994, as well as in February 1995, the suspension of military activities came at the height of intense network activity. Yet nothing has been disclosed so far by the Mexican government regarding the motivation for its actions in these cases, or how the activities of the network may have influenced them.

The activities described above have primarily concerned specific events in Chiapas and Mexico. In the majority of cases, protests and demonstrations have been aimed at drawing attention to human rights violations following, for example, the February 1995 army offensive and the Acteal massacre in December 1997. As indicated, these types of activities have been directed at an audience beyond the immediate network in order to raise awareness about events in Chiapas and to draw new groups and activists into the network. Awareness-raising also takes place through a different type of activity: practising Zapatismo at home.

In an earlier quotation from Dave McConnell, we saw how in the case of Pastors for Peace there is connection between EZLN solidarity work and earlier such work in the Central American region. Many of those involved in the network refer to Central American solidarity with Nicaragua, El Salvador and Guatemala as a predecessor of the transnational Zapatista solidarity network. On the other hand, there is also acknowledgement of significant differences between present solidarity work with the EZLN and Chiapas and that which took place in the 1970s and 1980s. Brian Dominick (2000) describes the differences as follows:

> The main difference is, at least for most of the younger or newer solidarity activists focusing on Chiapas, that the 'solidarity' is less material, and in other ways less explicit.... The new solidarity activist is looking here, to the community, to the 'belly of the beast,' for the site of action.... When people come back from a delegation to Chiapas, or an extended stay there, typically they want to figure out ways to apply what they've learned in Chiapas to community organizing here. And when they go down to visit Chiapas in the first place, they aren't going as teachers, but as students.

This way of approaching solidarity work also takes it beyond the traditional methods applied (e.g. direct aid), even though these methods, as evidenced by this chapter, are still present in the activities of the network.[4] In the words of Justin Paulson (2001), to be in solidarity with the EZLN, then, does not mean to

> simply lobby your government representatives to cease military aid to the Mexican state. It doesn't mean to simply write letters to your congressperson. It means to fight everywhere against what the EZLN is fighting against …: racism, sexism, homophobia, and a global economic order that guarantees the rights of capital while it takes away the rights, identities, and cultures of people. And it means to struggle everywhere for the future(s) of humanity.

This approach has to some extent been inspired and promoted by the EZLN. The EZLN acknowledges and accepts solidarity in the form of material aid and the presence of human rights observers, but at the same time it has been very explicit that solidarity also involves struggling at home against what is considered a neoliberal development model with global reach.[5] One of the objectives of the First Intercontinental Encounter for Humanity and against Neoliberalism in Chiapas in 1996 was precisely to extend the EZLN's political analysis of neoliberalism beyond the confines of Mexico and Chiapas and, accordingly, to give the resistance to neoliberalism a transnational dimension. Yet practising Zapatismo at home is not only a question of adopting the EZLN's critique of neoliberalism to the local and national setting of network activists; it is also about using EZLN organizing principles for local and national activities. Manuel Callahan (2000), an activist in the Austin (Texas)-based Zapatista Action (Acción Zapatista) group, describes the inspiration resulting from participation in the Continental American Encounter for Humanity and against Neoliberalism (Encuentro Continental Americano por la Humanidad y contra el Neoliberalismo) in Chiapas in April 1996:

> [W]hen we came back from the *encuentro* we felt, that's it, we got to have an *encuentro*, so we do, we have the Austin *encuentro*, fairly successful, a little over a 100 people showed up for three days, and we set it up like an *encuentro*, but we had our own questions … so we wanted to have an *encuentro* to create political space for various constituencies, to dialogue, interact, and develop different strategies, away from solidarity, that was what our goal was, so we wanted to introduce our critique of solidarity, and introduce our critique of activism.

In line with the EZLN's idea of creating space for critical discussions rather than directing them, the two continental and intercontinental encounters in Chiapas in 1996 were characterized by the very wide array of people they attracted. As is evident in the quotation above, it was this organizing principle that was at the heart of the Austin encounter in 1996, which was later followed up by similar events.

Institutional Politics:
Making the Politicians Listen

The organizations and groups described above are all civil society actors. While it is a fact that such authors account for the majority of network activists, we also need to be aware of the participation in the network of politicians and representatives of varying official institutions. In acknowledging this, we accept that network activities rarely take place only on the level of civil society. Activities thus also target states and governments, or their representatives, in order to induce their involvement in network-related activities. If we recall our distinction in Chapter 3 between core, periphery and transitory actors in the network, we may say that participation of, for example, politicians is in the main occasional and of a transitory nature. Such transitory participation does not come out of the blue. Mostly, it is the result of lobbying efforts on the part of network activists. The following discussion aims to show how politicians and official representatives have played a role in the network and how activists have been instrumental in facilitating this participation.

Since the uprising in 1994, there have been a number of resolutions and statements made by politicians, by officials and, in some cases, even by parliaments or parliamentary groups on the issue of Chiapas and the EZLN. One of the best-known and extensive examples of intervention by non-Mexican politicians in the conflict between the EZLN and the Mexican government are the Leahy and Pelosi Resolutions passed in the US Congress (in the Senate and in the House of Representatives respectively) in November 1999.[6] There is no doubt that the Acteal massacre in December 1997 and the ensuing expulsions of foreign observers, including many US citizens, from Mexico during 1998 were instrumental in attracting the attention of politicians in the USA and making them more attentive to the demands made by solidarity activists. The lobbying efforts leading to the Leahy/Pelosi resolutions were primarily carried out by some of the larger network organizations such as Global Exchange and the Mexico Solidarity Network. The Leahy Resolution (1999), which has the same wording as the Pelosi Resolution (1999), states that the Secretary of State should make sure that US military assistance and exports to Mexico are used for counter-narcotics purposes and not by Mexican security forces that have been implicated in human rights violations. This is point (1) of the five recommendations in the resolution. The resolution goes on to urge the Secretary of State to

> (2) encourage the EZLN and the Government of Mexico to take steps to create conditions for good faith negotiations that address the social, economic, and political causes of the conflict in Chiapas, to achieve a peaceful and lasting resolution of the conflict, and to vigorously pursue such negotiations; (3) commend the Government of Mexico for its renewed commitment to negotiations and for establishing a date for the United Nations High Commissioner for Human Rights to visit Mexico to discuss human rights concerns there; (4) give a higher priority in discussions with the Government of Mexico to criminal justice reforms that protect human rights, emphasizing United States concerns about arbitrary detention, torture, extrajudicial killings, and disappearances, and the failure to prosecute individuals responsible for these crimes; and (5) urge the Government of Mexico to implement the recommendations of the Inter-American Commission on Human Rights, particularly with regard to American citizens and others who have been summarily expelled from Mexico in violation of Mexican law and international law.

Even though the resolutions are primarily symbolic, they have been a major irritant for the Mexican government and a useful tool in the hands of network activists protesting against human rights violations in Mexico and Chiapas (Lewis 2000). As indicated earlier, the passing of the Leahy/Pelosi Resolutions was partly the result of the lobbying efforts of solidarity activists and organizations. In some cases, this involved inviting people and organizations from Chiapas to Washington DC to speak to politicians and provide them with information necessary for their work. David Martin (2000) of the Denver Justice and Peace Committee thus explains how this organization helped facilitate a US tour by representatives of CIEPAC, a Chiapas-based organization devoted to political analysis of the situation in Chiapas (see Chapter 3). The visitors from Chiapas had meetings with Representative Nancy Pelosi (D–CA) in October, one month prior to the presentation of the Leahy/Pelosi Resolutions in the US Congress. This initiative is an example of cooperation between second-level and third-level actors in the network (see Chapter 3). As such it is also an example of the fluid connections between the local, national and transnational levels in the network.

The presentation of the Leahy/Pelosi Resolutions in November 1999 coincided with the announcement of a visit to Mexico by the United Nations High Commissioner for Human Rights, Mary Robinson. Robinson's visit came just a few months after the visit by another UN representative, Asma Jahangir, a UN special rapporteur on extrajudicial executions. Both UN representatives launched significant criticisms of the human rights situation in Mexico and in particular criticized the judicial system (Ross 1999), as did a European Union parliament mission to Mexico in the spring of 2000 (Reuters 2000). The activity on the part of US politicians, as expressed in the Leahy/Pelosi Resolutions, was undoubtedly a factor in the Mexican government's decision to accept the visits by UN representatives.

Members of the US Congress, or their representatives, have also visited Chiapas on a number of occasions. In the summer of 1998, a delegation of four US congressmen and -women visited Chiapas, an event facilitated by a number of network organizations. Representative Luis Gutierrez (D-IL), speaking about his motivation for participating in the delegation, said that he had never before received information on the scale of that sent to him by network activists on issues pertaining to the conflict in Chiapas. In all, he received more than 3,000 letters (Enlace Civil 1998). The sending of messages and petitions to US congressmen and -women and Mexican politicians has been facilitated by the computer-mediated circulation of information on how to approach members of Congress and local politicians. Such information often contains both addresses and suggested messages.

Reactions from politicians and parliaments to the situation in Chiapas were especially widespread and vociferous in the wake of the December 1997 massacre in Acteal. In the immediate aftermath, political leaders and personalities, including Bill Clinton, Lionel Jospin, Kofi Annan, and former French first lady Danielle Mitterrand, all expressed concern with the situation in Chiapas (*La Jornada* 1997b). These voices were echoed in Europe by, for example, the European Union, the Catalan and the Basque parliaments, and the mayors of Venice and Dublin. These official reactions generally followed intense lobbying campaigns by network activists. There are, notably, strong network organizations in Spain (Colectivo de Solidaridad con la Rebelión Zapatista), Italy (Ya Basta) and Ireland (the Irish Mexico Group). The Italian organizations are particularly strong in comparison with other countries. Whereas politicians elsewhere did not begin to take the Chiapas question seriously until after the Acteal massacre in December 1997, Italian solidarity activists were able to mobilize as many as 120 Italian parliamentarians in February 1997 to sign a petition urging Mexican president Ernesto Zedillo to reconsider his position on the San Andrés Accords (*La Jornada* 1997a).

In Europe, the link between network organizations and political institutions has developed in the wake of negotiations between Mexico and the European Union on the establishment of a trade agreement.[7] Criticisms of this agreement have taken as their point of departure a clause on respect for democracy and human rights. When the negotiations began in 1995–96, the Mexican government opposed this clause on the grounds that it interfered with Mexican sovereignty. Eventually, however, it accepted the clause and negotiations proceeded. This type of EU pact is generally referred to as a fourth-generation trade agreement. Throughout the duration of the negotiation process there was a battle of words between the Mexican government and network activists on the issue of Chiapas and its repercussions for the trade agreement. In some cases, this involved the mobilization of parliamentarians in the respective member countries of the European Union. Again, some of the strongest voices of criticism came from Italy and its parliament, where a resolution stated that the Italian parliament would not ratify the agreement unless negotiations between the EZLN and the Mexican government were resumed (Petrich 1998).

When negotiations entered the final phase on 1 July 1998, Mexican foreign minister Rosario Green was keen to stress that the Chiapas conflict should play no part: 'I am convinced that Mexico has the institutions, the talent, the will on the part of the government to resolve this situation in Chiapas, and I don't believe we need foreign intervention' (cited in Reuters 1998). Network activists and organizations concerned with the human rights situation took the opposite view, believing that the democratic clause in the trade agreement would sanction the monitoring of the situation in Mexico (Mergier 1999). In the end, the Mexican government won this particular battle of information and misinformation, and the agreement was finally ratified, entering into force on 1 July 2000. Contrary to the wishes of network activists, the agreement contained only symbolic reference to respect for human rights. Yet their action was not futile; it had been an unprecedented opportunity to practise informational politics directed at both civil society actors and politicians and officials. This was the view of Kenneth Haar (2000) of the Red–Green Alliance (Enhedslisten), for example, expressed shortly after the ratification of the trade agreement in the Danish parliament in early 2000:

> Although the finale in Denmark was a defeat for many people concerned with the human rights situation in Mexico, the past months' work by a number of organizations has not been in vain. The debate on the EU–Mexico agreement has been the most intensive and thorough on a 'bilateral' agreement for many years. This is in large part thanks to a number of declarations from organizations in Denmark ..., reports and letters from Centro de Derechos Humanos Miguel Agustín Pro Juárez, Amnesty International, RMALC [Mexican Action Network on Free Trade], and last but not least the constant and inspiring effort by CIFCA [Copenhagen Initiative for Central America].

The Transnational Zapatista Counterpublic

Hitherto, the activities of the transnational Zapatista solidarity network have been discussed using the categories of civil society politics and institutional politics. This is, however, mainly an analytical distinction. In reality, the two types of politics are enmeshed. We will now discuss how they may be understood in a more integrated and dialectical manner by applying them to the concept of the public sphere, and to the derivative notion of transnational counterpublics. Habermas (1996: 360) describes the public sphere as a 'network for communicating information and points of view ...; the streams of communication are, in the process, filtered and synthesized in such a way that they coalesce into bundles of topically specified public opinions.' In the work of Habermas, the public sphere exists in the singular. This may, to some extent, reflect past reality. However, thinking about the public sphere in the singular today seriously impairs the concept's analytical precision. This becomes especially evident when we seek to transfer the concept of the public sphere from its original anchoring in the national state to the transnational sphere.

In a critique of Habermas, Fraser (1995) contends that to conceive of the public sphere in the singular is to overlook how the public sphere is penetrated by relations of inequality, despite the underlying liberal notion of formal equality. Discourses in the public sphere are dominated by actors who possess important social, material or political resources. Other actors, with a lower or marginal status in terms of political standpoint, material income, cultural or sexual identity, and so on, have less access to make their voices heard in the public sphere. These groups, consequently, tend to create alternative subaltern counterpublics.

It is thus a defining feature of modern societies that, rather than one, there exist several public spheres – or subaltern counterpublics – within civil society. Projecting Fraser's concept onto the present debate on transnational interaction, we may suggest the concept of transnational counterpublics as a transnational equivalent to the concept of subaltern counterpublics. The accentuation of plurality in the concept of transnational counterpublics does not necessarily imply that we cannot speak of a transnational public sphere in the singular as well. We may suggest this as an expression and convergence of opinions in national public spheres. Transnational counterpublics, in contrast, are more genuinely transnational. They are constituted by a range of geographically dispersed actors and are often centred around local or national issues considered to be of relevance also to people outside the geographical location, or around issues with a cross-border nature, as with certain environmental problems. Transnational counterpublics, in other words, are the social space of informal transnational movement networks.[8]

This recognition of the existence of transnational counterpublics is not to suggest that there are no longer dominant national public spheres. Rather, what is suggested is that these are increasingly surrounded and penetrated by transnational counterpublics. The latter comprise actors who lack sufficient resources to participate in the dominant public sphere, or whose issues of concern do not find a ready echo therein. On the other hand, they are not self-referential units existing independently of the transnational public sphere or of dominant national public spheres. On the contrary, there are significant overlaps and attempts by transnational counterpublics to sway opinion in these public spheres. It is still through the dominant public spheres that access to the material and political resources necessary for goal accomplishment is obtained.

In Chapter 3 we discussed how the infrastructure of the trans-national Zapatista solidarity network functions. This provided, as it were, an internal view of the network and focused on the roles played by core and periphery actors. In contrast, application of the transnational counterpublic concept to the network is intended to draw attention to the larger social context in which the network is embedded and to the external activities of network activists. This involves, in particular, an analysis of the relations between, on the one hand, core and periphery actors, and, on the other hand, transitory actors (see Chapter 3). By attempting to draw transitory actors (e.g. politicians) into the network, core and periphery actors reach out beyond the immediate network and engage with dominant public spheres. To the extent that network activists engage in such extrovert activities, we may speak of the Zapatista solidarity network as an empirical expression of a transnational counterpublic. The trans-national counterpublic concept thus in many ways breaks down the distinction between civil society and institutional politics.

The primary institutional actors that the network activists have sought to influence have been the Mexican government together with other governments and intergovernmental organizations with potential leverage on it; the most important of these is the US government, which has significant influence due to the two countries' membership of NAFTA and because it is Mexico's largest trading partner and an important creditor.[9] The European Union, for its part, has had a degree of influence on the Mexican government through the 2000 trade agreement, as discussed earlier. Network activists have also tried to influence the Mexican government directly through letter-writing campaigns and protests outside consulates. Yet, as the quotation by foreign minister Rosario Green showed, and as has been demonstrated by the expulsions of foreigners, Mexico resents foreign interference in its internal matters. It is thus difficult for civil-society-based network activists to influence the Mexican government directly. Consequently, there is a widespread conception that a more effective means is to mobilize governments and other official actors, who may have a degree of leverage when it comes to influencing Mexican politics.

Ensuring that such institutional actors serve the network's interests is no easy matter. It takes hard work on the part of activists to convince them to spend time and effort on a particular issue in a world that abounds with cases deserving attention. In order to get the message through, activists must employ a dual strategy of approaching relevant actors directly (including email, faxes and regular mail) and engaging with the dominant public sphere in their respective countries. Numbers are important here: the more people network activists can mobilize to engage in this type of action, the more impact they are likely to have. The information circuits of the network often facilitate this kind of action by issuing guidelines on how to approach institutional actors.

There is no doubt that this strategy is most effective when an issue is also visible in the public sphere. In this sense, there is a close relationship between the civil society politics of network activists carried out in the public sphere (e.g. demonstrations) and their engagement in institutional politics. When network activists stage happenings and protests in front of Mexican consulates and embassies, they become visible in the public sphere, in some cases attracting the attention of mainstream media. As we have seen, it has been far easier for network activists to gain the attention of these actors in more extreme situations (e.g. the Acteal massacre of December 1997). To the frustration of activists, it has been much harder to generate interest in the low-intensity conflict in Chiapas since 1994.[10] Nevertheless, computer-mediated communication enables this kind of information to reach a relatively large audience beyond the immediate network and outside the circuits of the mainstream media.

This constant circulation of information within the network and beyond enables activists to maintain uniform pressure on both relevant institutional actors and mainstream media journalists. Furthermore, it prepares the transnational Zapatista solidarity network should a situation arise that makes it easier to provoke media interest and bring about official intervention. Certain network actors, especially some of the larger organizations, try to maintain more regular relationships with mainstream media. Ted Lewis (2000) of Global Exchange expresses this position as follows:

> One of the areas where we have been quite successful for an organization of our character is in terms of being able to push issues to the media; there are a number of people on the staff who are quite savvy in terms of how to utilize the mainstream media to push our issues forward.... We don't take the position that many organizations on the left have done over the years, of just writing off the media, saying they are not worth dealing with; we actually very actively cultivate relations with reporters ... try to help them with stories ... and that comes back to you later in terms of them being willing to utilize some of the sources that you are suggesting.

Keeping mainstream media up to the mark by providing them with information is an example of the interaction between the transnational Zapatista solidarity network and dominant public spheres. There is, in addition, a close relationship between activities directed towards the mainstream media and those directed towards institutional actors. In other words, the higher the report rate in the mainstream media of issues related to Chiapas and the EZLN, the easier it is for network activists to get institutional actors to take an interest. The audience for mainstream media is much larger than that which receives information through the network information circuits. Institutional actors, who are often at the mercy of public opinion, are therefore relatively more susceptible and hence likely to respond to information published in the mainstream media.

These efforts at influencing mainstream media and institutional actors in a given country are obviously not carried out by the network as a whole. Rather, they take place through the activities of organizations physically located within the borders of the country, hence underlining the continued relevance of the state and the national context as the arena for contestation and politics. However, these actors rarely restrict their informational work to the level of their own nationally defined territory. We saw earlier how network activists attempt to influence the dominant public sphere in their respective home countries in order to motivate institutional actors to put pressure on the Mexican government in regard to its dealings with Chiapas and the EZLN. Yet network activists also engage in activities aimed more directly at the Mexican government: letters to Mexican politicians and officials; demonstrations and actions targeted at official Mexican visits abroad and staged outside consulates and embassies.

These activities represent more than attempts to influence Mexican politicians and officials. They also enter into the dominant Mexican public sphere. What characterizes the transnational Zapatista solidarity network, and transnational counterpublics in general, is that they also attempt to influence the dominant public sphere in specific target countries. In some cases this goal is pursued by the use of direct action, but in general the means are more indirect. The Mexican media culture today is relatively free, with a number of critical newspapers and magazines. When network activists abroad stage activities directed at Mexican symbols and representatives, this news often finds its way into the Mexican media, and, consequently, into the public sphere. In other cases, activists and scholars have contributed directly to Mexican newspapers such as *La Jornada* (see, e.g., Harvey 2000). This influence on the Mexican public sphere by network activists has also been evident in relation to the physical presence of foreigners in Mexico. The expulsions of foreigners from Mexico between 1998 and 2000 thus created something of a sensation in the Mexican media. The same may be said of certain visits by prominent foreigners, such as that of José Saramago, who visited Chiapas after the Acteal massacre and gave several interviews. To note that network activities overseas often enter the Mexican public sphere through the cooperation of Mexican organizations is to emphasize once again the close link between the national and the transnational.

Transnational counterpublics are not located in geographical space, but are, in a sense, nowhere and everywhere. It is when actors interact across borders through informational and physical networks that they come to form transnational counterpublics. As noted earlier, these interactions take place not only within the circuits of the

Figure 4.1   The transnational Zapatista counterpublic

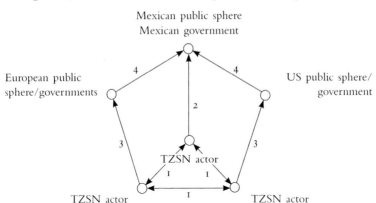

network infrastructure but also through dominant national public spheres. These relations are illustrated in Figure 4.1. The figure is obviously stylized inasmuch as it illustrates only a few of the countless interactions that exist in the empirical transnational Zapatista counterpublic. The US and European public spheres represent the primary public spheres with which network actors engage. The Mexican public sphere is, of course, the target of much network activity. The above discussion and Figure 4.1 indicate four different levels of interaction between the actors involved. These levels are all interrelated and are often indistinguishable except from an analytical point of view. The levels may be summarized as follows:

- *Level 1* Interaction between network actors as described mainly in Chapter 3.
- *Level 2* Interaction between network activists and the Mexican government. The activities are mainly attempts by activists to pressure the Mexican government to adopt new policies or to change policies on Chiapas and the EZLN. These activities may target Mexican authorities directly and/or take place at the level of the Mexican public sphere.
- *Level 3* Interaction between network activists and representatives of governments and intergovernmental organizations. These activities are mainly carried out by network organizations located in the

respective countries and are aimed at changing the policies of governments and intergovernmental organizations on Mexico. This type of activity may target governments directly or take place at the level of the public sphere

- *Level 4* Interaction between institutional actors and the Mexican government on issues regarding the situation in Chiapas.

The term 'transnational counterpublic' cannot be limited in its use to the infrastructure of the transnational Zapatista solidarity network. In other words, the transnational counterpublic is not only expressed in the interaction at level 1 in the above schema. To the extent that the network is also referred to as a 'transnational counterpublic', it is only so in its interaction with dominant public spheres and actors outside the immediate network. The transnational Zapatista counterpublic is thus expressed in all of the relations illustrated in Figure 4.1.

Notes

1. Samuel Ruiz, who resigned from the diocese of San Cristóbal de las Casas in 1999, was president of the National Commission for Intermediation (Comisión Nacional de Intermediación, or CONAI) from its establishment in December 1994 to its dissolution in June 1998. The objective of CONAI was to serve as a mediator between the EZLN and the Mexican government. The dissolution of CONAI was a result of the silence on the part of the EZLN and the increasingly aggressive attitude of the Mexican government in the wake of the December 1997 massacre in Acteal.

2. The consultation on the indigenous law referred to in the quotation took place in March 1999 and was announced by the EZLN (1998) in the Fifth Declaration of the Lacandon Forest. The original title of the consultation was the National Consultation on the Indigenous Law Initiative of the Commission of Concordance and Pacification and for the End of the War of Extermination (Consulta Nacional sobre la Iniciativa de Ley Indígena de la Comisíon de Concordia y Pacificación y por el Fin de la Guerra de Exterminio). The consultation was a response to the Mexican government's refusal to ratify and implement the original San Andrés Accords of 1996. The consultation took place all over Mexico and included about 3 million votes on questions pertaining to the rights of the indigenous people in Mexico. Prior to the vote, the EZLN had sent two representatives (one man and one woman) to each of Mexico's more than 2,500 municipalities. As suggested in the quotation, it also called for an international consultation on these questions (EZLN 1999a). This consultation, mainly addressed to Mexicans living outside of Mexico, received about 58,000 votes (EZLN

1999e).

3. The memo may be read in its entirety on the Mexico Solidarity Network website at www.mexicosolidarity.org/resource/roett.html.

4. The different types of solidarity are often practised by the same actors, but in some cases differing views on the meaning of solidarity have been the cause of conflict among network actors (see also Chapter 5).

5. During the extensive reorganization process of 2003 of the Zapatista communities, the EZLN criticized certain elements of transnational solidarity as being disrespectful and paternalistic. See also the discussion in the Conclusion.

6. The resolutions were submitted by Senator Patrick Leahy (D–VT) and Representative Nancy Pelosi (D–CA).

7. The agreement is available in its entirety at http://europa.eu.int/comm/trade/bilateral/mexico/fta.htm.

8. The transnational counterpublic concept contrasts in many ways with the concept of global civil society which has made its way into the social sciences as an appendage to that of globalization. There are at least three problems associated with the analytical use of the concept. First, and taking into consideration the history of the civil society concept, it is dubious to speak about a global civil society in the absence of a global state. Second, and as noted by Keane (2001: 28–29) and Eschle (2001: 73), global civil society too easily becomes a description of transnational civil society action in its totality (e.g. Lipschutz 1996: ch. 8; Falk 1999: ch. 9), thus overlooking variety and heterogeneity. Third, and in continuation of this point, the concept of global civil society often reflects a certain normative aspiration on the part of its proponents, and a desire to see a united and coherent global civil society responding to the problems associated, for example, with neoliberal globalization (Anheier et al. 2001: 11).

9. Following the so-called peso crisis in December 1994, which led to the devaluation of the Mexican peso, the US government made a US$20 billion loan to Mexico.

10. The low-intensity conflict in Chiapas involves a constant level of violence and repression on the part of paramilitary groups representing local financial and political interests. Moreover, the massive presence of the Mexican army in Chiapas is also the cause of regular incidents of violence and intimidation.

5

Global Consciousness

This chapter discusses the relationship between the EZLN's resonance outside Mexico and its ability to invoke a global consciousness, while at the same time remaining focused on the local and national roots of the uprising. In theoretical terms, the EZLN's invocation of a global consciousness allows it to anchor its transnational frame in a common belief system. This system should be understood not necessarily as shared social and cultural world-views, but rather as a shared perception of the interconnectedness of the world and of humanity. Global consciousness, in short, entails the ability and aspiration to see the world as a single place. Without a degree of global consciousness, it is not possible to analyse, for example, the spread of neoliberal and democratic ideas in a way that identifies global causes and implications; nor is it likely that a communications technology such as the Internet would be used to facilitate communication across borders. As argued in Chapter 1, the notion of a global consciousness constitutes the backbone of our definition of globalization. It does not, however, denote a static or stable way of perceiving the world. It is constantly produced and reproduced through the activities and inventions of social actors. The relationship between globalization and global consciousness is thus dialectical. In other words, globalization presupposes a global consciousness, but global consciousness is, at the same time, produced through the globalization process.

Developments in Transnational Solidarity:
From Altruism to Reciprocity

In what follows we consider the historical development of the notions of transnational solidarity and global consciousness, and demonstrate how these are interlinked. It is argued, in general and theoretical terms, that transnational solidarity is changing from a force based primarily on notions of altruism to a situation where it seems more precise to speak of reciprocal or mutual solidarity. This change involves an important development in the relationship between those who offer solidarity and those who benefit from it.

Forms of solidarity

There follows a typology of transnational solidarity based on both the sources of activity and the actors involved. Distinction is made between ideological, rights-based and material forms of solidarity. This typology is ideal-typical and hence does not reflect or encompass all empirical forms of solidarity.

Ideological solidarity

This form has its roots in the traditions of Marxism and socialism. It may be identified by reference to two historical examples. The first we will call *left internationalism*. This form of solidarity was prevalent especially in the first decades of the twentieth century. In its early form, left internationalism presented a cosmopolitan alternative to global capitalism (Drainville 1998: 47) through expressions such as 'workers of the world unite' (Waterman 1998: 236). Left internationalism built on a degree of global consciousness, which assumed that the working-classes all over the world faced similar conditions and similar prospects of social change. This form of internationalism was a motivating factor in transnational mobilization and participation in the Spanish Civil War on the Republican side. Left internationalism was, however, characterized by struggles over the definition of socialist strategy. Yet what interests us here is not whether left internationalism was built on unity or faction, but rather the fact that it was rooted in a degree of global consciousness. In general, left internationalism and solidarity were not conceived of as the voluntary actions of individuals and civil society organizations, but were structured from above through national parties and states with socialist governments. Despite its elements of global consciousness, this old internationalism thus had an explicitly national dimension (De Angelis 2000: 11). Since the end of the Cold War this form of solidarity has virtually disappeared (Drainville 1998: 47).

The second example of ideological solidarity, *Third World solidarity*, was prevalent in the 1970s. Rucht (2000) labels the movements engaged in this type of activity as 'distant issue movements'. These are typically located in the developed parts of the world, especially Europe and the USA. Distant issue movements, in Rucht's definition (2000: 79), are 'movements that mobilize for issues that are not related, or are only very indirectly related, to the situation of the mobilizing groups in their home countries.' Distant issue movements in the German context discussed by Rucht have changed significantly over the years. For the purposes of our discussion, we will focus on the nature of distant issue movements in the 1960s, 1970s and 1980s. These became especially common and active with the student movement of the 1960s and were concerned particularly with the consequences of structural inequalities between the developed world and the developing world (Rucht 2000: 81). This awareness reflected a growing global consciousness, where the world was analysed as one structure, expressed for example in persistent inequalities between different parts of the world. The attention to inequalities between regions and continents would have been inconceivable without a farily well developed global consciousness. In the 1970s, distant issue movements were highly politicized and often had revolutionary aims. As such, they considered themselves to be alternatives to established and state-led forms of development aid. The solidarity work thus consisted in aiding revolutionary and social movements struggling for socialist social change in their home countries, and accordingly it often reflected the bipolar conflict between East and West. During the 1980s, the radicalism of these movements gradually waned, and they adopted a more pragmatic and professional approach (Rucht 2000: 82). The actors involved in this form of ideological solidarity were mainly civil society organizations and groups working from a left-wing perspective. As will be discussed below, elements of this form of solidarity are present in contemporary mutual solidarity activities, albeit in a different way.

Rights solidarity

This form is concerned with human rights abuses and other kinds of human oppression that result from the actions of states or extra-legal forces. Rights solidarity work generally aims at putting pressure on human rights abusers. This may be done directly by lobbying the governments of the countries in which the violations take place; but often pressure is exerted through other governments or intergovernmental organizations expected to have a certain influence on the state in which the violations occur.[1] This type of solidarity is often embodied by transnational advocacy networks (Keck and Sikkink 1998; Risse and Sikkink 1999). Transnational advocacy networks primarily work on issues involving bodily harm to vulnerable individuals or inequalities in legal opportunity. This means that rights solidarity work is most common in cases where the violation of rights is the consequence of intentional acts on the part of specific individuals or states, and less common in cases where violations have more structural causes (Keck and Sikkink 1998: 27). Accordingly, rights solidarity is often less politicized than the ideological form. It generally attempts to maintain a neutral political position and take the side of victims of human rights violations without consideration of the specific political conflict to which the abuses may be related.

Rights solidarity has deep historical roots, which also reflect its foundation in notions of global consciousness. Passy (2001: 8) thus refers to the ideas of solidarity and human rights as rooted in ideas and thoughts associated with Christianity, the Enlightenment and socialism. The influence of Christianity and Enlightenment are especially visible in rights solidarity; they are both ideational currents rooted in an understanding of human beings as endowed with certain universal rights. These ideas would become enshrined in the Universal Declaration of Human Rights in 1948. In their account of an early movement of transnational rights solidarity, the antislavery movement from 1833 to 1865, Keck and Sikkink (2000) point to two major influences in this movement, which was strongest in the USA and Britain. The first was a religious influence, embodied particularly by Quakers as well as by Methodists, Presbyterians and

Unitarians. The second, prevalent mainly in the USA, was based more on liberal Enlightenment ideas of liberty and equality (Keck and Sikkink 2000: 38). These historical influences are also visible in contemporary transnational advocacy networks. The main difference between historical and contemporary transnational rights solidarity lies in the institutional references available to rights solidarity activists in present times, as well as in the increasing interdependence of states. This interdependence, often a result of trade and economical agreements, makes it difficult to commit human rights violations without being subjected to criticism from other states and transnational civil society organizations (Brysk 2000).

Material solidarity

This form is directed mainly towards victims of disasters and to underdevelopment. These may have natural or human causes. Natural disasters include phenomena such as droughts, earthquakes and floods. Man-made disasters are wars and other forms of violent conflict which turn large numbers of people into refugees either within or outside their own country. Underdevelopment is usually the result of a lack of resources or of neglect and incompetence by authorities. Problems of this type occur almost exclusively in the developing world. In the developed world, there exists a substantial sector of organizations that deal with disasters and underdevelopment issues. These are often bureaucratically structured and professional organizations. Some are partially state-funded; others are state development and aid organizations. Material solidarity reflects a global consciousness inasmuch as it constructs a world in which the fate of distant people can no longer be reduced to their 'own business'. Obviously, this form of solidarity is greatly enhanced and aided by the availability of images and information from faraway places.

Historically, this form of solidarity goes back at least to the foundation of the International Committee of the Red Cross following the Battle of Solferino in 1859. The Red Cross went on to play a major role in relief work, especially during World War I. The period following the end of World War II witnessed the birth of a large number of organizations whose objective was to deliver aid to populations suffering from the consequences of the war. These solidarity efforts were, to a considerable degree, carried out by organizations based in the USA and directed mainly at Europe. The large majority of these had a religious origin (Baglioni 2001: 222).

If we return briefly to the case of the Red Cross, the problems faced by this organization provide an interesting basis for understanding a number of fundamental changes in the nature of material solidarity. The work of the Red Cross is built on neutrality and relies on states' acceptance that it may intervene in specific conflicts. As observed by Baglioni (2001: 221), the idea of neutrality and state acceptance suffered an important loss of legitimacy during World War II and, later, in the Biafran War in 1968. This gave rise to a new model of material solidarity that did not tie itself to the direct acceptance of states. An example of this model is Médecins sans Frontières (Baglioni 2001: 224). Like rights solidarity, material solidarity is often carried out by organizations that take a neutral position in specific conflicts, thus placing themselves on the side of the victims.

Mutual solidarity: an emergent political paradigm?

In their description of the antislavery movement, Keck and Sikkink (2000: 52) note that it was characterized by the conspicuous absence of victims, who were largely considered unproblematic 'others'. The relationship between providers and beneficiaries in the transnational antislavery movement thus rested on a high degree of paternalism, seldom recognized by the activists involved. While a stronger force in earlier movements than in their contemporary counterparts, paternalism and inequality also exist to an extent in today's solidarity movements. This form we will term *altruistic solidarity*. The notion of altruistic solidarity draws, to some extent, on the preceding discussion, although the forms of solidarity described in the typology above cannot simply be subsumed under this label. Our discussion of altruistic solidarity, based on an ideal-typical understanding, will be used to identify the primary characteristics of what we have referred to as *mutual solidarity*.

Mutual solidarity is, in many ways, a continuation and extension of previous forms of solidarity, and therefore not a new historical form that replaces others. It has not developed in a void. Invoking a key contribution of resource mobilization theory, we may suggest that the mutual solidarity paradigm is developing in a context of extensive mobilizing structures. The debates that are increasingly visible in its emergence are thus taking place within already existing solidarity organizations.[2] Before we proceed, it should be understood that mutual solidarity does not rest on a well-developed theory: the concept is a combination of an emergent empirical reality and normative aspirations on the part of solidarity activists.

Altruistic solidarity denotes a one-way relationship between those who offer solidarity and those who benefit from it (Eterovic and Smith 2001: 198). Moreover, it reflects a situation where the provider of solidarity is supposed to be stronger than the beneficiary, who is weak and in need of help. This element is visible in most instances of rights and material solidarity. As noted by Waterman (1998: 235) and by Eterovic and Smith (2001: 198), altruistic solidarity is often found in the relationship between developed and developing countries. Waterman (1999: 8) refers to this as substitution solidarity:

> *Substitution* implies standing up, or in, for a weaker or poorer other. This is how international solidarity has been usually understood amongst Development Co-operators and 'First-World Third-Worldists.' By itself, however, a *Substitution Solidarity* can lead to substitutionism (acting and speaking for the other), and it can permit the reproduction of existing inequalities.

The notion of substitution thus implies a situation with a degree of inequality in the relationship between those who offer solidarity and those who benefit from it. This type of altruistic solidarity usually involves the transfer of different forms of resources from developed to developing countries. It is often the result of initiatives by activists in the rich world, but may also be inspired by direct calls from aggrieved groups and populations in the poor parts of the world. As noted by Eterovic and Smith (2001: 198), altruistic forms of solidarity are often rather non-political and do not fundamentally challenge the underlying causes of the grievances that inspire the solidarity effort.

Armed with the definition of altruistic solidarity as a one-way exchange between providers and beneficiaries, we may now define mutual solidarity as an emergent form of solidarity that involves a more reciprocal or two-way relationship (Eterovic and Smith 2001: 203) between providers and beneficiaries. Or, put differently, mutual solidarity may be seen as a form of solidarity that blurs the distinction between providers and beneficiaries. In regard to solidarity exchanges between the developed and developing worlds, this point echoes the argument in Chapter 1 that contemporary globalization lacks an obvious direction (Giddens 1994b: 96).[3]

A degree of global consciousness is present in all forms of transnational solidarity. The concept of mutual solidarity, however, denotes a 'higher' level of global consciousness than the solidarity forms described above: it constructs the grievances and aspirations of physically, socially and culturally distant people as deeply interlinked. This is probably most evident in regard to environmental problems and other border-transgressing risks. Awareness of risks that cannot be contained within borders has found expression in the emergence of a world risk society (Beck 1999). World risk society is also a self-critical society that is increasingly capable of analysing events in a global rather than local or national perspective. It is a planetary society where it is difficult to project social conflicts into the future or an external space (Melucci 1998). The increase in the reflexive capacity of people has, according to Giddens (1994b), led to a situation in which traditions are coming under pressure. This post-traditional society (Giddens 1994b: 96–7) is also:

> the first *global society*. Until relatively recently, much of the world remained in a quasi-segmental state, in which many large enclaves of traditionalism persisted. Over the past few decades particularly, influenced by the development of instantaneous global electronic communication, these circumstances have altered in a radical way. A world where no one is 'outside' is one where pre-existing traditions cannot avoid contact not only with others but also with many alternative ways of life. By the same token, it is one where the 'other' cannot any longer be treated as inert. The point is not only that the other 'answers back', but that mutual interrogation is possible.

Rights solidarity and material solidarity, as described above, generally build on a notion of distance between providers and beneficiaries in the solidarity exchange, rather than on the possibility of mutual interrogation. The providers are in one place, mainly Europe and the USA, where there is a rather high degree of stability, while the beneficiaries are located in a distant place with severe problems, which may be ameliorated through transnational solidarity efforts.

Seen in this light, altruistic solidarity may be defined as substitution (Waterman 1999: 8) and, in some ways, considered to reproduce the distance between providers and beneficiaries in the solidarity exchange. Mutual solidarity, in contrast, is a form of solidarity that, while it does not dissolve distance, emphasizes similarities between physically, socially and culturally distant actors, while at the same time respecting and acknowledging local and national differences. As indicated by the above quotation from Giddens (1994b), solidarity in general and mutual solidarity in particular are highly dependent on the availability of means of global communication. Without knowledge about events in other parts of the world, we could not speak about a global consciousness. At the same time, we cannot simply assume that global communications media will produce a global consciousness. The relationship is dialectical in the sense that the use of global communications media presupposes at least an incipient global consciousness and an interest in faraway events.

Mutual solidarity is not an inevitable outcome of contemporary globalization processes, although mutual solidarity, as indicated earlier, is intimately related to globalization. The potential for a mutual solidarity remains limited by a number of factors and inequalities, and as such is not fully realizable. Transnational solidarity in general, and mutual solidarity in particular, are thus essentially social constructs formed through a process of transcending the different distances at play in transnational interactions. By applying the notion of transcending distances, we also imply that even the successful construction of mutual solidarity does not dissolve these distances. Physical, social and cultural distances are immanent in all relationships between geographically dispersed groups and individuals, and will remain so. The concept of mutual solidarity, however, suggests that these distances will increasingly become constructed in a different manner that emphasizes similarities and common aspirations and problems, rather than differences that disable transnational encounters and dialogue. On the other hand, and as stated above, contemporary proponents of mutual solidarity also display a positive valuation of, and respect for, difference. Thus, mutual solidarity combines notions of universality and particularity. This is evident in the tendency to formulate mutual solidarity through a radical democratic matrix, critical of neoliberal development policies (see Chapters 6 and 7).

This latter point indicates that the concept of mutual solidarity denotes a somewhat politicized relationship between providers and beneficiaries in the solidarity exchange. In other words, distant social struggles are increasingly analysed with a point of departure in a more or less similar injustice frame (see Chapter 6) and master frame (see Chapter 7), thus blurring the very distinction between providers and beneficiaries in the solidarity exchange. We contended above that rights and material forms of solidarity are often characterized by a rather low level of politicization. If we accept the claim that mutual solidarity rests on a more politicized relationship between providers and beneficiaries, it may appear that mutual solidarity has more in common with the ideological form of solidarity described earlier. This form of solidarity, however, entails an often strictly binary analysis of the world and a division between 'us' and 'them'. This form of solidarity, referred to by Waterman (1999: 8) as identity solidarity, reflects some of the limitations and dichotomies imposed by the Cold War on political action. Those groups and organizations worthy of solidarity were, accordingly, those that were committed to the same strategies and goals as the provider of solidarity.

In contrast, mutual solidarity builds on a greater level of openness to different forms of social struggle. As indicated above, this openness is especially expressed in the formulation and framing of mutual solidarity through a radical democratic matrix. In other words, mutual solidarity entails a constant mediation between particularity and universality – that is, an invocation of a global consciousness resting on recognition of the other. We will now take a closer look at how the transnational Zapatista solidarity network contains important elements of an emergent mutual solidarity paradigm, and how this is partly the result of the EZLN's ability to mediate between particularity and universality.

The 'Politics of Overflowing'

In the coming discussion, we explore the different ways in which the EZLN has invoked and formulated a global consciousness, and how this is connected to the notion of mutual solidarity. This element of the transnational framing process is inherently communicative and entails constant mediation between particularity and universality. In the case of the EZLN, Subcomandante Marcos has served as the primary communicator between the EZLN and transnational activists. Accordingly, the following discussions focus rather strongly on his role in the transnational framing process.

'Asking we walk': the power of listening

It was noted above that a major difference between ideological solidarity and mutual solidarity is the fact that the former is often tied to a binary analysis of the world. We may also suggest, along these lines, that ideological solidarity is exclusive rather than inclusive. Mutual solidarity, in contrast, builds on inclusion and openness to other definitions and analyses of social struggle, while at the same time acknowledging the inherently interconnected character of these struggles. Extending these points to the EZLN, it is contended that the relative lack of definition of the EZLN and its goals, and its refusal to play the role of a vanguard, are key to understanding its ability to invoke a global consciousness and generate a mutual solidarity. As outlined by Subcomandante Marcos in an interview with García Márquez and Pombo (2001), the anti-vanguardist position entails a radical departure from both previous and existing armed movements in Latin America, as well as a somewhat ambiguous relationship with the armed element of the EZLN:

> [O]ur army is a very different army because it is proposing to cease being an army. The soldier is an absurd person who has to take up arms in order to convince the other …, and for this reason a move-ment has no future if its future is military. If the EZLN persists as an army, it is destined for failure…. And the worst that can happen … is that it comes to power and installs itself as a revolutionary army. For us, this would be a failure. What would have been a success for a political-military organization in the 1960s and 1970s … would be a failure for us. We have seen that in the end these victories are failures or defeats hidden behind their own disguise…. This is an oppressive power that decides for society from above…. The world, and Mexican society, are made up by differences, and the relationship between these differences has to be constructed with a basis in respect and tolerance, things that did not appear in any of the discourses of the political-military organizations of the 1960s and 1970s.

Social change through armed struggle is thus portrayed as inevitably leading to an authoritarian situation and benefiting only a minority of the population. This partly explains the EZLN's constant emphasis on civil society as the main force in creating social change. To the extent that the EZLN envisions a role for itself in social change processes in Mexico, this is as a force that opens spaces for the empowerment and politicization of civil society (Bellinghausen 1999).[4] The abandonment of the armed path to social change was, according to Subcomandante Marcos, a consequence of the encounter between the EZLN and what he refers to as *zapatismo civil* (Le Bot 1997: 306). Subcomandante Marcos explains this encounter in an interview with Monsiváis and Bellinghausen (2001):

> The EZLN prepared for January 1, but not for January 2.... The EZLN appears on January 1, starts the war and realizes that the world is not what it was thought to be, but something else. Anyway, since then the virtue of the EZLN, if we can call it that, has been the ability to listen.... In this moment, the EZLN says: 'here is something we do not understand, something new,' and with the intuition that the leadership of the EZLN had ..., we said: 'let us detain ourselves, here is something that we do not understand, that we did not foresee, and for which we did not prepare. The most important thing is to talk and listen more.'

As Subcomandante Marcos explained in an interview with Le Bot (1997: 241), the EZLN had worked with two scenarios prior to the uprising on 1 January 1994: either the uprising would be met with indifference or it would ignite a general uprising in the Mexican population. As the above quotation indicates, neither of these scenarios materialized. People did not want to join the armed struggle, yet they were not indifferent to the fate and message of the EZLN. What emerged instead was a demand that the parties of the conflict enter into negotiations, which they duly did after twelve days of fighting in January 1994.

The EZLN's decision to respond to these calls from civil society by listening echoes to some extent the experiences surrounding the formation of the EZLN in the 1980s. In the interview with Le Bot (1997: 142ff.), Subcomandante Marcos explains how the EZLN was formed through an encounter between, on the one hand, a small group of urban intellectuals with a revolutionary vision and, on the other, the indigenous communities of Chiapas. This handful of non-indigenous revolutionaries (including Subcomandante Marcos) came to Chiapas with a baggage of Marxist-Leninist orthodoxy that was soon challenged by the world-view and traditions of the indigenous communities. Initially, this group looked at the indigenous people as exploited peasants who needed to be shown the way to liberation (Higgins 2000). But this perception, explains Subcomandante Marcos, was gradually broken down, and in the end the indigenous communities turned out to be the teachers rather than the students (Le Bot 1997: 147–9):

> [W]e were not speaking with an indigenous movement that was waiting for a savior, but an indigenous movement with a long tradition of struggle.... In those days, we are speaking here about the period 85–87, we are beginning to learn.... So this organization, still within a Marxist-Leninist tradition, suddenly realizes that there is a reality that it cannot explain.... The virtue of this military organization lies in recognizing that it did not have the answer and ought to learn.... When the EZLN faces something new and realizes that it does not have a solution to the problem, that it has to wait and learn, it also stops being a teacher.

The dialogue between this urban group of revolutionaries and the indigenous communities was facilitated by a figure present in several of Subcomandante Marcos's writings: old Antonio (*el viejo Antonio*). While old Antonio may appear as a literary figure, Subcomandante Marcos emphasizes that he is a real person, who died of tuberculosis in 1994 (Le Bot 1997: 147, 153).[5] He recounts (Le Bot 1997: 154–5) that old Antonio served as a 'translator' between the urban intellectuals and revolutionaries and the indigenous communities:

> [O]ld Antonio is the bridge that gives the guerrillas in the mountains access to the communities. [H]is fundamental contribution is to make the Zapatistas understand the specificity of the indigenous question in the mountains of southern Mexico. [A]nd in the end, this is the tool that Marcos appropriates to communicate the indigenous world to the urban world. Old Antonio supplies the indigenous elements to the Zapatista discourse when it addresses itself to the outside.

Thus the experience of the encounter between the indigenous communities and non-indigenous revolutionaries was reflected in the encounter between the EZLN and a Mexican and transnational public following the uprising on 1 January 1994 (Le Bot 1997: 306). The major lesson the EZLN learned from the encounter with the indigenous communities and old Antonio was the need to listen (Subcomandante Marcos, quoted in Holloway 1998: 163):

> The original EZLN, the one that is formed in 1983, is a political organization in the sense that it speaks and what it says has to be done. The indigenous communities teach it to listen, and that is what we learn. The principal lesson that we learn from the indigenous people is that we have to learn to hear, to listen.

The focus on listening rather than giving orders and proposing solutions is captured in the EZLN phrase 'asking we walk' (*preguntando caminamos*). This principle defines a process and a method rather than a goal. As already indicated, this approach to social change differs widely from the one promoted by revolutionary movements of the twentieth century, which in the majority of cases proceeded with a well-defined recipe for how to obtain their objectives (Holloway 1998: 165). The principle of 'asking we walk' is closely related to the EZLN's radical democratic visions (see Chapter 7). Democracy is seen not only as an end but also as an integral part of the process of social change. This perspective makes it impossible to predefine the path of social struggle or revolution and to think of a defined point of arrival (Holloway 1998: 165). Our emphasis here on the lack of definition of the EZLN does not imply that it does not have long-term strategies and concrete goals, as evidenced for example in the struggle for constitutional reform in the area of indigenous rights. This definition, however, constantly 'overflows, thematically and politically. The definition of indigenous rights is seen not as an end-point, but as a start, as a basis for moving on into other areas of change, but also as a basis for taking the movement forward, a basis for breaking out' (Holloway 1998: 173). Had the EZLN limited itself to the quest for indigenous autonomy, the transnational resonance and applicability of the EZLN would have been much less conspicuous. The fundamental principle of the EZLN is, in other words, not to create a new identity or affirm an old identity in a negative manner by establishing a 'them' and 'us' dichotomy (Holloway 1996: 3).[6] As the above quotation suggests, the indigenous people are instead transformed into a universal symbol of exclusion. This is done in a way that invokes a global consciousness of the interconnectedness of human struggles, and opens up the way for a mutual solidarity that enables a variety of social struggles to articulate their particularity in a manner that simultaneously asserts and transcends identity (Holloway and Peláez 1998: 4).

Subcomandante Marcos: a window to the outside and the inside

The EZLN's lack of definition allows for a more universal formulation of the particularity of its struggle.[7] This is evident, for example, in the currency of expressions such as 'we are all Marcos' and 'we are all Zapatistas'. These expressions, used primarily by solidarity activists, are inspired by Subcomandante Marcos, who refers to himself not as a person but as a figure and a symbol. In a statement regarding the March for Indigenous Dignity in February/March 2001, Subcomandante Marcos thus made the following remarks (quoted from Johnston 2003: 85):

> When the dust raised by our uprising settles, people will discover the simple truth: in this whole struggle and thinking process, Marcos was just one more fighter. That's why I say: if you want to know who Marcos is, see who's hidden behind the mask, then take a mirror and look at yourself. The face you see there will be the face of Marcos, because we are all Marcos.

This statement underlines the symbolic nature of the figure of Subcomandante Marcos. This interpretation finds support in the much earlier, now famous, response of Subcomandante Marcos to a question concerning his sexuality (quoted from Holloway and Peláez 1998: 10–11):

> Marcos is a gay in San Francisco, a black in South Africa, an Asian in Europe, a Chicano in San Isidro, a Palestinian in Israel, an indigenous person in the streets of San Cristóbal … a peasant without land, an underground editor, an unemployed worker, a doctor with no office, a non-conformist student, a dissident against neoliberalism, a writer without books or readers, and a Zapatista in the Mexican southeast. In other words, Marcos is a human being in this world. Marcos is

every untolerated, oppressed, exploited minority that is resisting and saying 'Enough!'

Subcomandante Marcos thus embodies in many ways the constant mediation between particularity and universality in the EZLN discourse. Speaking about himself in the third person, Subcomandante Marcos (Le Bot 1997: 155) has described his own role as that of a window:

> Marcos is transformed into a figure that has nothing to do with who is behind, he is converted into someone who is used.... Marcos ... is a window used to look inside and to look outside. But it happens that the window is dirty and people start seeing themselves, and it is here that Marcos is converted into a symbol, in this thing that has been constructed since 1994.

As suggested in the latter part of the quotation, the role of Subcomandante Marcos was different prior to, and in the first months following, the uprising. In the period from 1 January 1994 until the dialogue between the EZLN and the Mexican government in the cathedral of San Cristóbal de las Casas in late February 1994, Subcomandante Marcos thus describes his main role as that of a military leader (Le Bot 1997: 155–6).[8] Through his subsequent roles as spokesperson, translator and window, Subcomandante Marcos has acquired some of the characteristics of a Gramscian organic intellectual, the role of which is to transmit ideas between different groups involved in social struggle, and to overcome the parochial and translate particularities into a more globally applicable and understandable language (Bruhn 1999: 43–4).

In the early days of the EZLN, the major issue for the leadership and Subcomandante Marcos was to construct a link between the indigenous people with their cultural traditions and historical symbols known and recognized by the Mexican public in general. As recounted by Stephen (2002: 256–7), this was partly accomplished through the construction of a hybrid figure, Votán Zapata, melding local indigenous myths with national Mexican myths:

> Most people in the Lacandon jungle had completed little more than one or two grades in elementary school where they no doubt heard of Emiliano Zapata and celebrated his birthday. Within the embryonic group which would form the EZLN ... a local interpretation of

Zapata was forged through the melding of that revolutionary figure with two Tzeltal mythical figures. The result was a hybrid: Votán Zapata who appears to have been fashioned by Marcos and some of the indigenous founders of the EZLN in Chiapas. The figure of Votán Zapata became a local icon who embodied the spirit of the new indigenous Zapatismo of Chiapas.

Later, in the years following the uprising, the figure of Votán Zapata was interpreted even more broadly as a universal symbol of struggle and oppression (Stephen 2002: 270):

[T]he figure of Votán Zapata is projected not only as a symbol of struggle for indigenous peoples of Chiapas, but for all people who have been living in misery, without rights, justice, democracy or liberty and who support the struggle to obtain these goals. Votán Zapata is universalized to be an icon for all who can support the cause of Zapatismo, but is also used to promote the EZLN's own particular struggle.

The role of Subcomandante Marcos as an organic intellectual or translator has undoubtedly been aided by the anonymity of the masks that he and the other regular EZLN members wear.[9] It is the mask that lends weight and credibility to expressions like 'we are all Marcos' and 'we are all Zapatistas', and to the EZLN's repeated rejection of any vanguard role or aspiration to power. But just as Subcomandante Marcos has stressed that the EZLN's lack of definition is not a viable strategy in the long term (Le Bot 1997: 306), there also may be an end to the masks that have become symbols of this position. In more recent interviews (e.g. Ramonet 2001), Subcomandante Marcos has thus alluded to the possibility that EZLN members will take off the masks and transform the EZLN into a non-armed political organization. However, he has stressed that the precondition for such a development is that the Mexican Congress accepts the COCOPA proposal on indigenous rights (see Chapter 7).

'A world in which many worlds fit': dignity and the EZLN

We will now explore further how the EZLN has been able to broaden the struggle of the indigenous people of Chiapas and Mexico to make it relevant for non-indigenous people outside the country. It is argued that this process must be understood partly through the concept of dignity (*dignidad*), a recurring theme in the EZLN's discourse, as well as in its attempts to articulate its struggle both nationally and globally.

In Mexico, oppression and racism aimed at the indigenous people has a long history, dating back to the conquest of the Aztec empire in the early sixteenth century. Notwithstanding the fact that the indigenous population is today formally endowed with the same rights as others, racism is still widespread. As Díaz Polanco (1997b: 151ff.) recounts, this paternalism has been evident in relation to the EZLN uprising. Observers like Octavio Paz were thus led to speculate that the uprising was the result of manipulation by external forces: that is, the indigenous people, who make up the majority of the EZLN, were not considered capable of staging an uprising and formulating a coherent criticism of the status quo.

A major aim of the EZLN has consequently been to alter society's perception of the indigenous people as second- or third-class citizens (EZLN 2001c).[10] Yet what is at stake is not merely the granting of certain rights so as to make the indigenous the 'same' as the non-indigenous people of Mexico. Rather, as noted by Harvey (1998a), the struggle of the indigenous people centres on the right to have rights. This is most clearly reflected in the quest for autonomy. For the indigenous people, autonomy entails the right to govern themselves, and, as such, the right to define their own rights in accordance with tradition and cultural practices. The issue of the cultural rights of the indigenous people has been absent from previous armed movements in Latin America. This absence has been criticized repeatedly by the EZLN and Subcomandante Marcos. It has also been linked to another lacuna in these earlier movements: the lack of respect for other minority groups, such as homosexuals and lesbians (García Márquez and Pombo 2001).[11] As Paulson explains (2001), a key to understanding the resonance of the EZLN beyond Chiapas and Mexico lies in the fact that

> its rhetoric is refreshingly progressive, free of orthodox dogma, not necessarily anti- or even non-Marxist, but not needing to invoke Marx's name throughout the communiqués. Nor did the EZLN feel the need to subordinate every struggle to the class struggle; the American and European liberals and non-orthodox leftists were ecstatic to see Marcos supporting gays and lesbians, for example.

As noted above, the struggle of the indigenous people has revolved around the notion of dignity.[12] The central role of dignity comes not from the urban intellectual element of the EZLN, but from the indigenous communities and their century-long tradition of resistance (Bruhn 1999: 49). It is therefore related closely to resistance and the desire to overcome oppression:

> The indigenous peoples who support our just cause have decided to resist without surrender.... And they have decided this because they have made theirs a word that is not understood with the head, that cannot be studied or memorized.... This word is DIGNITY. Respect for ourselves, for our right to be better, for our right to struggle for what we believe in, for our right to live and die according to our ideals. Dignity cannot be studied; you live it or it dies. It aches inside and teaches you how to walk. (1995c: 265)

Dignity is, accordingly, 'the right to define and defend one's own identity' (Bruhn 1999: 49). Yet dignity is also more than the right to defend one's *own* identity. During the March for Indigenous Dignity (Marcha por la Dignidad Indígena) in February/March 2001, the EZLN made a number of speeches en route to Mexico City. In a message delivered in Puebla, the EZLN (2001b) presented the following definition of dignity, which clearly transcends the question of indigenous identity:

> [D]ignity is a bridge. It needs two sides that, being different, special, and distant, are united in the bridge without ceasing to be different and special, but ceasing to be distant.... In the bridge of dignity there is the one and the other, and the one is not more or better than the other, nor is the other more or better than the one. Dignity demands that we are us. But dignity is not that we are only us. In order for dignity to exist, the other is necessary. Because we are always us in relation to the other.... Dignity is thus recognition and respect. Recognition of what we are and respect for what we are, yes, but also recognition of what the other is, and respect for what the other is.... So, dignity is a house that includes the other and us.... Dignity should be a world, a world in which many worlds fit.... Indigenous dignity is not dominating the other that is not indigenous.... Indigenous dignity is a bridge that needs the other side.... The March for Indigenous Dignity cannot be only for the indigenous. The March for Indigenous Dignity has to be the march for the indigenous and the non-indigenous.

The struggle for dignity is thus not reducible to the struggle for indigenous rights, or for social change in Mexico.[13] This global relevance of dignity was asserted in the invitation to the First Intercontinental Encounter for Humanity and against Neoliberalism (Primer Encuentro Intercontinental por la Humanidad y contra el Neoliberalismo) in Chiapas in 1996 (EZLN 1996b): 'Dignity is that homeland without nationality, that rainbow that is also a bridge, that murmur of the heart no matter what blood lives in it, that rebel irreverence that mocks borders, customs and wars.' Dignity, for the EZLN, can only be obtained through a relation to the 'other' based on recognition and respect for difference. Dignity, in other words, is only possible in 'a world in which many worlds fit' (*un mundo donde quepan muchos mundos*) – one of the EZLN's best-known expressions. Through the establishment of a linkage between the notion of indigenous dignity and the desire for 'a world in which many worlds fit', the EZLN constantly transcends the particularity of the indigenous people and projects their struggle into a universal and global arena. This is done on at least two levels: abstractly, through references to humanity and dignity; and on a more concrete level, through demands of a universal character, such as housing, food and health (Ceceña 1996). This 'humanness not articulated in any theory, ideology, or doctrine' (Higgins 2000: 371), and the related ability to make the ordinary and daily transcendent (Ceceña 1996), is what makes the EZLN unique.[14] The universality of the EZLN discourse is captured in the following interview with a solidarity activist (Galván 2001):

> The issues that the Zapatistas address are not specific to Mexico. When they speak of human dignity, their message is universal. When they list their specific demands, they address the basic needs of every human being: food, shelter, medical care, education, equal protection of the law, etc.... Their emphasis on the dignity of every human being bridges issues and borders and opens the door to a worldwide movement for humanity.

The key to understanding the resonance of the EZLN outside Mexico and Chiapas thus, to a large extent, lies in its ability to mediate between the particular and the universal, or, in Holloway's (1998: 173) words, to engage in a 'politics of overflowing'.

Conflicting solidarities and the limits of mutual solidarity

We have so far discussed the EZLN's ability to invoke a global consciousness and to mediate between the particular and the universal. This ability is, to a great extent, what has enabled the incipient emergence of a mutual solidarity paradigm around the EZLN and the transnational Zapatista solidarity network. Yet talk of mutual solidarity should not lead us to project a state of harmony. Indeed, it is important to identify and understand some of the currents of conflict present within the Zapatista solidarity network and the potential limitations of mutual solidarity. As already indicated in Chapter 4, the mutual solidarity approach to the EZLN and the solidarity network goes beyond the traditional methods used in such work. The mutual solidarity approach is nurtured by the EZLN. This was reflected, for example, in a speech delivered by the EZLN (1999h) at the closing ceremony of the Democratic Teachers and Zapatista Dream Encounter (Encuentro Magisterio Democrático y Sueño Zapatista) in Chiapas in August 1999:

> [W]e are also democratic teachers, and electrical workers, and university students, and workers in the city and the country, and artists, and intellectuals, and religious men and women, and neighbors, and homosexuals, and lesbians, and ordinary women and men, and children, and old ones, that is, rebels, dissidents, inconvenient ones, dreamers. Because of that, the most important thing we Zapatistas want to ask you is to see us as another democratic union section. That you do not see us as someone who must be helped, poor things, out of pity, out of alms, out of charity.[15]

With these remarks, the EZLN dissociates itself somewhat from the types of solidarity discussed earlier in this chapter as altruistic solidarity.[16] On the other hand, the EZLN is also aware of the potential benefits of more traditional solidarity forms such as rights and material solidarity. This form of solidarity is reflected in numerous projects to improve infrastructures and educational facilities in Chiapas. Moreover, it is visible in the more or less constant presence of human rights observers in Chiapas, as well as in the occasional visits by human rights observation delegations and their subsequent lobbying work directed at the Mexican government and the US and European governments (see Chapter 4). Thus the Zapatista solidarity network displays the simultaneous presence of mutual and altruistic solidarity. This fact does not necessarily present a problem, and in many cases the different types of solidarity are practised by the same activists. Nevertheless, the distinction also points to important fault lines within the network. Marc Tomsin (2001), a French network activist, thus remarks that:

> the network of solidarity with the Zapatistas looses itself in lobbying, in human rights observation, in the relationship with governments and parliaments, with international institutions. The network ought to direct itself to the organizations of social struggle, not to the powerful of the planet.

This point is echoed by Jeroen ten Dam (1999), a former member of the now dissolved Amsterdam-based Mexico Solidarity Committee, in his criticism of Zapatista solidarity in Europe:

> Day by day the European network is becoming an ever more bureau-cratically organised humanitarian aid organisation, that will do anything in the aid of the good cause.... The main focus of the European solidarity network has become putting pressure on the European Union and Parliament not to accept the preferential treatment treaty between the European Union and the Mexican government. The other focus is to pressure the United Nations to intervene in Chiapas (as either a mediator or human rights observer). Both the European Union and the United Nations are instruments of the governments of the world, and we see no reason to ask them favours. Asking them for favours is to passively accept their authority and existence. We do not accept that and never will.

These quotations suggest that there are significant differences within the network in terms of the understanding of solidarity. We now briefly turn our attention to a number of limitations in the realization of mutual solidarity. These reflect not so much on the internal differences in the Zapatista solidarity network, but rather on the inequalities in the relationship between providers and beneficiaries in the solidarity relationship.

Up until now, the concept of mutual solidarity has described a situation in which distance is increasingly transcended and where globalization has no obvious direction. As noted elsewhere, however, distance should not be measured only as a physical entity, but also in social and cultural terms. By including these parameters for measuring distance, we are also forced to recognize a number of obstacles and limitations to mutual solidarity. Johnston's (2003) work on solidarity with the EZLN provides a range of insights on this issue. Johnston particularly challenges accounts of globalization that point to the emergence of, for example, a cosmopolitan democracy (Archibugi et al. 1998), a world culture (Boli and Thomas 1999), and a cosmopolitan public sphere (Köhler 1998). According to Johnston (2003), accounts of this type convey the image of a level playing field where global citizens are free to exchange ideas and form solidarities. This image, Johnston suggests, is an illusion that obscures obstacles to constructing solidarities. Extending these observations to the transnational solidarity network surrounding the EZLN, Johnston notes that this is characterized by uneven geographical development and inequality. The participants in transnational solidarity with the EZLN thus 'continue to be divided by cultural barriers, linguistic gaps, tactical differences, and radically different lifeworlds' (Johnston 2003: 97). In the case of the EZLN and the transnational Zapatista solidarity network, this may be reflected in a situation where the solidarity dialogue takes place almost exclusively between the educated leadership of the EZLN and network activists, and to a lesser extent between activists and 'ordinary' people in the Zapatista base communities.[17]

Notes

1. Seen from the perspective of organizations and groups in the country where rights violations are taking place, the ability to mobilize other governments as well as intergovernmental organizations to exert pressure on their national governments is described by Keck and Sikkink (1998: 12) as a boomerang pattern.
2. See, for example, Smith et al. 1997 and McCarthy 1997 for a discussion of mobilizing structures in a transnational context.
3. This point does not indicate that influence coming from the developing world to the developed world is a phenomenon limited to present times. The transnational resonance of, for example, Che Guevara, who became a revolutionary icon in the USA and Europe in the 1970s, demonstrates that the example of the EZLN has important historical precursors.
4. This discussion will not be developed further in this chapter, but will be continued in more detail in Chapter 7.
5. See also Stephen (2002: ch. 6) and Higgins (2000) for a discussion of the old Antonio figure.

6. The page number refers to a downloaded version of the article.

7. While most network activists see the lack of definition of the EZLN as a strength and point of attraction, more traditional left-wing observers, such as Petras (1999: 41), tend to view it as a limitation.

8. The first dialogues between the EZLN and the Mexican government began on 21 February 1994, and took place in the cathedral of San Cristóbal de las Casas with Bishop Samuel Ruiz as mediator.

9. In an attempt to demystify the figure of Subcomandante Marcos, Mexican authorities revealed his 'true' identity in connection with the February 1995 offensive against the EZLN. Subcomandante Marcos was said to be one Rafael Sebastian Guillén Vicente, born and raised in the northern state of Tamaulipas and a former student and teacher in Mexico City. Subcomandante Marcos himself has never confirmed this identity, but has admitted that he comes from a middle-class background. The family and educational background of Subcomandante Marcos/Rafael Sebastian Guillén Vicente is traced in a book by de la Grange and Rico (1998) with the specific aim of discrediting him.

10. It should be noted that the EZLN does not speak for all indigenous people of Mexico. Even in Chiapas there are conflicts between indigenous groups who support the EZLN and those who do not. The Acteal massacre in Chiapas in 1997 was thus carried out by indigenous people affiliated with local power holders. At the same time, it is important to be aware that the indigenous people of Mexico are not a homogeneous group. There are fifty-six indigenous groups in Mexico, each with its own traditions and values.

11. In addition to its concern with the oppression of homosexuals and lesbians (e.g. EZLN 1999f), the EZLN has also been attentive to the oppression of women in Mexican society, which is characterized by deep-seated machismo. This has also been the case in the indigenous communities. Prior to 1994, grassroots organizing in, for example, Chiapas was marked by a predominantly male leadership (Harvey 1998b). This situation changed significantly with the EZLN uprising, which accorded women a prominent position within the movement. This position was made public in the Women's Revolutionary Law published as part of *The Mexican Awakener* (*El Despertador Mexicano*) (EZLN 1994a), a 'newspaper' issued by the EZLN on the day of the uprising. The prominent role of women in the EZLN is visible in the fact that many of its commanders are women.

12. The notion of dignity and its use in social struggle are not an invention of the EZLN (Holloway 1998: 160). It has also been used by previous armed and social movements.

13. It is interesting to note that the weight of the indigenous issue was contested within the EZLN's leadership prior to the uprising. As recounted by Subcomandante Marcos (who is not indigenous), the indigenous leaders in particular were keen not to portray the EZLN as an indigenous army (Le Bot 1997: 202).

14. Another aspect of the humanness referred to by Higgins (2000) is the EZLN's and Subcomandante Marcos's constant reference to their own shortcomings and analytical errors, reflected for example in the above descriptions of the meeting between the urban intellectuals and the indigenous communities,

and in the meeting between the EZLN and civil society in the wake of the 1994 uprising.

15. Translation from Spanish adapted from the Irish Mexico Group website at http://flag.blackened.net/revolt/mexico/ ezln/1999/marcos_teachers_close_aug.html.

16. During the reorganization process of 2003 of the Zapatista communities, the EZLN criticized certain elements of transnational solidarity as being disrespectful and paternalistic. See also the discussion in the Conclusion.

17. These points challenge in many ways the basic approach of this book. However, as stated in Chapter 1, the emphasis in the book is on facilitating rather than limiting and obstructing factors in the transnational framing process, and in the construction of transnational solidarity. This represents a choice of presentation rather than a disregard for the relevance of these issues. Accordingly, the question of limiting factors is only touched on briefly in the analytical chapters.

6

Neoliberalism

In this chapter we analyse how the EZLN has expanded and diffused its injustice frame in a way that has found echo beyond the borders of Mexico. This injustice frame is based on the concept and empirical reality of neoliberalism, and has been a central element in the formation of the transnational Zapatista solidarity network. The EZLN has used the concept of neoliberalism as a common denominator in the development of the injustice frame lying at the root of its uprising. This is visible on two levels. On the first, the frame is rooted primarily in the national and regional contexts of Mexico and Chiapas. On the second, the frame is broadened to the transnational arena. This latter phase has been most conspicuous since 1996, when the EZLN convened two encounters 'for humanity and against neoliberalism'.

'Sellers of the Homeland':
The National Dimension

At the root of the theoretical argument concerning neoliberalism as a potential transnational injustice frame lies an empirical fact: the almost global extension since the 1970s and 1980s of neoliberal ideas and policies. This is obviously not to suggest that the spread of neoliberalism has been uniform on a global scale. Even if it is accepted that neoliberalism denotes a process with global ramifications, it is useful to bear in mind that policies are filtered through national specificities and regional diversity (Otero 1996: 3). This raises again the issue of global consciousness, for it is that which allows people to recognize similarities in the spread and consequences of neo-liberalism despite obvious local and national differences.

As we have noted on several occasions, the original framing litera-ture takes its point of departure in a nationally defined context. The above reservation concerning the uneven nature of globalization and neoliberalism requires us to refer back to the theoretical discussions in Chapter 2 in order to register certain qualifications relating to the use of the injustice frame in the analysis of transnational framing. It was contended in Chapter 2 that injustice frames typically display three components: recognition of a problem; acknowledgement that the problem may be ameliorated through collective action; and solu-tion proposals (Gamson et al. 1982; Snow and Benford 1988). In a transnational context, however, the use of neoliberalism as the basis of injustice frames lies mainly in the recognition of the problem and in the acknowledgement that social action may lead to change and, to a lesser extent, in proposed solutions.

Physically, socially and culturally distant actors engaged in trans-national framing processes may thus make use of the concept of neoliberalism as a broad framework that allows them to discern similarities in the social and political problems they experience. But it does not necessarily follow that this analysis will lead to the definition of common solutions. In this sense, our transnational use of the concept of injustice frames departs somewhat from its original interpretation. Integrating the components of recognition, action and solution would make it difficult to pursue our argument from Chapter 1 that globalization as a process is essentially created by local and national actors. To speak of common solutions, in other words, would project our discussion into the arena of a coherent and global civil society, and understand global resistance as a unitary force. Yet it is dubious to speak about a global civil society in the absence of a global state, just as it is empirically untenable to think of resistance in terms of a coherent global movement. An approach along these lines would also risk overlooking the fact that national states and intergovernmental organizations remain central sites of authority even for transnational social actors. While neoliberalism may be recognized as a process affecting the majority of the world's population, and standing in need of action and change, solutions to the problem are mostly defined on a national level.

In terms of our case, this serves as a useful reminder that, despite its transnational ramifications and repercussions, the EZLN is a national movement seeking change mainly on the national level (e.g. EZLN 1995a). Or, rather, we are reminded that the EZLN injustice frame moves simultaneously on national and transnational levels. The national aspect of the injustice frame has been brought to the fore, *inter alia*, by Johnston and Laxer (2003: 70–71):

> While states enforce globalism, the EZLN struggles to reclaim the Mexican state as an expression of national will. Nationalism plays a constitutive role in Zapatismo, a factor not always understood or recognised within solidarity networks outside Mexico.... The Zapatistas' emphasis on Mexican nationalism is particularly salient when juxtaposed against Mexico's loss of sovereignty through globalism.... The power of nationalism, albeit in a sophisticated, multi-national variant, is also exceptionally important to the Zapatista struggle.

The EZLN's use of the concept of neoliberalism is largely anchored in the loss of national sovereignty referred to in the quotation from Johnston and Laxer above. This loss of sovereignty has been closely associated with the entering into force of NAFTA on the day of the EZLN uprising. In a widely circulated statement, the EZLN (1994f: 64) early on described NAFTA as 'nothing more than a death sentence to the indigenous ethnicities of Mexico, who are perfectly dispensable in the modernization programme of Salinas de Gortari'. The basis for this harsh judgement of NAFTA lies in particular in the predicted impact of the trade agreement on Mexico's small maize producers, many of whom are indigenous. Under NAFTA, all import quotas and tariffs are to be phased out over a fifteen-year period. Considering that the average yield in Mexico is 1.7 tons per hectare compared to 6.9 tons in the USA, the removal of tariffs and quotas is likely to drive many indigenous maize farmers out of business (Harvey 1998a: 181).

Carlos Salinas de Gortari, referred to in the above statement, was president of Mexico from 1988 to 1994 and is usually seen as the symbol of neoliberal reform in Mexico. President Miguel de la

Madrid (1982–88), had already embarked on a neoliberal development path following the Mexican debt crisis in 1982, which was soon to be followed by debt crises in a number of other developing countries. But it was Salinas de Gortari who locked Mexico into a neoliberal development model and speeded up reforms, not least as a result of the decision to enter NAFTA with the USA and Canada (Centeno 1994: 15ff.). These reforms included the privatization of nationally owned corporations and the reform of Article 27 in the Mexican Constitution. As mentioned earlier, the reform of Article 27 was a major motivation for the EZLN uprising, who considered it (EZLN 1994d) 'a betrayal to the fatherland'. In this sense, the EZLN focuses strongly on the consequences of neoliberalism in the national Mexican context. This is indicated already in the name of the EZLN as an army of national liberation. For the EZLN, neoliberalism thus entails the demand on countries to open their borders to the free circulation of capital. This development is considered to lead to instability (EZLN 1999e):

> Those rapacious and migratory birds that are international financial capital have come to nest in Mexican lands. But it will only be for a moment. The overvaluation of the Mexican peso and the lowering of interest rates are good food for those parasites, but they can only lead to their advantage if the bubble bursts. The profit comes from the 'crack', not from stability.[1]

These lines were clearly written in the light of the financial crisis of 1997, which hit Asia especially, and contributed in large part to the free movement of speculative financial capital.[2] In order to expose and criticize this situation whereby Mexico's national borders are opened to financial capital by a neoliberal national government of *vendepatrias* (sellers of the fatherland) (EZLN 1994d), the EZLN has from the beginning made widespread use of notions of history and nation. The EZLN, in other words, has consciously inserted the uprising into the long history of social struggle in Mexico. This anchoring in Mexican history is evidenced by the opening lines of the EZLN's first public statement, the Declaration of the Lacandon Forest (EZLN 1994b):

> We are a product of 500 years of struggle: first against slavery, then during the War of Independence against Spain led by insurgents,

then to avoid being absorbed by North American imperialism, then to promulgate our constitution and expel the French empire from our soil, and later the dictatorship of Porfirio Diaz denied us the just application of the Reform laws and the people rebelled and leaders like Villa and Zapata emerged, poor men just like us.... We are the inheritors of the true builders of our nation. The dispossessed, we are millions and we thereby call upon our brothers and sisters to join this struggle as the only path.[3]

Nowhere is the national dimension in the EZLN clearer than in the reference to Emiliano Zapata in the name of the movement. To refer to Zapata is to refer to the Mexican Revolution (1910–19). Following from its self-perception as an inheritor of the Mexican Revolution, the EZLN disputes the right to appropriate the symbols of Mexican history. The PRI, considered by the EZLN to be its main opponent at the time of the uprising, also makes use of the revolution as a source of legitimacy. This is obvious already in the name of the party (the Institutional Revolutionary Party). The PRI came into being in 1929 in an attempt to unite the many factions of the revolution into a revolutionary family. The figure of Emiliano Zapata was later appropriated for this purpose by the PRI and turned into a co-founder of the political regime. When, for example, President Salinas de Gortari announced the reform of Article 27 in the Mexican Constitution, he deployed an image of Emiliano Zapata in the background (Rajchenberg and Héau-Lambert 1998: 23).

The EZLN, on the other hand, considers the PRI's neoliberal policies to have betrayed the revolution and the ideas of Emiliano Zapata. On the seventy-fifth anniversary of the death of Zapata, the EZLN (1994d) made the following remarks that clearly refer to the appropriation by the PRI of the figure of Zapata:

Today, 10 April 1994, is the 75th anniversary of the assassination of General Emiliano Zapata.... Today the usurper Salinas de Gortari, who named himself 'President of the Mexican Republic', lies to the Mexican people saying that his reforms to Article 27 of the constitution reflect the true spirit of General Zapata. The supreme government lies!.... The right to land for those who work it can never be given up and the war cry 'Land and Liberty' lives on without rest in Mexican lands. Under the cloak of neoliberalism which casts shadows on our soils, peasants who struggle for their agrarian rights are imprisoned and murdered.[4]

In an interview with Blixen and Fazio (1995), Subcomandante Marcos, alluding to the agrarian reforms under Salinas de Gortari, elaborates further on the connection between neoliberalism and the nation:

> Those who defend the national project are either assassinated or thrown out. The neoliberal project demands this internationalization of history; it demands that national history is erased and made international; it demands the erasing of cultural borders…. Neoliberalism's main error is to think that one can go against history … and to make believe as if here there was never a history, a culture or anything.

It is clear that the EZLN's use of neoliberalism as an injustice frame is closely tied to the consequences of neoliberalism in a national Mexican context. The EZLN rarely makes specific suggestions as to how the problems associated with neoliberalism may be ameliorated. Yet, as evidenced in the account below (EZLN 1997b), a focus on neoliberalism as a development model erasing the history and culture of Mexico naturally points in the direction of a strengthening of the national state as the obvious response:

> The Zapatistas think that, in Mexico … the recuperation and defence of national sovereignty is part of an anti-neoliberal revolution…. The Zapatistas think that the defence of the national state is necessary in view of globalization, and that the attempts to slice Mexico to pieces come from the governing group.[5]

This stance has led the EZLN to lend moral support to a wide range of causes opposing privatization initiatives in Mexico. Two prominent examples of anti-neoliberal protest that have attracted support have been the student strike at the National Autonomous University of Mexico (Universidad Nacional Autónoma de México, or UNAM) (EZLN 1999c), and the protests against plans to privatize Mexico's archeological sites (EZLN 1999i).[6]

The strike in 1999 at UNAM, Mexico's public university with about 300,000 students, was a response to government plans to charge tuition fees and introduce restrictions in the time of study.[7] Access to free and public education was one of four pillars on which the post-revolutionary political system (i.e. the PRI) built its legitimacy (Basáñez 1996: 189ff.).[8] These pillars all reflected to some extent the popular demands of the revolution symbolized by Emiliano Zapata and Francisco 'Pancho' Villa.[9] Accordingly, and once again stressing the EZLN's concern with the cultural and historic heritage of Mexico, the initiatives proposed by the government have been viewed by the EZLN and the students at UNAM as a betrayal of some of the popular demands emerging from the revolution. The issues raised by the privatization of tuition fees fit well into the EZLN's critique of neoliberalism, which was already established at the time of the strike in early 1999, and the EZLN provided the student movement with an important point of reference and inspiration.

The EZLN has also been engaged in initiatives protesting against plans to privatize Mexico's archeological sites. The concern with this issue obviously reflects, to some extent, the fact that the EZLN is mainly made up of indigenous peasants of Mayan descent.[10] In a speech at the National Meeting in Defence of the Cultural Heritage (Encuentro Nacional en Defensa del Patrimonio Cultural), held in Chiapas and convened by the EZLN, Subcomandante Marcos (EZLN 1999i) pointed out the effects of neoliberalism in regard to the history and culture of Mexico:

> Those who govern now pretend to put a price tag on the cultural history of Mexico and convert the national historical heritage into a privatized collection piece ..., to convert it into a Disney World of the ancient.... For those who govern us today, if history cannot be traded in the stock market it does not have any value. And if the cultural heritage cannot be sold it is something useless and annoying.

This brings us back to the discussion regarding the use of neoliberalism as an injustice frame in transnational framing processes. The focus on the national consequences of neoliberalism by the EZLN may be taken to suggest that the injustice frame presented by the EZLN has a limited reach beyond Mexico. The distinction between the three components of the injustice frame – recognition, action and solutions – may help us refine this perception. Put differently, the transnational resonance of the EZLN injustice frame lies primarily in the first two dimensions, recognition and action, and to a lesser extent in the third dimension, solutions. While the EZLN has hinted at a solution within the context of Mexico – namely, the recuperation of national sovereignty – it has not done so with regard to countries outside Mexico. It is true that the EZLN has suggested that neoliberal politics should be countered by a loose and informal transnational network of social activists. This, however, does not denote a solution per se but rather a recognition that neoliberalism affects people all over the world, albeit in different guises, and that social action may lead to social change. Solutions, on the other hand, must take place within the local and national contexts of activists.

The 'Fourth World War' against 'Humanity': The Transnational Dimension

The EZLN began giving its injustice frame a specific transnational dimension in 1996, when it convened two encounters 'for humanity and against neoliberalism' in Chiapas.[11] The subsequent broadening of the frame should not be seen as a move away from the national dimension described above. Rather, the two dimensions are present simultaneously. Similarly, the argument concerning the transnational leap of the injustice frame after 1996 is not meant to suggest that the EZLN had hitherto lacked this dimension, or that people outside Mexico were not attentive to the international relevance of neo-liberalism constituted as an injustice frame. As early as November 1994, Cecilia Rodriguez (1994), in a speech to the USA-based Native Forest Network, made the following link between the EZLN and neoliberalism:

> The struggle of the Zapatistas runs clearly and directly against the policies of neo-liberalism.... It is neo-liberalism which the Zapatistas are fighting against, in the midst of progressive forces which are unable to identify their enemy, and the failures of rigid Marxist dogma, and this is the global significance of their struggle, this therefore makes their front line your front line as well.

The early linkage between the EZLN and neoliberalism was in large part due to the coincidence between the uprising and the coming into force of NAFTA on 1 January 1994. The great majority of observers (e.g. Morton 2000; Ayres 2003) have focused accordingly on the coincidence between the EZLN uprising and the coming into force of NAFTA being the result of strategic considerations on the part of the EZLN. Whether the choice of date was in fact so conscious is difficult to verify. In an early interview (EZLN 1994f: 144), Subcomandante Marcos referred instead to more practical reasons for the choice of date, while acknowledging the usefulness and symbolic value of the coincidence. Whether or not the choice of date was a deliberate attempt by the EZLN to gain attention, it is beyond doubt that the 'Zapatistas' decision to attack on the NAFTA's implementation date provided an international link for what might otherwise have been seen as a local or at most national conflict' (Bob 2001: 20).[12] At the same time, Mexico's participation in NAFTA also provided the EZLN with a certain amount of protection, as the agreement exposed Mexico to closer scrutiny from its northern neighbours and increased the visibility of Mexican politics (Nash and Kovic 1996: 180). As discussed in Chapter 4, the participation of Mexico in NAFTA has also provided, in particular, US and Canadian solidarity activists with an important lever in their attempts to influence politicians, as well as the North American public in general.

As briefly mentioned in Chapter 3, the coincidence between the EZLN uprising and the coming into force of NAFTA served to draw special attention to Chiapas from activists in the USA, Canada and Mexico who had been involved in activities opposing NAFTA in the early 1990s (Bob 2001). Cleaver (1994: 21–2) notes the importance of these dormant and already existing networks:

> So when the Zapatista Army marched into San Cristóbal and the other towns of Chiapas, not only did those already concerned with the struggles of Indigenous peoples react quickly, but so did the much more extensive organizational connections of anti-NAFTA struggles. Already in place were the computer conferences and lists of the anti-NAFTA alliances. For many, the first information on their struggles came in the regular postings of the NAFTA Monitor on 'trade.news' or 'trade.strategy' either on Peacenet or through the Internet.

The case of NAFTA is especially interesting because it is a free-trade agreement involving both developed (USA, Canada) and developing (Mexico) countries. As suggested by the quotation from Cleaver above, opposition to NAFTA had resulted in the formation of transnational alliances, especially between workers and unions in the three countries. The anti-NAFTA activities had, however, been initiated mainly by activists in the USA and Canada. Accordingly,

Carr (1999: 52), for one, has worried about the asymmetrical character of cross-border labour contacts: 'The vast majority of these initiatives have been launched from the north ... and reproduce consciously and unconsciously elements of chauvinism, paternalism, patron-clientelism and protectionism.'

Seen in the light of such observations, the resonance of the EZLN in for example Canada and the USA is especially noteworthy as it points to the reverse situation. Transnational activities involving movements in developing countries have typically taken the form of unidirectional solidarity. Activity surrounding the EZLN has been conspicuous precisely because it has developed from a unidirectional relationship between the EZLN and solidarity activists (altruistic, or rights and material solidarity) to one of mutual solidarity and exchange (see Chapter 5). As indicated earlier, this development should be understood in relation to the encounters in Chiapas in 1996. While NAFTA provided an early connection between the EZLN and critics of neoliberalism, the encounters significantly changed the EZLN's role in the solidarity network: initially the focus of solidarity for transnational activists, it would become an internationally recognized node of special influence in a critique of neoliberalism extending beyond the borders of Mexico. While the Zapatista solidarity network existed in an incipient form prior to 1996, the following phase denoted a qualitatively new development. This has been characterized by greater maturity and deeper politicization, pointing ahead in many ways to the transnational justice and solidarity network that first emerged in full force in Seattle in 1999.

It may appear from the above account that the EZLN has in a sense 'chosen' its new role as a node of special influence through the initiative of the encounters. Whereas it is true that such a role is gained through innovative action by specific actors, this should not blind us to the fact that, as well as being chosen, it is also to some extent 'given'. The role as a node of special influence should thus be considered in relation to existing or emergent cycles of contention (Tarrow 1998) and master frames (Snow and Benford 1992). Consequently, the location of the EZLN uprising at the beginning of an emergent cycle of contention that came to fruition in Seattle in 1999 is vital in understanding why the EZLN has become a node of special influence in the transnational Zapatista solidarity network, and to some extent also in the transnational justice and solidarity network.[13]

The EZLN's interpretation of neoliberalism as a global phenomenon was developed mainly in the two declarations of La Realidad. The First Declaration was issued in January 1996 to announce the first intercontinental encounter; the Second Declaration was issued at the end of the encounter, in August 1996. The EZLN used the encounter to present neoliberalism as a threat to humanity as a whole. At the April 1996 American preparation for the intercontinental encounter, the EZLN (1996d) stressed the interconnectedness of the world and its own global reach, by stating that it is a 'world-wide system that enables crime to turn itself into government in Mexico. It is a national system enabling crime to rule in Chiapas. Fighting in the mountains of South Eastern Mexico, we fight for Mexico, for humanity and against neoliberalism.' Neoliberalism's threat to humanity, evident already in the name of the encounter, invokes a global consciousness projecting problems beyond the borders of Chiapas and Mexico. This impression was further enforced by the EZLN's (1996b) definition in the First Declaration of La Realidad of neoliberalism as a world war against humanity:[14]

> During the last years, the power of money has presented a new mask over its criminal face. Disregarding borders, with no importance given to races or colors, the power of money humiliates dignities, insults honesties and assassinates hopes. Re-named 'neoliberalism', the historic crime of the concentration of privileges, wealth and impunities, democratizes misery and hopelessness. A new world-war is waged, but now against the entire humanity.... With the name of 'globalization' they describe this modern war which assassinates and forgets.... A new lie is sold to us as history. [T]he lie about the victory of neoliberalism.... Instead of humanity, it offers us stock market value indexes, instead of dignity it offers us globalization of misery, instead of hope it offers us emptiness, instead of life it offers us the international of terror.

In an address to the International Civil Commission for Human Rights Observation (Comisión Civil Internacional de Observación por los Derechos Humanos), which visited La Realidad and Chiapas in November 1999, Subcomandante Marcos elaborated on this definition. In this address, later published in *La Jornada* (EZLN

2001e), Subcomandante Marcos defined neoliberalism as a fourth world war (the Cold War being the third). The main combatants in this war are considered to be neoliberal globalization and humanity. Neoliberal globalization, argues Subcomandante Marcos, is forcing the penetration of market rationality into more and more social relations. This development involves increasing homogenization, and the corresponding eradication of difference and identity as valuable characteristics of humanity. Considering that identity is to a large extent tied to national cultures, nation-states and ethnic groups, with their cultural particularities, are among the first victims. These two aspects – the expansion of market rationalities and the eradication of difference – form the basis of the EZLN's interpretation and critique of neoliberalism. This interpretation does not differ significantly from that of the Mexican context, as presented above. Thus, in many ways, the EZLN has simply broadened its national interpretation to the international arena.

A distinction was made in Chapter 2 between four different types of framing process. It was emphasized that our concern with the transnational framing process underlying the formation of the Zapatista solidarity network would largely involve the first three processes: frame bridging, frame amplification and frame extension. The EZLN's broadening of its national injustice frame to the transnational context may be considered an instance of frame bridging. Frame bridging was described in Chapter 2 as the attempt to mobilize sectors of the public who lack an organizational base for expressing discontent, around some of the social movement's concerns and grievances. For the purposes of this study, however, we must qualify this definition. Those overseas activists who embraced the broadened EZLN injustice frame were already involved in activities springing from a critique of neoliberalism, and therefore did not lack an organizational base. This was evidenced, for example, in the early connection between anti-NAFTA activists and the EZLN, and in the fact that the EZLN uprising was in many cases embraced by organizations already challenging neoliberalism. As noted by Stephen (2001), the resonance of the EZLN injustice frame outside Mexico thus had much to do with the choice of concept:

> The Zapatistas, like many poor, indigenous, rural people in the world, understood long before westerners did that free trade and other aspects

of neo-liberal policy were not working for them. They didn't call it neo-liberalism. They called it people coming in to take over their resources without consulting them. This is a really old colonial issue. So once the leadership of the EZLN like Marcos, and others in the command who had long-term experience in peasant movements and negotiating the government in Mexico found a new label, neo-liberalism, they used it, and connected with other global movements.

The concept of neoliberalism has its roots in the 1980s, when it was used by people and organizations in the USA and Europe to criticize, in particular, the policies pursued by Ronald Reagan in the USA and by Margaret Thatcher in Great Britain. By choosing the concept of neoliberalism as the axis of its injustice frame, the EZLN deployed an already well established and widely acknowledged point of reference, well suited to give the EZLN's injustice frame resonance beyond the borders of Mexico. Referring back to our distinction between the recognition, action and solution components, we may say that the choice of the concept of neoliberalism significantly strengthened the recognition component of the EZLN injustice frame.

Returning to our discussion of frame bridging, it is fair to say that the EZLN's injustice frame not only resonated with already existing organizations and groups but also served to motivate people who had hitherto lacked an organizational base. This leads to another important qualification concerning our use of the framing concept. A successful frame is considered to be one that attracts new activists to the social movement. Yet in a transnational framing process, such as that underlying the formation of the Zapatista solidarity network, success on the part of the EZLN in broadening its injustice frame obviously does not mean that its ranks swell. To the extent that the EZLN's transnationalization of its injustice frame draws new people into solidarity activism, this takes place through other organizations and groups already involved in network activities, or through the formation of new ones.

In our exposition of the transnational dimension of the EZLN injustice frame, we have focused on the organization's definition of the problems associated with neoliberalism. In contrast, the Second Declaration of La Realidad, presented at the closing ceremony of the intercontinental encounter in 1996, paid more attention to the potentials of transnationalizing resistance to neoliberalism. The EZLN (1996e) called for the creation of a

> collective network of all our struggles and particular resistances. An intercontinental network of resistance against neoliberalism, an inter-continental network of resistance for humanity. This intercontinental network, recognizing differences and knowing similarities, will seek to meet with other resistances all over the world. This intercontinental network of resistance will be the medium through which the different resistances can support each other. This intercontinental network of resistance is not an organizing structure, it does not have a leading or decision-making centre, it does not have central leadership or hierarchies. The network is all of us who resist.

The above quotation leads us back to the theoretical arguments outlined above, where it was argued that the EZLN injustice frame did not propose solutions. The quotation may appear to contradict this point, as it proposes a concrete initiative for struggling against neoliberalism in its different guises. However, it should not be con-sidered a solution per se. Rather, it draws up a framework within which solutions may be sought.

The fact that a movement gives its injustice frame a transnational dimension does not necessarily mean that this frame is received and understood by a transnational audience. This underscores the observa-tion in Chapter 2 that transnational framing processes always involve a sender–recipient relationship. We have so far looked at injustice frames mainly from the point of view of the sender, the EZLN. In the remainder of the chapter, the focus is on the way the EZLN injustice frame has been received outside Mexico and how it has been understood and applied by non-Mexican actors.

The 'Ultimate Underdogs':
The Left after the Cold War

The end of the Cold War marked the beginning of an identity crisis within the radical left.[15] In the Latin American context, and beyond, this tendency was reinforced by the 1990 electoral defeat of Nicaragua's Sandinistas. Whether or not those on the radical left had supported Soviet bloc socialism, its demise precipitated the need to rethink the foundations of their position.[16] In his epitaph for the radical Latin American left, *Utopia Unarmed*, Castañeda (1994: 240–41) notes that

> the most damaging effect of the Cold War's conclusion on the Latin American left lies in the generalized perception of defeat.... This sense of defeat is derived from the left's perceived or real connection with existing socialism. For the left, the fall of socialism in the Soviet Union and Eastern Europe represents the end of a stirring, effective, nearly century old utopia. Indeed, the very notion of an overall alternative to the status quo has been severely questioned.

Speaking also from within a Latin American context, Vilas (1996: 265–6) has referred to similar tendencies towards a deradicalization of the left:

> The Latin American left appears motivated by the need to adapt to the new scenario emerging out of recent global and regional political changes – the end of the cycle of the Central American revolutions, the crisis of Cuban socialism, the acceleration of global financial integration, the end of the cold war system – rather than by its overall transformation. In fact, the changes in that scenario are leading the left to modify its own ideological orientations, programmes, organizational structures and range of action.

This retrenchment of the radical left after the end of the Cold War does not lie in the fact that the original causes underlying its existence have vanished or diminished. According to a study by the UN Economic Commission for Latin America and the Caribbean (CEPAL), more than a third of Latin American households, corresponding to 211 million people, lived below the poverty line in 1999. Mexico lies above this average, with 38 per cent of its households living below the poverty line. Comparing urban and rural households, the study shows that poverty is considerably more widespread in rural areas (Economic Commission for Latin America and the Caribbean 2001). If we consider rural Chiapas, the home state of the EZLN, we are consequently met with even more extreme indicators of poverty. In some municipalities, more than two-thirds of households are without electricity, while more than half lack drinking water (Harvey 1998a: 184). It should be noted that these numbers are well above the averages for Mexico, as well as for the state of Chiapas as a whole. The inhabitants of the municipalities mentioned by Harvey (1998a), Ocosingo, Altamirano and Las Margaritas, are at the same time predominantly indigenous. This points to the fact that not only in Mexico but all over Latin America the indigenous people live under socio-economic conditions very much worse than those of society in general. Considering, at the same time, that Chiapas is one of Mexico's poorest states, the indigenous people who form the basis of the EZLN belong to the most marginalized sector of the Mexican population. Their severe plight was reflected by the EZLN (1994b) in the Declaration of the Lacandon Forest, where eleven demands were made, among them concrete demands for work, housing, land, food, and health.

The fact that the EZLN uprising took place despite these conditions has attracted considerable sympathy and astonishment from transnational activists. Considering this apparent paradox, Kerry Appel (2000) comments that

> it is them, the most excluded people in the world, the indigenous Mayan men and women from the marginalized …, poverty stricken communities, with little or no education, little or no food or resources, little or no rights of recognition that have risen up and said, we can change the world, and have put themselves and their lives on the line in order to do that.

This view of the EZLN finds echo on a website calling for the formation of a so-called Zapatista Bloc at the anti-FTAA protests in Quebec in April 2001 (Zapatista Bloc 2002):[17]

> Because of the symbolic nature of their revolt, their ability to draw connections between local oppression and international structures of institutionalized violence and repression, and their stance on indigenous rights and autonomy, the Zapatistas have been an important part of the struggle against global capitalism. The Zapatistas, the ultimate underdogs, have constantly and effectively battled not only with arms but also with words, ideas and visions for a sustainable and just future. The Zapatistas have inspired the mobilization of civil society in Mexico and around the world in the fight for democracy, liberty and justice.

The paradoxical appearance of the EZLN is a common thread in many accounts of its resonance beyond the borders of Mexico. These accounts, in turn, often make reference to Fukuyama's (1989) insistence on the end of history, which seemed to leave little or no room for alternatives to liberal democracy and neoliberal capitalism. Justin Paulson (2001) thus situates the importance of the EZLN uprising in a post-Cold War setting characterized by a radical left on the retreat and without a promising alternative to the end of history:

> In terms of time, the EZLN sprang into public view three years after the collapse of the USSR. [T]he 'End of History' had been declared; the Labor Movement was relatively weak, especially in the United States; NAFTA was being enacted; etc. For both the activist left and the academic left, the early 1990s was a period of retreat and of resigned capitulation to neoliberalism. What was so surprising about the Zapatistas was that they weren't supposed to be there! What's a National Liberation Army doing when there aren't supposed to be any more National Liberation Armies?.... The EZLN has reminded people that there is still reason to struggle.... I think for a lot of people, seeing indigenous women armed only with sticks opposing heavily armed soldiers and tanks was something of a wake-up call: 'if they can do it, I can do it too.' Not only in sympathy, but in solidarity.

The EZLN itself also seems to be quite aware of this contribution. Commenting on the relationship between the EZLN and the transnational solidarity activists, Subcomandante Marcos (Le Bot 1997: 260) sums up the EZLN's contribution to the faltering radical left

> Perhaps Zapatismo helped them remember that it was necessary to struggle and that struggling is worth the effort.... It is a kind of agreement: they obtain from Zapatismo what they need, this reminder, this trampoline to jump again, and the communities obtain this support, this help guaranteeing their survival.

These quotations seem to convey the impression that the radical left had not died out in the wake of the Cold War, but rather that it found itself in an identity crisis, lacking focus and direction. Moreover, this crisis was not the result of the disappearance of the conditions usually considered to underlie the social indignation of the radical left. This leads us to return briefly to the earlier discussion of the three components in an injustice frame – recognition, action and solution. What seems to emerge from the quotations above is that the trenchancy of the EZLN injustice frame derives to a significant extent from the action component. This refers to the fact that an injustice frame provides a rationale for, and motivation to engage in, social action to ameliorate certain problems. The above quotations depict the time of the EZLN uprising as characterized not by the absence of just causes for a radical left, but by a lack of self-confidence and conviction that action and struggle are possible and effective. As Paulson and others suggest, the symbolic power of the EZLN uprising was strengthened by the fact that it took place despite the adverse conditions surrounding the movement. In many ways, then, it seems fair to say that there was already an existing recognition of the social consequences of neoliberalism present at the time of the EZLN uprising that could be activated through a frame bridging process. It was thus noted earlier by Stephen (2001) that the EZLN primarily gained resonance from its injustice frame by applying to it the concept of neoliberalism. This was crucial: the concept of neoliberalism was already in use, especially in Europe and the USA, as a common denominator for economic and political developments since the early 1970s.

We referred somewhat earlier to the lack of concrete solutions on the part of the EZLN with regard to the problems associated with neoliberalism. Thus, we may now propose that the EZLN injustice frame resonates mainly due to its action and recognition compo-nents; in relation to solutions, it is effectively silent. The absence of concrete solutions points us back to the discussion on the EZLN's anti-vanguardist position in Chapter 5. While acknowledging the effects of neoliberalism as a worldwide phenomenon, the EZLN considers variation and diversity in the forms of resistance to neo-liberalism to be valuable rather than problematic:

> [N]ot only in the mountains of South Eastern Mexico is there resist-ance and struggle against neoliberalism. In other parts of Mexico, in Latin America, in the United States and Canada, in the Europe of the Maastricht Treaty, in Africa, in Asia, and in Oceania, the pockets of resistance multiply. Each one has its own history, its differences, its similarities, its demands, its struggles, its accomplishments.... This is a model of pockets of resistance, but do not pay too much attention to it. There are as many models as there are resistances.... So draw

the model you prefer. In regard to the pockets, as well as in regard to the resistances, diversity is richness. (EZLN 1997b)

Paradoxically, perhaps, it is largely the EZLN's insistence on the diversity of social struggles that has given it the role of a node of special influence in the transnational justice and solidarity network which came to fruition in the Seattle protests in 1999. This inspiration is a recurrent thread in the accounts and self-perceptions of activists in the transnational justice and solidarity network who see themselves as inspired by the EZLN. Speaking to an audience at the protests against the IMF/World Bank meeting in Prague in September 2000, Andrew Flood (2000) of the Irish Mexico Group outlined the major inspirations stemming from the EZLN:

> [T]his movement [the transnational justice and solidarity network] has no single starting point. That said … I will point to one of the places we are coming from. I believe there is a debt to be acknowledged to the people who declared '*Ya basta!*' to the new economic order on the 1st of January 1994. I'd trace my involvement in this new anti-capitalist movement to Mexico and to the '1st encounter for humanity and against neoliberalism,' held in Zapatista camps in Chiapas in 1996.… [I]f we were to pick a point where the movements against neoliberalism moved from the single campaign/issue to global anti-capitalism perhaps that point is found in the jungles of the Mexican South East some four years ago. This 'historical' introduction is relevant to where we are going. Some left parties who don't understand this history are trying to take control of the movement in the hope of building their organisations, of becoming our leadership.… The protests lack the guiding hand of the party not because we have not realised the need for one but because many of us have explicitly rejected the experience of this authoritarian method of organisation.

In referring to the EZLN's inspiration as lying in opposition to vanguardism and bureaucracy, Flood also points to a number of potential lines of division within the transnational justice and solidarity network. These may be said to run roughly between those working from an anarchist point of view and those taking a more traditional organizational and party-oriented angle. This distinction recalls the discussion in Chapter 5 concerning the lines of conflict within the Zapatista solidarity network.

Chiapas in Seattle: Overlapping Networks

We will now take a closer look at the way the EZLN injustice frame has been received and used by activists outside Mexico. The EZLN's role in the formation of the transnational justice and solidarity network is acknowledged by the large majority of activists engaged in Zapatista solidarity work, the majority of whom consider themselves to be part of that network. The importance of this role is disputed, however. Tom Hansen (2000), director of the Mexico Solidarity Network, represents the more sceptical view:

> I do think that there is a broad progressive transnational network that is based around some very fundamental critiques of globalization.... I think that Zapatista support groups are ... part of this broad transnational movement, but I don't think that the Zapatistas are leading this movement or are even the inspiration for the majority of the movement. There are other international networks that are much more developed than the Zapatista support network, for example, the Hemispheric *Social Alliance*, *Jubilee 2000* or *Grito de los Excluidos*, to name a few.... I would like to be able to give the Zapatistas their due credit without overly romanticising their contribution.

Referring to the Seattle 1999 protests, Luis Espinosa-Organista (2000) of the Denver Peace and Justice Committee attributes more importance to the EZLN:

> [T]he EZLN or the Zapatista movement is not in itself responsible ... but it had a huge influence on those protests that happened, I am not saying that they are the authors but I am saying that the awareness there is in the world about globalization and the impacts of the economy comes from the analysis of the Zapatistas.

David Martin (2000), director of the Denver Justice and Peace Committee and a participant in the Seattle and Washington protests against the WTO and the IMF/World Bank, describes how Chiapas and the EZLN had a very visible presence in Seattle and Washington:

> I have been to the Seattle protest against the WTO and I went to the one in April against the IMF/World Bank and supporters of the Zapatistas are everywhere. For instance, in the morning of November 30 [in Seattle] we went to shut down the convention centre, our

parade was led by indigenous people from Chiapas, Global Exchange actually brought people from Chiapas. [I]n [Washington] D.C., one of the major protests on the day before the attempt to shut down the IMF/World Bank meeting was at the Mexican consulate … you see people dress like anarchists but you also see people dress like Zapatistas. It is interesting to me because it is such a dominant segment of this movement against the IMF, World Bank, WTO.

Despite their differences, the above quotations register the EZLN's role in the transnational justice and solidarity network. In many ways, this role has its origins in the 1996 intercontinental encounter in Chiapas. As noted by John Ross (2001),

> International solidarity increased in 1996 with the *Intergaláctica* [the first intercontinental encounter], which placed the EZLN in the vanguard of the just-beginning-to-burgeon anti-globalization movement. Suddenly, the Zapatistas were players on a much larger battlefield and Chiapas became a mandatory way stop on the road to the new resistance that first exploded in Seattle, 1999.

The 1996 intercontinental encounter, along with the similar continental American encounter in the spring of the same year, heralded a situation where the Zapatista solidarity network started overlapping increasingly with other transnational networks. These converging networks would later become an important part of the dynamic leading to the WTO protests in Seattle in 1999 and to the subsequent transnational wave of anti-neoliberal protest. As argued in Chapter 1, in our distinction between the three analytical levels of the book, this points to the fact that Zapatista solidarity is a subnetwork in the larger transnational justice and solidarity network. The latter is in many ways centred around the rejection and critique of neoliberalism. Accordingly, it is the EZLN's transnationalization of its injustice frame, described above, that has drawn Zapatista solidarity into the transnational justice and solidarity network and led to increasing diffusion and overlap between the networks.

This development also reflects a reconsideration of the nature of solidarity among activists, which has led to its increasing politicization. Accordingly, as noted by Marc Tomsin (2001) of the Paris-based Committee of Solidarity with the Peoples of Chiapas in Struggle (Comité de Solidarité avec les Peuples du Chiapas en Lutte), solidarity is not considered to be 'a "job": it is a component of international resistance'. This definition of solidarity points at the same time to some of the fault lines within the Zapatista solidarity network that were briefly touched on in Chapter 5. Reflecting on the people and organizations involved in EZLN solidarity work, and echoing our discussions in chapters 4 and 5, Brian Dominick (2000) makes a similar observation on the political dimension of solidarity:

> The most visible ones are conducting 'direct solidarity,' which is to say they are sending material aid or observers or educators and other delegations and caravans to Chiapas itself. That's a great contribution and I couldn't be happier that it's taking place. However, my interest has always been bringing a customized version of Zapatismo home to the US and Canada, to inform our own resistance struggles, explicitly in solidarity with Chiapas, but also raising hell here at home. There are lots of ways to rebel.

The quotations above illustrate the divisions that exist within the transnational Zapatista solidarity network. These seem most apparent between those who make use of the EZLN injustice frame in a mutual solidarity context and those who adopt a less politicized and more rights and material solidarity oriented stance. As Dominick (2000) suggests, this latter difference is in many ways an analytical distinction, as network activists rarely consider the two forms of solidarity to be mutually exclusive. The large majority of activists engage in both.

Our particular interest here lies in the visibility of the EZLN injustice frame within the transnational justice and solidarity network. The influence of the EZLN and the 1996 encounters on the network can be seen at work in some of the main actors: for example, Peoples' Global Action (PGA) and the Italian Ya Basta (not to be confused with the Ya Basta! website).[18] Peoples' Global Action is a transnational network of people and groups, the hallmarks of which are

> A very clear rejection of capitalism, imperialism and feudalism; all trade agreements, institutions and governments that promote destructive globalisation.... A confrontational attitude, since we do not think that lobbying can have a major impact in such biased and undemocratic organisations, in which transnational capital is the only real policy-maker. (2001a)

PGA does not consider itself an organisation in a traditional sense:

The political analysis and call to action of PGA are reflected in its manifesto, a dynamic, evolving document that will be revised at each PGA conference. PGA has no members and does not have and will not have a juridical personality. No organisation or person represents the PGA, nor does the PGA represent any organisation or person. PGA will limit itself to facilitating co-ordination and exchange of information between grassroots movements through conferences and means of communication. (2001a)

Peoples' Global Action was officially formed in February 1998 in Geneva, but it is in many ways an outcome of the discussions on neoliberalism at the intercontinental encounters in Chiapas in 1996 and in Spain 1997. This is clearly reflected in the following account from the PGA website:

> The sense of possibility that this uprising gave to millions of people across the globe was extraordinary. In 1996, the Zapatistas, with trepidation as they thought no-one might come, sent out an email calling for a gathering, called an '*encuentro*' (encounter), of international activists and intellectuals to meet in specially constructed arenas in the Chiapas jungle to discuss common tactics, problems and solutions.... This was followed a year later by a gathering in Spain, where the idea for the construction of a more action focused network, to be named Peoples' Global Action (PGA), was hatched. (2001b)

As already mentioned, the Second Intercontinental Encounter for Humanity and against Neoliberalism in Spain 1997 was a follow-up to the 1996 Chiapas intercontinental encounter, but was not convened by the EZLN. This second encounter was instrumental in moving the incipient transnational justice and solidarity network away from the EZLN as such. The encounters of 1996 and 1997 heralded a phase whereby the Zapatista solidarity network would become increasingly fused with other informal transnational networks.

Another example of the fusion between the Zapatista and justice and solidarity networks is the Italian Ya Basta:

> The Zapatista movement is a popular resistance movement, which aims to defend the right to survival and self-determination of the indigenous peoples of Chiapas. In the summer of 1996 thousands of people from all over the world gathered in the rebellious South East of Mexico, to support the Zapatista movement and their presence and to take part in the global meeting of liberation movements, that

was known as the First Intercontinental Meeting for Humanity and Against Neoliberalism. A group of Italian delegates (many of whom were activists from the Social Centres) decided to establish an association that would be a useful tool for supporting the Zapatistas' fight in Chiapas and their struggle against neoliberalism in Europe. (Ya Basta 2001)[19]

Today, Ya Basta is closely associated with the so-called White Overalls, who have played a significant role in the larger network's protests in recent years. The White Overalls, who use foam padding and helmets to protect themselves in clashes with police during demonstrations, have become a powerful and visible symbol of the worldwide protests against the WTO (Seattle 1999), the IMF and World Bank (Washington DC, April 2000 and Prague, September 2000), the FTAA (Quebec, April 2001), the European Union (Gothenburg, June 2001), and the G8 (Genova, July 2001). While Ya Basta has become increasingly involved in other struggles, it maintains a close relation with the EZLN struggle in Chiapas. What is particularly interesting about Ya Basta is not that it was formed in response to the EZLN uprising, but that it has become a central and vociferous actor in the transnational justice and solidarity network, thus expanding its activities way beyond support for the EZLN. Nevertheless, during the EZLN March for Indigenous Dignity to Mexico City, in February and March 2001, the EZLN was accompanied by the White Overalls (Petrich 2001). This return of Ya Basta to Chiapas and Mexico in the form of the White Overalls illustrates today's reciprocal relationship between the EZLN, the Zapatista solidarity network, and the transnational justice and solidarity network.

Notes

1. Translation from Spanish taken from the Irish Mexico Group website at http://flag.blackened.net/revolt/mexico/ezln/1999/marcos_newton_may99.html.

2. The statement echoes to some extent Ignacio Ramonet's (1997) article 'Disarming the Markets' in *Le Monde Diplomatique* in December 1997. The article took as its point of departure a critique of financial globalization and called for a number of initiatives aimed at restricting the free circulation of financial and speculative capital. Among these was a call for the formation of a movement under the name of ATTAC (Action for a Tobin Tax to

Assist the Citizen).

3. Translation from Spanish taken from the Ya Basta! website at www.ezln. org/documentos/1994/199312xx.en.htm.

4. Translation from Spanish taken from the Ya Basta! website at www.ezln.org/ documentos/1994/19940410a.en.htm. The reference to president Salinas de Gortari as a usurper reflects a widespread perception that the PRI's victory in the presidential elections in 1988 was fraudulent. The legitimate victor of the elections was considered to be Cuahtémoc Cárdenas of the left–centre coalition FDN (Frente Democrático Nacional/National Democratic Front). After the elections, the FDN was dissolved and the PRD (Partido de la Revolución Democrática/Party of the Democratic Revolution) was formed by Cárdenas and Porfirio Muñoz-Ledo. The PRD is currently Mexico's third largest party.

5. Translation from Spanish taken from an English version available at www. geocities.com/CapitolHill/3849/marcos_7pieces.html.

6. Also in 1999, the EZLN issued statements of support for electricity workers opposing privatization plans for Mexico's electricity sector (EZLN 1999b).

7. The protests in 1999 joined a long tradition of critical and political student activities. The best-known instance of student protest in Mexico is the 1968 army and police massacre of protesting students on the Plaza de las Tres Culturas in Mexico City. The number of deaths has not been made public and the incident was never investigated in depth by the authorities.

8. The other pillars, according to Basáñez (1996), were agrarian reforms, the corporative system, and the rule that no president may be re-elected after the constitutional six-year term.

9. Zapata and Villa are referred to as symbols of the popular demands because they never achieved power in a political sense. The two peasant leaders, who operated independently of each other (Zapata in the south and Villa in the north of Mexico), did gain considerable military momentum in 1914 and entered Mexico City and an empty presidential palace in December 1914. But Villa and Zapata were not able to fill the political vacuum and the revolution was 'taken over' by Obregón; hence Gilly's (1971) reference to the Mexican Revolution as an interrupted revolution. Even if the Mexican Revolution did not lead to the establishment of a socialist government, the demands for land reform, made especially by Zapata, found echo in the 1917 Mexican Constitution.

10. The majority of the EZLN is made up by people belonging to four ethnic groups: Choles, Tojolabales, Tzeltales and Tzotziles.

11. Meetings along these lines have subsequently been held in Spain in 1997 and in Brazil in 1999. The meeting in Spain, the Second Intercontinental Encounter for Humanity and against Neoliberalism (Segundo Encuentro Intercontinental por la Humanidad y contra el Neoliberalismo), was seen as a follow-up to the intercontinental meeting in Chiapas. The meeting was not called by the EZLN, but the encounter in Spain did have the participation of two representatives from the Zapatista communities in Chiapas. In December 1999 Belém, Brazil, hosted the Second American Encounter for Humanity and against Neoliberalism (Segundo Encuentro Americano por la Humanidad y contra el Neoliberalismo). This was a follow-up to

the continental American meeting staged in Chiapas in April 1996. This encounter was not organized or convened by the EZLN, but the EZLN endorsed and encouraged the initiative in June of 1999 (EZLN 1999g).

12. The page number refers to a typescript version of the article sent as an email attachment.

13. The notions of master frames and cycles of contention are discussed in more detail in Chapter 7.

14. In Chapter 1, we discussed the problems associated with the equation of neoliberalism and globalization. The EZLN, it should be noted, to a large extent makes use of the concepts in this interchangeable manner.

15. The term 'radical left' is used to denote a left wing different from that associated with social-democratic parties and the adoption of 'third way' strategies. Organizations and people on the radical left are critical of these strategies and opt for a more profound critique of democracy and capitalism/neoliberalism than is found within the social-democratic parties today. The term 'radical left' does not refer to a coherent line of thought but encompasses a wide variety of political standpoints.

16. This is not to suggest that such trends only became apparent after the end of the Cold War. In Europe, similar discussions had been present since the late 1970s and early 1980s. This debate took place, *inter alia*, around the so-called New Left and often pointed to the emergence of so-called new social movements as the bearers and creators of new political identities thought to be less rooted in class.

17. There are current negotiations to extend NAFTA to a new free-trade agreement, the Free Trade Area of the Americas (FTAA), to include all countries in Central America, the Caribbean, and South America, except, of course, Cuba. Negotiations were initiated shortly after the implementation of NAFTA and are scheduled to conclude in 2005. In line with these visions, the Mexican government under Vicente Fox has launched plans to create a development project involving the area between Puebla in Mexico and Panama. This plan, commonly known as the Plan Puebla Panama, has already drawn significant criticism from social activists within and outside Mexico.

18. See Starr (2000) for a description of the linkage between the EZLN and the transnational justice and solidarity network.

19. The quotation has been corrected and edited at a few points to improve readability.

7

Democracy

This chapter focuses on the relationship between democracy and the transnational framing process underlying the formation of the Zapatista solidarity network. The issues taken up here have a special kinship with those aired in Chapter 6: the EZLN's critique of neoliberalism cannot be seen in isolation from its approach to democracy, since this critique is formulated in what is referred to here as radical democratic terms. In Chapter 2 we discussed the spread of democratic and human rights ideas, since the late 1980s in particular. This development, it was argued, has established democracy as a master frame with an almost global reach. A master frame is understood here as a broad ideational reservoir from which social movements derive the foundations for social critique and proposed solutions. Adhering to the master frame provides social movements with legitimacy and support in their relationship with the external environment. Hence, the framing processes in which social movements engage are more likely to be successful if they are built on an existing master frame. In relation to the EZLN, the engagement with democratic ideas, however, does not involve concurrence with, or acceptance of, what we may describe as the dominant form of democracy: liberal democracy. On the contrary, it implies a critique of liberal democracy and an alternative vision based on a more radical perception of democracy. Thus the EZLN engages in a struggle over the definition of democracy in a time when the liberal variant has gained ascendancy.

Radical Democracy at Work:
The Mexican Context

The combination of armed struggle and democracy in the EZLN may appear incongruous. This challenging paradox has prompted Castañeda (1995) to label the EZLN armed reformists, and Touraine (1996) to refer to Subcomandante Marcos as an armed democrat. These characterizations all make implicit reference to the strategies adopted by traditional armed movements in Latin America and elsewhere, from which the EZLN, however, is considered to differ significantly – a point reiterated by the EZLN itself (e.g. García Márquez and Pombo 2001). Today, the armed aspect plays a more symbolic role, and the EZLN is best seen as a political movement struggling on the level of ideas rather than that of armed confrontation (Castañeda 1995; Kampwirth 1996).

The EZLN's transformation since the 1994 uprising is especially evident in its adoption of a democratic frame. This frame was less apparent in the early days and was not in evidence in the martial rhetoric of the first public statement (EZLN 1994b). Democracy was not absent from the EZLN ideational reservoir, though, and it soon began to assume more prominence. Returning to the different types of framing process, considered in Chapter 2, we may suggest that the EZLN engaged in a frame amplification process. Frame amplification serves to highlight certain aspects of a movement's ideational ballast considered to have resonance with an external audience. The coming discussion aims to demonstrate how this amplification process has resulted in the formation of a radical democratic master frame, and how the EZLN's radical democratic ideas have been practised on the local and national levels of Chiapas and Mexico, respectively.[1]

Liberal versus radical democracy

There are numerous interpretations of what democracy is and should be. For analytical purposes, and acknowledging the risk of oversimplification, we can say that contemporary struggles over the definition of democracy revolve around the distinction between liberal and radical democracy. The EZLN is considered to represent a radical democratic vision that criticizes and challenges liberal democracy. It is around this interpretation that we may discern the formation of a radical democratic master frame.

The concept of liberal democracy obviously refers to its roots in the philosophical tradition of liberalism. There, liberal democracy is a specific form of government, and a complex of civil and political rights. Government based on liberal democratic principles is considered to display the following characteristics (Sørensen 1993: 13): extensive and regular competition (in the form of fair elections) among individuals, organizations and political parties for political positions; an inclusive level of participation where no (adult) social groups are excluded; a level of civil and political liberties such as freedom of expression, freedom of the press, and freedom to form and join organizations.

The idea of radical democracy is not rooted in a specific theoretical and philosophical tradition, as is the case with liberal democracy. The concept is mainly normative and refers only to a limited extent to empirical examples. We may speak of three lines of normative thinking on radical democracy,[2] although this is an analytical distinction that overlooks significant overlaps. These are referred to as the broadening, the delegation, and the deepening of democracy.

The broadening of democracy refers to the extension of democratic principles to more and more societal areas. This perspective has two dimensions: the first denotes a situation in which the economy is under some degree of democratic control (Wood 1995; Fotopoulos 1997); the second denotes a situation with an element of democratic control in all areas of decision-making (Mouffe 1993). The delegation of democracy refers to the creation of autonomous spaces with a level of authority to govern independently from the state. This does not necessarily entail secession from the state. This view mainly entails the aspirations of minorities who feel excluded or repressed by the state (Esteva 1999, 2001). The deepening of democracy refers to the empowerment of civil society through social action. This perspective has two important dimensions. First, it points to a normative ideal where an active, organized and politicized civil society is seen as a vital part of democracy (Lummis 1996).[3] Second, it rests on the notion of civil society as a sphere penetrated by power relations (Gramsci 1971) or by the colonization of system rationalities (Habermas 1987) – a situation which can only be changed through social action on the level of civil society. In this sense, we may also speak of civil society as the target of social action (Cohen and Arato 1992).

Democracy in this radical perspective is generally seen as an unfinished project and as something that may be obtained only through social action and struggle. Notions of radical democracy are therefore highly political as they denote a significant critique of existing liberal democratic arrangements. As such, the idea of radical democracy clashes with any proclamation of liberal democracy as the end of history, and places itself squarely within a leftist political framework. In what follows, we continue discussion of the differences between liberal democracy and radical democracy, by analysing the EZLN's democratic vision and critique from a point of departure in the three-component framework of radical democracy laid out above.

The broadening of democracy

To approach the EZLN understanding of democracy we have to take into account the duality of its position. The EZLN distinguishes between two democratic levels: one based in civil society and the other based in the political institutions. Shortly before the presidential elections in Mexico in July 2000, the EZLN (2000) issued a communiqué outlining its view on the relationship between the civil society and institutional dimensions of democracy:

> For the Zapatistas, democracy is much more than the electoral competition or the alternation of power. But it is also the electoral dispute if it is clean, equal, honest, and plural. Therefore we say that electoral democracy does not exhaust democracy, but it is an important part of it.… The time of elections is not the time for the Zapatistas.… We want to find a politics that goes from the bottom to the top, one in which 'to rule by obeying' is more than a slogan, one in which the power is not the objective.… In the Zapatista idea, democracy is something that is constructed from below and with everyone, including those who think differently than we do. Democracy is the exercise of power by the people all the time and in all places.

Here the EZLN does not renounce electoral democracy or dismiss the gains and advantages of liberal democracy. Its definition of democracy seems to revolve around the concept 'to rule by obeying' (*mandar obediciendo*). This vision is influenced by the traditions of decision-making within indigenous communities (Harvey 1998a: 208–9). The type of democracy enacted in the Zapatista indigenous communities is different from that offered by liberal democracy, a difference especially marked in the way democracy in Zapatista communities is based on continuous consultation and debate aimed at the establishment of consensus. Subcomandante Marcos (Le Bot 1997: 281), however, acknowledges that this version of democracy has certain limitations: 'I think that this form of democracy is only possible in community life. It works in an indigenous community …, but I do not think that it is transferable or generalizable to other contexts.' Nevertheless, Subcomandante Marcos also notes that what is transferable from this vision of democracy is the close control subjected by the community to those in power (Le Bot 1997: 281). The basic ideas of this model should find their way also to the national level. In an interview with Durán de Huerta (1999: 271–2), Subcomandante Marcos describes the idea 'to rule by obeying' and its implications for democracy beyond the community level. This should involve a system that allows for a permanent evaluation of a government's work and entails the possibility of reversing political decisions if they are not made in accordance with the mandates given by the electorate.

The notion of 'ruling by obeying' is tied to the relationship between citizens and government. Yet the idea of broadening democracy also moves the question of democracy beyond the purely political and into the realm of the economy. This is most clearly seen in the EZLN's interpretation of neoliberalism as fundamentally at odds with democracy (Gilbreth and Otero 2001: 24–5):

> The Zapatista uprising contributed to an expansion of democracy in the domain of political society but also beyond it, into civil society and the cultural sphere. In addition, it has sought to expand democratization to the economic realm in order to address the social costs of neoliberal market reforms.… The exacerbation of socio-economic disparities following free-market reforms provoked the EZLN to question the relationship between economic marginalization and political exclusion and the extent to which this hampers democracy.

The EZLN, accordingly, does not make a watertight distinction between political and civil rights and social and economic rights, as do most versions of liberal democracy. Social and economic marginalization is dehumanizing and limits the opportunities to make meaningful use of civil and political rights. In the EZLN radical democratic vision the socio-economical aspect is thus considered to be an indispensable ingredient in any notion of democracy (Johnston 2000). We will not dwell further on the issue of neoliberalism as it has already been extensively discussed in Chapter 6. The main point here is that the EZLN's version of radical democracy and the broadening of democracy relate not only to politics in a narrow sense, but also to the economic sphere.

The delegation of democracy

It was noted above that the EZLN's notion of 'to rule by obeying' was rooted in indigenous traditions of decision-making. Here we must register two qualifications. First, indigenous traditions of decision-making vary according to region and ethnic group. It is not possible, in other words, to speak about one indigenous tradition of decision-making. Second, and in continuation, decision-making structures in Zapatista base communities are not necessarily similar to those of other indigenous communities. Indigenous and Zapatista decision-making structures should thus not be interpreted as one and the same thing (Stephen 2002).

Bearing these complexities in mind, we will limit ourselves here to discussion of the democratic practices within Zapatista communities. Stephen (2002) defines the main pillars of democracy in Zapatista communities as: 'to rule by obeying' – that is, to govern by listening, obeying the ideas of the community; consultation with base communities through community assemblies in which everyone has the chance to speak, including women and children; the use of local and regional councils to communicate opinions formed at the community level; respect for difference – that is, the ability to reach solutions that allow for variation and difference of views; governance as service. Leadership tasks are seen as a service to the community and not as a chance to gain personal advantage.

The major efforts of the EZLN have gone into securing a degree of autonomy for the indigenous people in order to establish a legal recognition of, *inter alia*, these indigenous practices of government and decision-making. This drive towards autonomy should be viewed as opposition to historical attempts to assimilate the indigenous population in Mexico, as well as in Latin America in general. This was evident in the nation-building projects in the centuries following the violent conquest of Latin America (Díaz Polanco 1997a: 7ff.). More recently, this tendency was seen in the 1950s and 1960s under the influence of modernization theories of development that seemed to aim at the eventual disappearance by assimilation of ethnic groups (Stavenhagen 1996: 23).

There are two factors to consider in regard to the EZLN's quest for autonomy for Mexico's indigenous people. First, as indicated above, the EZLN's demands for autonomy do not represent the aspirations of all of Mexico's fifty-six ethnic groups. Nevertheless, it is reasonable to say that the demands echo the wishes of a large part of the indigenous population. At the third meeting of the National Indigenous Congress (CNI) in 2001, which drew representatives from forty-two of Mexico's ethnic groups, the delegates expressed strong support for the EZLN's demands on indigenous rights (SIPAZ 2001b). Second, the search for autonomy should not be equated with a search for secession from the Mexican state (Esteva 2001). As we saw in Chapter 6, the EZLN has an eminently national character and engages, rather, in debates concerning the appropriation of national Mexican symbols and history.

The EZLN's aspiration to autonomy has revolved round a proposal prepared in late 1996 by COCOPA (Comisión de Concordia y Pacificación/Commission of Concordance and Pacification), a forum made up of Mexican legislators. The COCOPA proposal was an attempt to revive the peace process that had been stalled since the signing of the San Andrés Accords between the EZLN and the Mexican government in February 1996. The negotiations began in March 1995, and were encoded in the Law of Dialogue, Conciliation and Dignified Peace in Chiapas, which established the EZLN as a legitimate social actor with specific and legitimate demands. The COCOPA proposal built on the San Andrés Accords, and was accepted by the EZLN in 1996, but rejected by then president Ernesto Zedillo (1994–2000). The COCOPA issue reappeared in the new political climate following the PAN and Vicente Fox's rise to presidential power in December 2000. Fox put the question of indigenous rights high on his agenda and sent the COCOPA proposal to Congress. This was followed in February and March by efforts by the EZLN to generate a public debate on the issue of indigenous rights and the COCOPA proposal. This resulted in the March for Indigenous Dignity, which ended in Mexico City, where EZLN commanders delivered speeches in the Mexican Congress, advocating approval of the proposal. However, the expectations and awareness raised by the EZLN march and the new political signals from the Fox government were disappointed when the Mexican Congress approved a proposal that differed significantly from the COCOPA one. This was later approved by the Mexican state parliaments, but only after an unprecedented and heated debate. The proposal led the EZLN (2001d) immediately to break off any contacts with the government until the COCOPA proposal is constitutionally recognized.[4]

The deepening of democracy

The concept of civil society is vital to understanding the EZLN's radical democratic vision.[5] The focus on civil society in the radical democratic conception differs significantly from the role accorded to it in a liberal democratic framework. In order to bring out this difference, it is suggested that we distinguish between civil society as, respectively, the terrain and the target of social movements (Cohen and Arato 1992). The main difference between liberal and radical democracy thus lies in the fact that the latter views civil society not only as a terrain but also as a target of social action. This entails an emphasis on the politicization of civil society, which involves both traditional political questions concerning the distribution of power and resources within society, and the issue of what counts as political and who gets to define the rules of the political game (Alvarez et al. 1998).

This interpretation should not be taken to imply that civil society politics takes place independently of the state. On the contrary, considering that the state is the guarantor of an independent civil society, any notion of civil society politics is seen here as integrated with the state. In this we follow Cohen and Arato's (1992) distinction between politics of identity, politics of influence, politics of inclusion, and politics of reform. Applying this argument to the case of the EZLN, we can argue that it has moved on all of these levels simultaneously. In what follows, we will concentrate on the politics of identity and of influence, which in conjunction are referred to as civil society politics. Before proceeding, it may useful to consider briefly the other two kinds of politics in regard to the EZLN. The first, a politics of inclusion, has been encoded in the Law of Dialogue, Conciliation and Dignified Peace, referred to above. This document establishes a relationship between the EZLN and the government, and asserts that the EZLN represents the demands of a portion of the Mexican population. The second, a politics of reform, has been visible in the San Andrés negotiations and the unsuccessful attempt to make the Accords constitutional.

The EZLN's role as a force that opens up social and political space and engages in civil society politics has been evident in the wide range of initiatives involving Mexican and non-Mexican civil society actors. The most important are the following: the National Democratic Convention (Convención Nacional Democrática, or CND) in Chiapas in 1994; the National Consultation for Peace and Democracy (Consulta Nacional por la Paz y la Democracia) in 1995; the First Intercontinental Encounter for Humanity and against Neoliberalism in Chiapas (Primer Encuentro Intercontinental por la Humanidad y Contra el Neoliberalismo) in 1996; the visit of 1,111 civilian Zapatistas to Mexico City to celebrate the formation of the FZLN in 1997; the National Consultation Concerning the Legal Initiative on Indigenous Rights of the Commission of Concordance and Pacification and for an End to the War of Extermination (Consulta Nacional sobre la Iniciativa de Ley Indígena de la Comisíon de Concordia y Pacificación y por el Fin de la Guerra de Exterminio) in 1999; and the March for Indigenous Dignity (Marcha por la Dignidad Indígena) in 2001 aimed at the approval of the COCOPA proposal on indigenous rights.

Although these initiatives have had different objectives, they have one in common: to activate and politicize civil society by creating public space. In the above-mentioned instances, the EZLN has either served as facilitator between Mexican and non-Mexican civil society actors, or invited civil society actors to vote on different issues, or invited civil society actors to participate in events sponsored by the EZLN. On the one hand, these initiatives directed towards the empowerment and activation of civil society have had the aim of giving voice to a range of social forces that have been excluded by the political system in Mexico. In this respect, the EZLN's idea of democracy and civil society is largely an extension of the liberal conception of these ideas. The EZLN's demands, however, do not stop at this but strive instead to forge a fundamental change in the relationship between those who govern and those who are governed. For the EZLN, such change cannot come from above through democratic reform.

It is only when we view the EZLN's interpretation of civil society through the notions of the politics of identity and of influence that its radical democratic project becomes evident. This interpretation places us within a Gramscian framework (Gilbreth and Otero 2001: 8–9, 19):

> Rather than making war to take power and impose its vision from above, the EZLN sought to open political spaces in which new actors in civil society could press for democracy and social justice from below. This view was consistent with that of the new Latin American left, which conceptualized power as a practice situated both within and beyond the state and exercised through what Gramsci referred to as 'hegemony,' the dissemination of beliefs and values that systematically favoured the ruling class…. In expressing this view the EZLN established a cultural strategy that called into question the PRI's hegemony by reinterpreting national symbols and discourses in favour of an alternative transformative project…. In Gramsci's (1971) terms, the EZLN changed its strategy from a 'war of movements' challenging state power through the force of arms to a 'war of positions' contesting the moral and intellectual leadership of Mexico's ruling class.[6]

Whereas a war of movement may be fought by a small number of rebels, a war of position necessarily involves a larger portion of society than a few specific movements.[7] The EZLN's cultural strategy referred to in the quotation would thus not have been conceivable without the participation of a wide range of civil society actors. This strategy of social change renounces any role of leadership or vanguard for the EZLN. Instead, the EZLN engages in the formulation of the relationship between particularity and universality. This relationship is central to the notion of radical democracy as advanced by Laclau and Mouffe. These authors' emphasis on plurality and particularity does not entail a rejection of universalism. Rather, the notion of radical democracy proceeds from a view where the universal is increasingly particularized (Mouffe 1993: 13). Difference is acknowledged and accepted on the grounds that respect for difference rests on a notion of universality that grants everyone the right to be different (Laclau 1996: 49). This universal right to be different should, according to Laclau and Mouffe, be continuously contested and constructed through a democratic matrix. This empowerment of particularities and identities through a democratic matrix and a politicized civil society lies at the heart of the EZLN's radical democratic vision and its idea of a deepening of democracy.

The Struggle 'inside' Democracy: The Global Context

Our discussions have so far taken their point of departure in the national Mexican context, where the EZLN's radical democratic ideas have been most visibly played out. We now turn to the implications of the EZLN's radical democratic vision outside Mexico. In so doing, we return to the theoretical argument concerning the transnational framing process and the concept of master frames. We do so to establish a link between the EZLN's resonance outside Mexico and its engagement with the democratic master frame.

The distinction between liberal and radical democracy allows us to expand the notion of master frames by splitting it into two related concepts: latent master frames and action master frames. In the context of this study, the dominant latent master frame is constituted by general ethical and political ideas of democracy. Drawing on this latent master frame provides social movements with a degree of legitimacy in a more abstract manner. Action master frames, in turn, are derived from latent master frames, but are specifically elaborated by social actors with the aim of establishing a 'guide' for contentious social action. On a more general level, we may thus explain the resonance of the EZLN outside Mexico as the result of its adherence to the latent democratic master frame. However, this insight is not precise enough as an analytical tool. We therefore have to take a closer look at how the EZLN has made use of the latent democratic master frame to construct a concrete radical democratic action master frame. Unless we also adjust our analytical focus on this level, we will not be able to identify the political and contentious content of the EZLN's vision of democracy or to see the relationship between the EZLN's critique of neoliberalism and its radical democratic aspirations. The discussion below aims to identify traces of this radical democratic action master frame outside Mexico. This investigation will be conducted within the transnational Zapatista solidarity network as well as within the transnational justice and solidarity network.

The end of the Cold War as a political opportunity

Several attempts have been made to map the development of democracy in modern times. In the present study we focus on the democratic changes that have taken place since the 1980s and after the end of the Cold War. Our discussion of democracy in Chapter 2 indicated that the end of the Cold War provided social movements with new political opportunities. These were a product of the cessation of the bipolar conflict, which had had a restrictive effect on contentious social action. This provided authorities with legitimacy and a wide degree of manoeuvre in dealing with instances of contention. In particular, the scope for social ideas and actions to be deemed Soviet- and socialist-inspired was rather wide. This also limited significantly the reach of the concept of democracy. During the Cold War the West tolerated authoritarian and non-democratic governments so long as they were seen as a bulwark against the spread of socialist ideas (Shaw 2000: 135). Obviously, the end of the Cold War went a long way towards eliminating the legitimacy of this rationale (Donnelly 1993: 133).

It follows that contentious social movements are now able to engage in struggles over the definition of democracy without being categorized as Soviet sympathizers and as legitimate targets of repression. The EZLN, as well as most actors in the transnational Zapatista solidarity network, display an overtly democratic discourse, but, as we have seen, one that challenges the ideas of liberal democracy. The almost global dominance of democratic ideas and the fact that political authority is increasingly anchored in the adherence to democracy also means that contentious social movements with a democratic agenda are provided with a certain 'protection' (Schmitter 1996: 34). In the EZLN's case, participation in NAFTA has meant that Mexico is put under scrutiny from its northern neighbours (Nash and Kovic 1996: 180). Even though NAFTA is a purely economic arrangement, the USA and Canada have to pay attention to the democratic behaviour of Mexico in order not to arouse criticism from domestic media and public.

In other words, authoritarian regimes are having an increasingly hard time, as they can no longer refer to the imperatives of the Cold War as sources of legitimacy. In contrast, contentious social movements have access to a large number of global and regional institutions that serve as guarantors of democracy and human rights, and may be used as allies by social movements that criticize, for example, the conditions of democracy in their home countries (Shaw 2000: 167). This also means that there is no legitimacy outside democracy. Consequently, few groups place themselves in an explicitly anti-democratic framework. Where the ideological fault line during the Cold War divided social movements and governments into liberal democrats and socialists, the current world order is based, rather, on a division between democratic and non-democratic forces.[8]

We can now turn our attention to the master frame concept and its relation to democracy. The discussion will concentrate on latent master frames. These, as noted elsewhere, provide social actors with a broad ideational reservoir or toolbox from which to derive and construct concrete action master frames. The latent master frame in the contemporary situation is made up of democratic ideas, broadly defined. During the Cold War it was possible to identify two competing latent master frames: the liberal democratic and capitalist aspirations of the West, and the socialist ideals of the Soviet bloc. A glance at any contentious action during the Cold War reveals that legitimating ideas and visions were largely derived from one of these frames.

It is useful to make a distinction between two competing latent master frames in the present discussion. The one represented by the West is still largely based in notions of liberal democracy and capitalism. The other – obviously no longer represented by the Soviet bloc or by socialist ideas – is taking shape around resistance to notions of democracy. Representatives of this master frame usually take their point of departure in fundamentalist and nationalist ideas, examples being the American Militia movement, the neo-Nazi movement, and certain Islamic movements such as al-Qaeda. Inherent in this resistance is opposition to the globalization of democracy that has shaped recent decades.

This is not the place to pursue the arguments pertaining to this anti-democratic latent master frame. What interests us here is the democratic latent master frame and the way it is currently used by social actors with a contentious, but fundamentally democratic, agenda. This is not a coherent master frame with a basis in a widespread consensus regarding the content of democracy. As demonstrated earlier, important struggles over the meaning of democracy are taking place with a point of departure in the democratic latent master frame (Alvarez et al. 1998).

Frame levels: an analytical distinction

Action master frames may be defined as master frames that provide social actors with a set of more or less well defined ideas to be used in the construction of specific social movement frames. *Latent master frames*, in contrast, should be seen as a passive reservoir of ideas. Action master frames are developed by social actors who have operationalized the content of the latent master frame in such a way as to create a new and innovative action master frame serving as the basis of specific movement frames (see Figure 7.1).

Action master frames, however, are not purely strategic constructs, but the result of a process of social construction involving a wide range of social actors. Returning to our discussion of networks, we may refine this point by suggesting that the development of action master frames is intimately linked with the formation of informal transnational movement networks. That is, such networks presuppose the existence of an action master frame that may serve to tie the different nodes or participants together. This is not to assume a step-by-step model where the action master frame comes first, and the networks logically follow. As indicated above, action master frames are not strategic constructs, but are rather developed in a dialogical process involving a broad range of social actors.

Returning to the case of the EZLN and the Zapatista solidarity network, this means that the EZLN's radical democratic frame cannot be considered a coherent ideational complex developed by the EZLN and presented for ready use to non-EZLN activists. Rather, the frame has been shaped in dialogue between the EZLN and solidarity activists. The explanatory thrust of the master frame argument is accordingly more dynamic than it may appear at first sight. It is not, in other words, sufficient to claim that the formation of the Zapatista solidarity network has resulted from the EZLN's adherence to a democratic master frame. In the process of relating to the latent democratic master frame, the EZLN has engaged in a struggle over the definition of democracy with deep philosophical roots. This struggle, in turn, has resulted in the creation of a radical democratic action master frame, which may be seen as the outcome of the EZLN's relation to the latent frame. As suggested above, the EZLN's radical democratic action master frame is the result of dialogue with other social actors that were already engaged in this type of debate at the time of the uprising. The EZLN frame should thus be viewed as a variant of the general concern with the formulation of a radical democratic perspective within the left today.

It may be useful at this point to sum up the different levels of the framing concept outlined above: latent master frames, action master frames, and movement frames. In the contemporary situation, the most important latent master frame is rooted in democratic ideas. Latent master frames constitute a reservoir of ideas from which action master frames may or may not be created. Action master frames, in turn, have a political and oppositional content and are created through a dialogic and non-strategic process involving a wide range of social actors. There is a close relationship between action master frames and the formation of informal transnational movement networks. Movement frames are strategically developed by specific social movements in order to attract support and legitimacy. Action master frames serve as an ideational toolbox for the construction of movement frames.

Action master frames may in some cases be conducive to what Tarrow (1998) has defined as cycles of contention. These are not static and one-way relationships where cycles of contention are started by specific social actors who have developed a forceful action master

Figure 7.1   Frame levels and cycle of protest

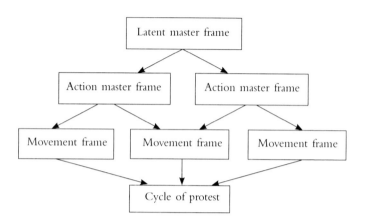

frame. In fact, cycles of contention are an expression of several action master frames with points of overlap. This draws us back to our distinction in Chapter 1 between social movement organizations, informal transnational movement networks, and transnational fields of synergy. Cycles of contention, in other words, occur at the level of transnational fields of synergy and express the increasing convergence of several informal transnational movement networks and, ultimately, of several social movement organizations.[9] The term 'convergence' does not imply the formation of coalitions. It rather points to a situation in which social actors at the social movement organization and individual levels increasingly guide their actions with a point of departure in related action master frames. In the present context, we may speak about a variety of action master frames constructed around a radical interpretation of the latent democratic master frame. To the extent that grievances rooted, for example, in issues of ecology, poverty, gender and race are formulated on the basis of related radical democratic action master frames, it becomes plausible to speak about the emergence of a cycle of protest. The relationship between the different frame levels and the notion of a cycle of protest is illustrated in Figure 7.1.

These thoughts echo Mouffe's (1993) and Laclau's (1996) ideas on radical democracy as expressed through the establishment of democratic equivalences. In relation to transnational fields of synergy and cycles of contention, we may suggest that these processes involve a degree of identity transformation through a democratic matrix. In Mouffe's words (1993: 18):

> These struggles do not spontaneously converge, and in order to establish democratic equivalences a new 'common sense' is necessary, which would transform the identity of different groups so that the demands of each group could be articulated with those of others according to the principle of democratic equivalence. For it is not a matter of establishing a mere alliance between given interests but of actually modifying the very identity of these forces.

In a similar vein, Laclau (1996: 57) speaks of chains of equivalence integrating the particular and the universal. This process may move along two paths:

> The first is to inscribe particular identities and demands as links in a wider chain of equivalences, thereby giving each of them a 'relative' universalization.... The second is to give a particular demand the function of universal representation – that is to give it the value of a horizon giving coherence to the chain of equivalences and, at the same time, keeping it indefinitely open.

What interests us here is that the EZLN may be considered to represent a particular demand with the function of universal representation, or, in the words of Gerlach (1987), a node of special influence. This point may have relevance on the level of informal transnational movement networks and action master frames, as well as on the level of transnational fields of synergy and cycles of contention. While it is obvious that the EZLN plays such a role within the transnational Zapatista solidarity network, it is of course to stretch the argument to say that this is also the case on the level of the transnational justice and solidarity network. Nevertheless, it is argued that important elements of the EZLN radical democratic action master frame may be identified also within parts of the transnational justice and solidarity network that are not directly influenced by the EZLN.

These points raise an important distinction with relevance for the remainder of the chapter. The following discussion and analysis of traces of the EZLN action master frame takes place on two levels. At the first level, we identify situations and settings outside Mexico where the EZLN radical democratic action master frame may be said to have had a direct influence on social action. At the second level, we discuss how the EZLN action master frame is compatible with ideas and actions of social actors who are not directly inspired by the EZLN frame. This distinction allows us to demonstrate how the EZLN frame has had a direct impact on the actions of social activists outside Mexico, and how, at the same time, it resonates well with existing radical democratic currents.

Direct democracy and decentralization: EZLN influence

We will now trace the influence of the EZLN radical democratic action master frame within the Zapatista solidarity network. As discussed in Chapter 4, an important element in the EZLN's influence beyond Mexico's borders is its impact on ideas of organization at local, national and transnational levels. The importance of the intercontinental encounter in 1996 in spurring the diffusion of EZLN ideas to settings outside of Mexico has been noted. The encounter heralded the expansion of radical democratic ideas, developed mainly in national and regional contexts, to the transnational level. At the closing ceremony, the EZLN presented its vision of the organization of transnational struggle against neoliberalism as a network without hierarchies or leaders (EZLN 1996e). This approach to organizing is seen by the large majority of network activists as an important value in itself. In the words of an anonymous interviewee and network activist, the diversity within the transnational Zapatista solidarity network is thus seen as a quality rather than a problem:

> There are groups with differing politics and projects, but I don't see any serious divisions that hamper anyone's work. For example, some organizations are more Zapatista-centred and others are more church-centred (they support the diocese in San Cristóbal and indigenous communities, not the armed struggle). I think this is due to the loose nature of the network and the diverse nature of solidarity groups' responses to the situation in Chiapas. This bottom-up type of organization is actually encouraged by the Zapatistas and allows for diverse types of work with less conflict.

Consequently, the relationships between groups, organizations and individuals participating in transnational networks are between independent and autonomous actors who share concerns but are not subsumed under the leadership of one or more specific actors. While this perception of the Zapatista solidarity network is echoed by the majority of activists, critical voices have not been absent. These can serve to focus our attention on some of the more serious differences that persist within the network. Jeroen ten Dam (1999), former member of the now dissolved Mexico Solidarity Committee from Amsterdam, has thus levelled a strong critique at what he considers to be authoritarian tendencies within the transnational Zapatista solidarity network and especially within the European network of solidarity activists:

> In the summer of 1997 the Second International Encounter for Humanity and against Neoliberalism took place in Spain. The organisation also came in for a lot of criticism. Even with the preparations it became clear that a small group of *apparatchiks*, mainly from Madrid and Zaragoza, had imposed their idea (which was an almost identical copy of the First Encounter in 1996) of how the Encounter should be organised. Groups with a more critical view and different ideas were not given any space to venture their opinions, but strangely enough most of these critical groups did in the end drop their criticisms.

The vision of organization as a loose network of autonomous groups, heralded by some as the empirical nature of the transnational Zapatista solidarity network and criticized by others as an illusion, is a common normative trait in much of contemporary social action and also in the transnational justice and solidarity network. This approach has visible similarities with the EZLN's radical democratic vision, discussed earlier in the chapter. However, it is worth cautioning that this approach has obviously not been invented by the EZLN but draws on a number of inspirational currents. Most notable are those stemming from anarchist thought and the so-called new social movements of the 1970s and 1980s. These ideational currents with which the EZLN radical democratic action master frame is related are touched on below.

As discussed in Chapter 4, one of the conspicuous characteristics of transnational solidarity with the EZLN is the awareness that it goes both ways. The following quotation from David Martin (2000) regarding EZLN-inspired social action in Denver suggests that one of the inspirations coming from the EZLN and Chiapas to activists outside Mexico lies exactly in the EZLN radical democratic action master frame and its contributions to direct democratic or grassroots organization:

> with the example of the Zapatistas you can talk about grassroots democracy and local control and local democratic practices … and I think that is what we are trying to do here in terms of organizing coalitions for economic justice, we are saying we need to get the power into the hands of grassroots organizations and have more democratic forms of government … what we are trying to do is create … grassroots democratic structures so that we can start building momentum to even have more influence politically, but also practice democracy amongst our own groups before we try to exercise power.

Kerry Appel (2000) echoes Martin's comments by stating how it is the organizing efforts of the EZLN rather than the armed aspect that lie at the core of the movement:

> [A] lot of people come to the Zapatista struggle because they are enamored with this idea of armed indigenous resistance, they want to go down and volunteer, they want to go down and join, they want to pick up a gun, but the guns have almost nothing to do with the Zapatista struggle, they haven't fired a shot since January 12th 1994, they only retain their guns so the Mexican government will continue to take them seriously as a force they need to talk to, but the main activity of the Zapatistas is just organizing, organizing, organizing, locally, nationally, and internationally, talking, having *consultas*, having *encuentros* … the hard boring stuff, so a lot of the people go to the Zapatistas because of this glamour, and they will say, is there any way I can join the Zapatistas, I want to run around the mountains with a mask on and a gun, and the Zapatistas will say no, if you want to help the Zapatistas, go home and fight for justice in your own lands, because if there is justice in your own lands, there will be justice here as well because it is all the same struggle.

The last part of the quotation directs our attention to the widespread belief within the Zapatista network that solidarity with the EZLN involves radical democratic organizing for social change in the local and national settings of network activists. As indicated, this perception comes to some extent from the EZLN, which ceaselessly stresses the mutual character of solidarity. That this call is so widely echoed underlines the success of the EZLN in extending the relevance of its local and national struggle beyond the borders of Mexico. Applying the theoretical terms used in this chapter, we may say that the transnational resonance of the EZLN is a result of the elaboration of a radical democratic action master frame, which provides a number of concrete visions on how to practise radical democracy, especially at the local level. As briefly mentioned in Chapter 4, the Zapatista network organization Zapatista Action (Acción Zapatista) of Austin, Texas, has drawn on the EZLN radical democratic master frame in an attempt to apply the EZLN's idea of *encuentro* to the local setting of Austin. Manuel Callahan (2000) of Zapatista Action explains the inspiration from the EZLN as follows:

> [W]e wanted to introduce this whole strategy of *coyuntura* … it is a strategy of analysis that allows for everybody in the room to make a contribution to the collective analysis of the various forces that are operating, and develop a strategy that is collective, and that everybody feels a part of…. They use it in Chiapas …, and the other thing we want to introduce is the notion of councils, which we weren't very clear of, we had this vague notion of how councils were operating in Chiapas … we were still having trouble getting some really good material on how the Zapatistas actually organized themselves and used education as a vehicle to organize all the levels of the Zapatistas … so we are kind of testing it on ourselves, experimenting what we vaguely have a sense of is happening in Chiapas.

As demonstrated by the quotation, the EZLN radical democratic action master frame is considered by many network activists to have its origins in the decision-making structures of the indigenous communities that form the basis of the EZLN. In other words, the perception of democracy in the indigenous communities seems to fit well with the anarchist and new social movement currents already present in activist circles, especially in the USA and Europe. It is worth recalling here our reservation that democratic processes in the indigenous communities influenced by the EZLN do not necessarily reflect decision-making practices in other indigenous communities outside the EZLN's influence. At the same time, and as suggested by the above quotation, the understanding of democratic practices in indigenous communities is not always substantial, and information on how democracy actually works in the Zapatista communities is scant.[10] What is of interest here, however, is not whether the EZLN and indigenous inspiration for radical democratic activities are rooted in perfect knowledge of the way democracy works in Chiapas. The core of our concern is the fact that the EZLN and its indigenous form of democracy have become a symbol of radical democracy beyond Mexico's borders. This is reflected in the comments by an anonymous interviewee to a question about the main contributions of the EZLN:

> Democratic and collective values ... are what the EZLN has to contribute to activism outside of Mexico.... In modern day Mayan culture, the authorities serve by obeying the directives of their community assemblies. If the authorities do not obey they are recalled.... Thus, the model of political leadership is from the bottom up. It is the negation of the predominant (top-down) structure in US organizations.

In comments such as this, there may be an element of romanticizing of the EZLN and the indigenous approach to democracy. First, and as noted earlier, a notable weakness concerns the tendency to conflate democratic practices in Zapatista communities with those of indigenous communities in general. Second, and according to Comandante Tacho of the EZLN, even Zapatista communities vary in regard to decision-making (Le Bot 1997: 295). Third, there is also a tendency to overlook anti-democratic structures within Zapatista base communities. These potential problems in applying the EZLN radical democratic action master frame will not be further discussed here. Rather, they serve to point our attention to a fact mentioned earlier, namely that the EZLN action master frame is not an immutable ideational complex presented by the EZLN for ready use, but also a result of the way the EZLN radical democratic ideas are received and moulded by transnational activists. The aim of the present discussions has, accordingly, been to demonstrate how elements of the EZLN radical action master frame are visible in the actions and self-perceptions of Zapatista network activists and not to assess whether these activists use the action master frame 'correctly'.

Beyond Mexico: challenging liberal democracy

We will now broaden the discussion to the transnational justice and solidarity network. The aim is not to show direct application of the EZLN action master frame, but rather to establish an argument pointing to similarities between this frame and those who guide social action within the transnational justice and solidarity network.

Lichbach and Almeida (2002: 26), in their study of the WTO protests in Seattle in 1999, describe how the protesters were extremely diverse, basing their protest on concerns and grievances tied to everything from material interests to social identities and global ideals. In light of this diversity of interest, it may seem risky to try to identify similarities. Nevertheless, it is contended here that the struggle over definitions of democracy constitutes such a unifying factor. This view is echoed by Smith (2001: 16), who notes that,

> If one had to identify a common thread among the demands of activists in this movement, it would be a demand for democracy. As governments seek to coordinate policies at the global level, they have systematically excluded ever greater numbers of people from decision-making. Against this exclusion, activists call for greater access to information about the free trade agreements that governments are negotiating. Many were surprised to learn that even their elected legislators could not obtain a copy of the negotiating text for the Free Trade Area of the Americas (only a heavily censored version of the text was released, months after the Quebec summit). These agreements have an enormous impact on everyday life in local communities, and so the members of these communities are beginning to demand a say in their negotiation.

This interpretation is largely shared by Lori Wallach, one of the key figures in the protests in Seattle. In an interview with Moisés Naím (2000: 4) of *Foreign Policy*, Wallach suggests the following diagnosis and cure for the democratic deficit in institutions that embody neoliberal policies, for example the WTO and the IMF:

> There would be a global regime of rules that more than anything create the political space for the kinds of value decisions that mechanisms like the WTO now make, at a level where people living with the results can hold the decision makers accountable. Right now, there are decisions, value-subjective decisions, being shifted into totally unaccountable, international realms where, if the decision is wrong, there's no way to fix it.[11]

This emphasis on the extension of democracy as a strategy for social change is also reflected in the ideas that have inspired the World

Social Forums held since 2001.[12] The forums are open to everyone who is critical of neoliberalism, and in many ways they continue the ideas and spirit of the two intercontinental encounters held in Chiapas and Spain in 1996 and 1997.[13] This relationship is evident in the guiding principles of the World Social Forum (2001):

> The World Social Forum is a plural, diversified, non-confessional, non-governmental and non-party space that, in a decentralized, networked fashion, interrelates organizations and movements engaged in concrete action at levels from the local to the international to build another world.... The World Social Forum asserts democracy as the avenue to resolving society's problems politically. As a meeting place, it is open to the pluralism and to the diversity of activities and ways of engaging of the organizations and movements that decide to participate in it, as well as the diversity of gender, race, ethnicity, and culture.

The last three quotations partially echo the EZLN's demands for a democracy built on the principle of 'to rule by obeying' – that is, a democracy with less distance between those who govern and those who are governed and affected by political decisions, and with a more effective democratic control over the market. This comparison must, however, be qualified in a number of ways. First, we should remember that the EZLN has mainly used the concept 'to rule by obeying' in the national context of Mexico. Second, the EZLN's fundamental critique of neoliberalism and its demands for the protection of the Mexican state and nation may seem to entail a rejection of the international institutions of neoliberalism rather than a demand for further democratization of these institutions. The point here, however, is not to discuss whether or not the EZLN democratic vision of 'to rule by obeying' is directly applicable on a transnational level, but to register that it has important overlaps with some of the radical democratic aspirations within the transnational justice and solidarity network.

It is, of course, too simple to take the comments advanced in the above quotations as common denominators for the democratic aspirations of all participants in the transnational justice and solidarity network. Smith and Wallach reflect a specific position where international institutions such as the WTO and the IMF are not fundamentally questioned. Rather, demands go in the direction of subjecting these institutions to closer democratic scrutiny and opening them to the influence of civil society actors. In relation to the EZLN radical democratic action master frame, this critique of democracy is located primarily in the dimensions of the deepening and broadening of democracy and its proponents may be described as global transformers (Held and McGrew 2002: ch. 8). Another important current in the transnational justice and solidarity network, corresponding to the category of radicals in Held and McGrew (2002: ch. 8), consists of activists working from an anarchist point of view. Yet as noted by Epstein (2001: 1), the anarchist inspiration in the transnational justice and solidarity network is not necessarily built on strict adherence to the theoretical roots of anarchism:

> For contemporary young radical activists, anarchism means a decentralized organizational structure, based on affinity groups that work together on an ad hoc basis, and decision-making by consensus.... Many envision a stateless society based on small, egalitarian communities. For some, however, the society of the future remains an open question. For them, anarchism is important mainly as an organizational structure and as a commitment to egalitarianism.

Contrary to the quotations from Smith and Wallach, anarchist tendencies seem to put more emphasis on democracy within and between groups and organizations, and less on the democratization of what are largely considered to be illegitimate international institutions. Polletta (2001: 26) describes the consensus-oriented decision-making procedures in the New York branch of the anarchist-inspired Direct Action Network, which plays an important role in the transnational justice and solidarity network:

> I had seen the group's decisionmaking style in action at one of its Sunday meetings. Participants sat in a circle and were called on by two facilitators who also kept track of the agenda. A time-keeper alerted the group to the fact that it had used up the time allotted for an issue; in this meeting, participants 'consensed' that they would devote ten more minutes to discussion. A difficult question about whether to fund a project – a hundred or so dollars – required two extensions in this meeting. Tempers flared during the discussion, and people signaled their intention to block what seemed to be an emerging consensus. The solution slowly hammered out was that DAN [Direct Action Network] would not fund the project and people instead would contribute voluntarily. There was consensus and a hat

was passed around and quickly filled. The next issue was taken up. Again, discussion seemed to go round and round; again, consensus was eventually reached.

Apart from its ideological and theoretical roots in anarchism, this approach may also be identified in the new social movements of the 1970s and 1980s. The debate on new social movements is extensive and will not be taken up here. It is, however, useful to consider briefly in the present context the movements' vision of direct democracy. Scott (1990: 27) sums up the characteristics of the new social movements:

> Anti-authoritarianism shifts the emphasis towards direct or grassroots democracy, and away from formal representative democracy.... Representative democracy is distrusted because it weighs power in favour of the representatives who enjoy extensive autonomy, and away from those who they represent, who must, by and large, rely on the integrity of those who act in their name and call on their, largely passive support. This critique of formal democracy is turned not merely upon existing social institutions, but also upon the social movements who have allowed themselves to be drawn into institutionalized politics and have developed large bureaucratic and oligarchical organizational forms in the process.

This approach to the question of democracy is significantly different from that offered by Smith and Wallach above. What is interesting is not the differences and the tensions they may cause, but the fact that this anarchist and grassroots approach to democracy is also echoed in the EZLN radical democratic action master frame. The similarities here are not so much in the concept of 'to rule by obeying', but rather in the conception of autonomy defended by the EZLN. In terms of the EZLN frame, the anarchist current resembles the delegation dimension.

Notes

1. It should be stressed that the EZLN does not explicitly make use of the concept of radical democracy as a description of its political project and visions.
2. It is acknowledged that these positions display fundamental differences. This is especially the case with the work of Cohen and Arato (1992) and the

work of Laclau (1996) and Mouffe (1993). Cohen and Arato build on a Habermasian framework, while Laclau and Mouffe build on a critique of Habermas.

3. At first sight, this view may not appear to differ significantly from liberal democracy, which also presupposes an active civil society as the foundation for democracy. In the perspective of liberal democracy, however, civil society is made up by interest groups that do not question social, economic and cultural values in fundamental ways. In contrast, radical democratic visions of civil society focus on civil society as an arena of conflict and politics and the development of contentious identities.

4. The approved proposal and the original COCOPA proposal differ in a number of respects. The most important seem to be the following: the new proposal does not recognize the indigenous communities as entities with legal rights; the new proposal denies the indigenous people the right to their lands and territories and thus to the use of the natural resources in these areas; the new proposal does not include indigenous rights at the level of the national constitution, but only at the state level (SIPAZ 2001c). Despite the fact that indigenous autonomy has not yet been enshrined *de jure* in the Mexican Constitution in the form desired by the EZLN and other parts of the indigenous population of Mexico, the formation of autonomous municipalities in Chiapas means that *de facto* autonomy is currently being practised in a number of areas with EZLN influence, albeit in a climate of constant conflict and violence.

5. Civil society as an idea has a long history, which is beyond the scope of this chapter. The modern use of the concept relates mainly to the democratic transitions in Eastern Europe and Latin America (Cohen and Arato 1992). In regard to Mexico, an important point of reference is the civil society organizational efforts in Mexico City following the 1985 earthquake (Monsiváis 1987).

6. See also Bruhn 1999, Johnston 2000, and Morton 2000 for Gramscian interpretations of the EZLN.

7. We cannot, however, apply Gramsci's framework to the EZLN without some qualifications. Gramsci was basically a Marxist revolutionary, who saw the working class as the leader of a new counter-hegemony. The aim of the counter-hegemony was therefore to pave the way for the subsequent takeover of the state by the working class (Laclau and Mouffe 1985: 69). In the context of the EZLN, Gramsci's thinking may be more usefully applied along the lines of Cohen and Arato's (1992) concept of self-limiting radicalism. Social movements that display a self-limiting radical character have abandoned the revolutionary aspirations inherent in Gramsci's thinking, and do not consider the working class (or other classes or groups) the natural leadership or vanguard in social struggles from a socialist perspective.

8. This distinction has obviously been enforced as a result of the 11 September 2001 terrorist attacks in New York. During the Cold War, governments had extensive freedom to repress Soviet or socialist-inspired social movements. In the contemporary situation, a similar freedom may now be awarded to anti-terrorist activities.

9. The question of when informal transnational movement networks and the action master frames on which they rest establish the degree of overlap

and convergence that allows us to speak of the existence of a transnational field of synergy is obviously a question of utmost importance. This question, however, falls outside the immediate aim of the discussions in this book, concerned as we are here with the formation of informal transnational movement networks that constitute a 'lower' level of analytical abstraction than the transnational field of synergy concept.

10. See, however, the interviews with Subcomandante Marcos, Comandante Tacho and Mayor Moisés in Le Bot 1997. See also articles and reports at the Irish Mexico Group website at http://flag.blackened.net/revolt/mexico. html.

11. The page number refers to a downloaded version of the article.

12. The forums have been supported by *Le Monde Diplomatique* and Bernard Cassen. The ideas underlying the forums also reflect to some extent the views of the organization ATTAC, of which Cassen is president, and its demands for more democratic control over the market. As mentioned in Chapter 6, ATTAC's formation was inspired by an article by Ignacio Ramonet (1997), editor-in-chief of *Le Monde Diplomatique*.

13. The EZLN and Subcomandante Marcos have spoken about the forums in positive terms and in a way that resembles the discourse surrounding the intercontinental encounter in Chiapas in 1996.

8

The Internet

This chapter focuses on the role of the Internet, or computer-mediated communication, in the formation of the transnational Zapatista solidarity network. Its main argument is that the Internet provides a qualitatively new communication medium with a significant facilitating impact on the potential for establishing transnational forms of social interaction.[1] This potential is especially evident in the Internet's ability to establish resonance and exchange between the everyday experiences of senders and recipients in the transnational framing process.

In Chapter 3, significant emphasis was also laid on the role of the Internet in the transnational Zapatista solidarity network. We mainly looked there at the way the Internet has facilitated the informational infrastructure of the network. That is, the chapter provided a view from within the network. In consequence, less attention was paid to the way the Internet has facilitated the formation of the Zapatista solidarity network. This aspect will be pursued here, while at the same time we will draw on some of the insights provided by Chapter 3. Overall, the book takes the view that the Internet has a largely positive and facilitating effect in regard to transnational framing processes. The last part of this chapter, nevertheless, considers some of the potential obstacles and problems in the relationship between the Internet and transnational interaction.

The Internet as Social Space

In Chapter 2, it was claimed that framing processes are more likely to be successful if there is a degree of resonance between the everyday experiences of senders and recipients in the framing process. It was emphasized, at the same time, that such resonance should be expected to be more problematic where there is great physical distance between senders and recipients. This is obviously the case with the transnational Zapatista solidarity network. Yet physical distance is rarely the only kind of distance at play in transnational framing processes. In the case of the relationship between the EZLN and the Zapatista solidarity network, distance should also be measured in social and cultural terms. The EZLN is made up mainly of impoverished indigenous people. In contrast, the large majority of network activists are non-indigenous people in the rich parts of the world, mainly Europe and the USA.

While traditional forms of communication technology such as telephone and fax to some extent enable social actors to cross physical distance, they are less useful in regard to the crossing of social and cultural distance. We referred earlier to the resonance between the everyday experiences of senders and recipients in framing processes as a central ingredient in a successful frame. This kind of resonance, as suggested above, faces particular problems in cases where there is not only significant physical but also social and cultural distance between the actors involved. Transnational framing processes, in other words, presuppose the existence of communications technologies with a potential for bridging these distances. This chapter argues that the Internet and computer-mediated communications hold an important potential in that respect. What should be highlighted is not merely the conspicuous advance in the speed and in the reduction in costs associated with the Internet; though the Internet has indeed given rise to a range of quantitative changes in the form of communication. The thrust of the argument here lies, rather, in the qualitative changes brought about by the Internet. That said, these qualitative changes cannot be meaningfully separated from the quantitative changes referred to above. The relationship between them is, instead, dialectical (Cleaver 2000b).[2]

The Internet is a social construct shaped by the social actors who make use of it (Slevin 2000: 7). Of course, the Internet is also a technology in a more objective sense. But the way technologies are put to use by social actors is not predetermined. Accordingly, the significance of the Internet in the formation of the Zapatista solidarity network is an outcome of the interplay between the EZLN and the actors who make up the network. The transnational framing process underlying the formation of the Zapatista network thus involves a sender and a recipient. In our case, the sender is the EZLN, while the recipient is the multiplicity of organizations and groups outside Mexico who have responded to the EZLN and the situation in Chiapas in one way or another. The relationship between the sender and the recipient in framing processes may be understood through the conceptual pairs private–public and direct–mediated (Diani 2001). A central argument is that the Internet blurs, and to a large extent collapses, these distinctions. If we accept this claim, it also means that we have to look at the Internet as something more than a medium in a traditional sense – that is, as more than simple relay of information from one actor to another.

The Internet is obviously not the first example of an information technology enabling the crossing of physical distance, yet it has certain qualities that make it more than a quantitative continuation and improvement of earlier means of communication. It is not merely a tool. The Internet thus creates opportunities for transnational framing that cannot be understood through the optic of traditional communications technologies. The Internet differs from traditional forms of communication inasmuch as it has the potential for creating social space (Harasim 1993; Poster 1997) – a space where social actors can 'meet' irrespective of their physical location. This argument obviously challenges long-held convictions in the study of social movements regarding shared physical space as a precondition for the formation of social movements (Diani 2001).[3] Of course, traditional means of communication such as telephone and letters also involve to some extent a shrinking of physical distance. The main difference between the Internet and such traditional means of communication lies in the fact that the Internet has the potential for shrinking social and cultural, as well as physical, distance.

In Chapter 2, it was suggested that the potential of the Internet lay in its ability to reach a larger audience at much lower cost than is possible through telephone and letter-writing activities (Slevin 2000: 74). Moreover, it was mentioned that the relative ease with which computer and modem equipment can be used by 'ordinary' people greatly enhances its potential for use in activities of social action and transnational framing. The main difference, though, lies not in the fact that larger numbers of people can be reached in a cheaper and more effective way, but in the opportunities for continuity and co-presence in computer-mediated forms of communication. This is partly due to reduction of the time lag between sending and receiving information.

This reduction of the time lag is obviously also a feature of, for example, telephone and fax communication, but these media differ from the Internet in the highly personalized communication they permit. The Internet, in contrast, enables many-to-many communication (Kollock and Smith 1999: 3) on an almost instantaneous basis. Harry Cleaver (2000), a network activist and a theorist on the uses of the Internet within the Zapatista solidarity network, draws out some of the advantages of the Internet as compared to political organizing in earlier decades:

> [T]he way I put it now is, that it took six years to build the anti-war movement in the 60s, it took six months to build the anti-war movement in the Gulf War, and it took six days to build an anti-Mexican government movement in 1994.... It is quite clear that the Internet is making possible a level of organization, a speed of organization, that we have never seen before ... and for me, who worked on an underground newspaper in the 60s heavily involved in the anti-war movement, who remembers how slow everything was, the guys who would send us shit anonymously by mail, we would get it and write stories about it, and then it would take a week to produce the paper, and then we had to get out and distribute it, and if we wanted to send it to the East Coast, we would have to package it and find somebody to distribute it, and now all that shit is happening like that, it is a qualitative difference that has to do with a quantitative change ... just like the Zapatista mobilization against the Mexican government, in Mexico 200,000–300,000 people would gather at the Zócalo, but around the world it was happening in 40 countries and 100 cities, and it was having effect, and it would not have been possible without the Internet.

If we return to the argument about the Internet as a social space, this circumstance is expressed in a number of different ways. In the case of the Zapatista solidarity network, the listserv Chiapas-L provides an example of a discussion forum where debates can go on continuously and indefinitely and with the participation of an unlimited number of people, in contrast to what is possible, for example, in newspapers. Moreover, huge archives of material can be made available on the Internet. An archive of this type is maintained by the Chiapas95 listserv (described in Chapter 3) as well as by the Chiapas-L listserv. The existence of archives of this sort makes it possible for users of the Internet to establish a degree of continuity between the past and the present. Such continuity, of course, is an important element if we are to understand the Internet as a social space. Material circulated on and via the Internet is obviously not always organized in archives as in the cases of Chiapas95 and Chiapas-L. This does not mean that it disappears. In most cases, material remains accessible on the Internet beyond the immediate time of distribution.

Websites also provide a stable space on the Internet. Websites are living things in the sense that they have a past as well as a present. They continuously develop, reflecting events in the real world as well as the attitudes of the people who maintain them. Seeing websites as living things obviously involves the possibility that websites 'die' or become defunct over time. The reception of information via the Internet is thus rarely an isolated action. It takes place in an already existing social space marked by the traces of prior activities and with a stable presence in the form of listservs, archives and websites. It is clear, then, that the Internet cannot be sufficiently understood if it is perceived simply as a tool. Harry Cleaver (2000) puts it this way:

> My position is that we are the Internet, it is not the computers, it is not the wires, it is the communications that flow and change, we are the Internet, so it is not a tool. I don't like the term virtuality, because there is nothing virtual about working the Internet, the Internet … is the people who are communicating with each other, and we construct that, so I think of the Internet as a space…. Every time you send a new email linkage it's a new space, a new website is a new space…. There is nothing virtual about that, it is real people setting up computers, talking to each other, and that interacts with

the rest of their lives, just like going to a demonstration interacts with the rest of their lives.

It was argued in Chapter 2 that the Internet blurs the sender–recipient dichotomy that dominates traditional mass media such as newspapers and television. This argument emerged from the distinction between direct and mediated forms of communication (Diani 2001). Information distributed and received through the media is obviously an instance of mediated information. So far, we have only discussed the differences between the Internet and communications media such as telephone and fax. These are, however, highly personalized media of communication. Media such as television and newspapers, in contrast, are mass media: media where the distribution does not take place on a personalized level and where the recipients of information are not defined except in more abstract terms.

Information distributed through mass media communication does not reach its audience before it has passed through a filter where news and information are subsumed under specific standards on what is newsworthy and what is not (Slevin 2000: 73–5). In the worst case this may lead to the distortion of information, but in most cases it means that news is left out because it is not considered to be interesting for the reader or the viewer. Before the arrival of the Internet, media such as newspapers and television were the only mass media options available to social movements. If social movements were to reach a wider audience than could be reached through telephone and letter-writing campaigns and through direct forms of communication such as demonstrations and the distribution of flyers, newspapers and television were unavoidable stations along the way.[4]

The Internet tends to dissolve the distinction between personalized and mass media communication. The Internet can be seen as both. Internet- or computer-mediated communications may take place between two people sending emails to each other. In other cases, information and communication on the Internet involves multiple recipients, as in the case of mass communication media. As discussed in Chapter 2, this type of communication takes place, for example, through listservs and websites. Despite the fact that the Internet also enables forms of mass communication, it does so in a way that is significantly different from that of traditional forms of mass communication.

The main difference is that the Internet is a medium that allows for a high degree of unmediated communication. While this may, at first, appear to be a contradiction in terms, it points, in fact, to the aspect of the Internet that holds the greatest potential for social movements and other social actors. The Internet is, in many ways, the first communications medium that enables distributors of information to reach a large undefined audience (as do traditional mass media) without, at the same time, having to conform to conventional mass media standards. In Chapter 3 we described how the Internet-based informational infrastructure of the Zapatista solidarity network rests on the notion that the information distributed through the circuits of the network is more authentic due to the absence of media filters. The Internet, then, allows people to relay information over great physical distances to a large and worldwide audience; furthermore they are able to do so in the form that they find most fitting. Also in contrast to traditional mass media, communication on the Internet is able to take place on a many-to-many basis (Kollock and Smith 1999: 3). This type of communication is exemplified by listservs such as Chiapas95 and Chiapas-L where there are many recipients (the list subscribers) as well as many senders of information. The latter circumstance is due to the fact that such listservs act as gateways for a large number of different informational sources.

Another important aspect of the Internet in regard to social action is the difficulty of censoring Internet-distributed information. It is thus almost impossible for governments to maintain control over flows of information on the Internet. While newspapers and television may, to some extent, be controlled and censored this is more difficult with the Internet, especially as communication can now take place via satellite and cellular phones. These points echo the arguments of RAND researchers Ronfeldt and Arquilla (1998), where the EZLN uprising is presented as the primary example of a social netwar, which, to a significant degree, revolves around information (see Chapter 1). Although these authors don't reduce the social netwar to the Internet (1998: 11), it is clear from the study that in so far as it facilitates the distribution of uncensored information, the Internet should be expected to play a central role in social netwar conflicts.

The arguments presented so far are those with the greatest relevance to transnational framing processes. It was argued above that successful frames presuppose a degree of resonance between the everyday experiences of the senders and recipients engaged in the process. It was also suggested that this resonance was a rather unlikely prospect considering the distances involved, or unlikely, at least, from the viewpoint of traditional means of communication. The thesis of this book is that the Internet provides social actors with unprecedented means for communication across physical, social and cultural distances. The Internet does not dissolve these distances, of course; it does, however, have the potential to make them less of an obstacle to transnational framing processes. Distance, at least in its social and cultural dimensions, is often a mental construct resting on lack of knowledge. When actors far away from Mexico are able to gain an insight into the everyday lives and experiences of people in Chiapas, through accounts relayed by the people directly involved, physical distances lose their salience.

The importance ascribed to the Internet above should not be confused with the technological euphoria that seems to prevail in some quarters of the Zapatista solidarity network. The danger does exist of armchair activism (Paulson 2001) and of a flattened picture of realities on the ground in Chiapas and Mexico generally (Hellman 1999).[5] Activists and researchers alike should be sensitive to this. Another necessary qualification concerns the continued relevance of physical encounters in transnational framing processes and the dialectical relationship between computer-mediated and physical activities (Slevin 2000: 79). This chapter argues, accordingly, that transnational framing does not only take place through the Internet. As shown in Chapters 3 and 4, the transnational Zapatista solidarity network has a significant physical dimension, although it is true that this is often closely related to its computer-mediated aspects. Thus transnational framing also takes place when people go to Chiapas and meet with actors at the local level. These qualifications should not, however, divert our attention from the fact that the Internet has played a significant role in the formation of the Zapatista solidarity network. The remainder of the chapter pursues this argument through a more empirically informed discussion of the use of the Internet in the relationship between, on the one hand, the EZLN and EZLN-related actors, and, on the other hand, the transnational Zapatista solidarity network.[6]

'We Denounce...'

In the period following the Mexican army offensive in Chiapas in February 1995, the media were full of stories about the EZLN and the Internet. The conspicuous role of the Internet in the events surrounding the February 1995 offensive attracted the attention of people and organizations that had hitherto viewed the EZLN uprising as an anachronistic and traditional armed movement. Special attention in this regard was directed to the role of Subcomandante Marcos. In one of the earliest accounts of the importance of the Internet to the EZLN, Todd Robberson (1995) of the *Washington Post* engaged in the following speculations about Subcomandante Marcos and his use of computer technology and the Internet:

> [T]he rebel leader typically would write his voluminous communiqués on a laptop computer, which he carried in a backpack and plugged into the lighter socket of an old pickup truck he used when travelling between the remote Zaptista strongholds of La Garrucha and Guadaloupe Tepeyac. Today, both villages are firmly under Mexican army control, while the whereabouts of Marcos and his followers remains a mystery. Nevertheless, Marcos' communiqués continue to flow unimpeded through cyberspace, usually reaching readers in countries as distant as Italy, Germany and Russia faster than they can be published by most Mexican newspapers.... If Marcos is equipped with a telephone modem and a cellular phone, it would be possible for him to hook into the Internet even while on the run, as he is now.

Later in the same year, the account by Robberson was reflected in numerous other articles fascinated by the apparent paradox of an impoverished indigenous army using sophisticated communications and information technology (e.g. Doyle 1995; Watson et al. 1995). While these articles only allude to the possibility of Subcomandante Marcos and the EZLN being online, they also seem to have been the source of some misunderstanding about the role of the Internet in the EZLN. In late February 1995, the *Christian Science Monitor* (1995) had thus distorted the story to the following account:

Marcos, it turns out, is online. Punching out communiqués on a laptop computer powered from the cigarette lighter in his car, and then passing them along via modem and cellular phone, Marcos has connected with peace and human rights activists over computer bulletin boards.

The myth concerning the EZLN and Subcomandante Marcos being online is joined by that surrounding the Ya Basta! website initiated by Justin Paulson in March 1994. As Paulson states in an interview conducted by Pablo Espinosa (1996) for *La Jornada*, the website is not run by the EZLN itself; nor is it the official voice of the EZLN. Nevertheless, he notes (2001) that the EZLN agreed to let him use the 'ezln.org' domain name in 1996. The mythical status of the Ya Basta! website obviously stems from the fact that it was the first website devoted entirely to the issues of the EZLN and Chiapas (see Chapter 3).

While the story about Subcomandante Marcos writing on a laptop computer powered by the lighter socket of a truck is not entirely implausible, there is no evidence as such that either the EZLN or Subcomandante Marcos have direct access to the Internet through modem or cellular phones.[7] Harry Cleaver (1998a: 628) has the following to say about the EZLN and the Internet:

> It is important to note that the EZLN has played no direct role in the proliferation of the use of the Internet. Rather, these efforts were initiated by others to weave a network of support for the EZLN. Although there is a myth that EZLN spokesman Subcomandante Marcos sits in the jungle uploading EZLN communiqués from his laptop, the reality is that the EZLN and its communities have had a mediated relationship to the Internet. The Zapatista communities are indigenous, poor and often cut off not only from computer communications but also from the necessary electricity and telephone systems. Under these conditions, EZLN materials were initially prepared as written communiqués for the mass media and were handed to reporters or to friends to give to reporters. Such material then had to be typed or scanned into electronic format for distribution on the Internet.

The job of putting the EZLN on the Internet, then, is carried out by activists in the transnational Zapatista solidarity network and by Mexican newspapers and magazines. EZLN communiqués, at least in the early days of the uprising, were often transported from EZLN villages in Chiapas to, for example, the *El Tiempo* magazine in San Cristóbal de las Casas. *El Tiempo* would then pass on the information and communiqués to national newspapers such as *La Jornada* and *El Financiero*.[8] The role played by *La Jornada* is especially important. In Chapter 3, we learned that in late 1994 Justin Paulson (2001) gained permission to reprint articles from *La Jornada* in return for helping the newspaper get online. The fact that EZLN communiqués were (and are) usually printed in *La Jornada* obviously gave Paulson and the Ya Basta! website a privileged position in terms of distributing EZLN communiqués and declarations via the Internet.[9]

The EZLN's 'presence' on the Internet is thus clearly one mediated and facilitated by network activists. Yet this does not mean that the EZLN is not conscious of the potential of the Internet, although the EZLN and Subcomandante Marcos have made few statements directly addressing its significance. Thus the popular myths referred to above have never been directly contradicted or confirmed by the EZLN and the issue remains a rather grey area. In an interview with Le Bot (1997: 348–9), Subcomandante Marcos does make the following general remarks regarding the importance of the Internet:

> A new space, a novel space, that was so new that no one thought a guerrilla could enter into it, is the information superhighway, the Internet. It was a terrain not occupied by anyone…. There are people who have put us on the Internet and Zapatismo has occupied a space that no one had thought of. The Mexican political system has gained its international prestige thanks to its informational control…. The fact that it has been possible to distribute this type of news on a channel that cannot be controlled, efficiently and fast, is a very serious blow … because the information is everywhere at the same time.

Subcomandante Marcos points out that the EZLN has a presence on the Internet mainly through the efforts of the transnational Zapatista solidarity network. He also raises another issue: the considerable degree of informational control that the Mexican state has always exercised. This situation only began to change significantly in the 1990s: the EZLN uprising and the use of the Internet clearly demonstrated that censorship was becoming increasingly difficult.

The importance of undistorted information obviously has the greatest bearing on the internal situation in Mexico, but it also has significant implications for the transnational framing process. If we accept that this process rests on the availability of information, a situation in which a government is able to repress the information flows from a given country represents a serious obstacle. For example, accounts of the everyday experiences of the indigenous communities of Chiapas would have had little chance of reaching a non-Mexican audience had the Mexican government been able to exercise effective control over information flows. We will now move on to discuss how EZLN-related actors (i.e. the Zapatista base communities in Chiapas) have directly addressed audiences outside Mexico through the Internet. This will be not so much an analysis of the content of these communications as an assessment of the way the Internet has been used by EZLN-related actors to give people outside Mexico insight into the everyday lives and experiences of people on the ground in Chiapas.

The EZLN leadership, and especially Subcomandante Marcos, have on several occasions issued statements and communiqués directed specifically to actors outside Mexico: for example, to the US public and US politicians (EZLN 1994c), to European gatherings of network activists in Brescia (EZLN 1995d) and Paris (EZLN 1996c), to the European March against Unemployment (EZLN 1997a), to Mumia Abu-Jamal (EZLN 1999d) and Leonard Peltier (EZLN 1999j), and to international civil society (EZLN 1996g) in general.[10] In fact, most EZLN communiqués are addressed, *inter alia*, to international civil society. Of course, these communications have not exclusively taken place through the Internet; in many cases they have also been published in traditional mass media such as newspapers. There again, anything significant published on Chiapas and the EZLN in newspapers and magazines has eventually found its way onto the Internet and through the computer-mediated information circuits of the Zapatista solidarity network. The Chiapas95 listserv, for instance, is full of articles from newspapers and magazines.

It is useful to make a distinction here between the EZLN and EZLN-related actors regarding use of the Internet. Official declarations and communiqués issued by the EZLN leadership are often couched in general and metaphorical language. As such, they convey less forcefully information about the everyday lives and experiences of the people of Chiapas. Nevertheless, statements by the indigenous communities in Chiapas have been very numerous, as the archives of the Chiapas95 and Enlace Civil listservs show.[11]

It has been noted that the activities of the Zapatista solidarity network have been most intense in relation to certain extreme events such as the army offensive in February 1995 and the Acteal massacre in December 1997. This does not imply that Chiapas has otherwise been without violence. On the contrary, Chiapas has experienced a high general level of violence both before and since the 1994 uprising. It has been the consequence of both the heavy army presence and the activities of numerous paramilitary groups. This remains the situation today: incidents of intimidation and violence occur almost daily. The mainstream media rarely report this low-intensity warfare. The great advantage of the Internet in this situation is that it connects Chiapas to an audience to whom it can relate these occurrences without the information having to pass through the filters of mainstream media. At the same time, this kind of direct and arguably more authentic information provides the rationale for activists to connect to the informational infrastructure of the Zapatista solidarity network.

The denouncements issued by the indigenous Zapatista communities in Chiapas are distributed externally largely through Enlace Civil and, to a lesser extent, the FZLN.[12] In Chapter 3 the FZLN and Enlace Civil were cast as second-level actors in the solidarity network, while the indigenous communities of Chiapas occupied the first level. In many cases, denouncements are transmitted from the FZLN and Enlace Civil to third-level actors, such as the listservs Chiapas95 and Chiapas-L, and from there to the fourth and fifth levels. Denouncements all reflect the problems the Chiapas communities face on a daily basis. Internet distribution reaches a worldwide audience within a very short time. Although telephonic and fax communications share this quality, the Internet has the potential to reach more people, at the same time, at a much lower cost, and with considerably less effort in terms of working hours and technical knowledge. Moreover, Internet-distributed information is easily passed on by its immediate recipients by the simple forwarding of emails.

There follow three examples of the hundreds of denouncements issued by indigenous Zapatista communities and distributed via the Enlace Civil listserv. All reflect instances of low-intensity conflict:

In the *ejido* of Arroyo Granizo, municipality of Ricardo Flores Magón in rebellion, on October 16, 1999, we publicly denounce the acts committed by paramilitaries in this community. For a year they have come to the community, threatening at every moment ... that they are not afraid of anyone and that they have relations with the military and other communities of the region. (Municipio Autónomo en Rebeldía Ricardo Flores Magón 1999)

We denounce the illegal acts committed in the community of Yibeljoj in the municipality of Chenalhó, Chiapas. Today, May 25 [2000] at 6 o'clock in the morning two pick-up trucks from the judicial police, two from the federal police, and a truck from the Mexican Army ... arrived to detain Antonio Santiz Gutiérrez accused of having stolen an AK-47 fire arm.... [I]t is not the first time that this group has intimidated the population. Moreover, it is known that they are the ones directly responsible for the Acteal massacre.... After the detention a group of women organized to stop the trucks, closing the road with wood and a human barrier, and succeeding in regaining the detained. At this moment the paramilitaries retired shouting that they would return shortly with more people. (Municipio Autónomo de San Pedro Polhó 2000)

On Wednesday, April 21, 2001, more than thirty soldiers, shooting into the air, arrived in the community of Nuevo Mariscal, they stopped in the centre of the community, threatening with their weapons and asking for the authorities of the community ..., informing them that they were going to stay in the village for more than three days. To this day [April 23] the military presence continues in the communities where the people are afraid of what the soldiers might do.... The people cannot go out to work or do what they normally do. (Municipio Autónomo en Rebeldía Ricardo Flores Magón 2001)

Denouncements distributed through the FZLN and Enlace Civil originate primarily in indigenous communities that sympathize with the EZLN. Second-level actors in the informational infrastructure of the Zapatista solidarity network, such as Indymedia–Chiapas (see Chapter 3), provide an outlet for the indigenous communities of Chiapas in general. The communication efforts of Indymedia–Chiapas are mainly Internet-based. While the denouncements distributed through the Enlace Civil listserv are rarely translated from Spanish to English, Indymedia–Chiapas generally provides an English translation of statements and documents.[13] Indymedia–Chiapas (2001b) describes its purpose and functioning on its website in the following terms:

We emerged as a direct response to the EZLN's call for the creation of alternative media and communication networks. Indymedia–Chiapas provides a space for the indigenous communities of Chiapas to distribute their written, photographic, video and audio material at the state, national and international level.... Only with the support and participation of *compañeros* and *compañeras* from the indigenous communities in Chiapas (many already trained in communication skills) can we achieve our goal of Indymedia–Chiapas becoming a tool and weapon for the people. For this purpose, one of the first steps that we took as Indymedia–Chiapas was to open a semi-permanent office in San Cristóbal de las Casas, where people from indigenous communities are free to produce and publish their work on the Indymedia website. It is equipped with computers, scanners, printers, Internet access, and technical support to facilitate access to the Indymedia–Chiapas web page.

Enlace Civil and Indymedia–Chiapas thus both strive to provide the indigenous people of Chiapas with a way of being heard beyond the borders of Mexico. This vision obviously rests on an understanding of the mainstream mass media as being of limited value in this regard. The incidents described in the quotations above are serious and disturbing for the people who live under these conditions. But from a mainstream media perspective they are still small incidents, the likes of which occur every day in a number of countries around the world. That is, they are rarely sufficiently newsworthy to make it through the filter of the mass media, and even when they do they are rarely presented in the words of the people involved. As the quoted denouncements show, accounts are often delivered in a straightforward and simple language. This reflects the reality of Chiapas: most indigenous people only have Spanish as a second language and rarely any formal education. Accordingly they cannot formulate denouncements that meet journalistic standards.

However, this task is often carried out by second- and third-level actors within the Zapatista solidarity network who put the reported events into a language and format more likely to reach a wider audience. Yet, as we have seen, these actors are at the same time conscious of the need to let the people involved make themselves heard with their own voices and to pass on information in its raw form via the Internet. In many cases, this type of information may pass through all levels in the informational infrastructure of the network, as discussed in Chapter 3. The messages and statements distributed through the Enlace Civil listserv will sometimes end up, for example, on the Chiapas95 listserv, and from there go out to recipients on the fourth level of the informational infrastructure. It is obviously also possible that people there may receive messages and denouncements directly from a second-level actor such as Enlace Civil. It was illustrated in Figure 3.2 that information distributed through the Zapatista solidarity network does not necessarily travel in a linear manner from one level to the next but may jump levels. Regardless of the mode of distribution, the information is there and potentially available to anyone with a computer and modem. The Internet thus provides an unprecedented means for people to get acquainted with the everyday lives and experiences of people living thousands of miles from their own homes.

Connectedness: An Illusion?

We have so far focused on the benefits of the Internet to the EZLN and support actors in Chiapas. We turn now to the other end of the sender–recipient relationship in the transnational framing process: the activists in the transnational Zapatista solidarity network. A useful point of departure is the debate inspired by Judith Adler Hellman's (1999) article 'Real and Virtual Chiapas: Magic Realism and the Left', which appeared in *Socialist Register 2000*. This adopts a sceptical stance towards the value of the Internet for EZLN soli-darity activities. It consequently prompts us to reconsider some of the above arguments. Hellman (1999: 174ff.), for instance, points out that information about Chiapas and the EZLN distributed via the Internet comes from a very limited number of sources, much of it drawn from *La Jornada* or selected by Harry Cleaver through the Chiapas95 listserv. Hellman's observation thus contradicts in many ways the claim that the great benefit of being connected to the computer-mediated Zapatista solidarity network is the availability of more authentic and independent information than can be obtained through the mainstream media. In the *Socialist Register 2001*, Justin Paulson (2000: 282–3) of the Ya Basta! website presents a critical reply to these arguments:[14]

[T]here are literally scores of Web-pages, dozens of mailing lists and archives – not to mention dozens of 'mainstream press' sources that now report regularly from Chiapas and are available online – that spread information over the Internet. Every one of these has different standards for distribution of information, fact checking, and so on. [T]here isn't one person (Cleaver or anybody else) who oversees what gets printed on each Web-page or what information gets spread around and what doesn't get 'selected or distributed.'

Moreover, in response to Hellman's assertion regarding the centrality of *La Jornada* as a source, Paulson (2000: 283) notes that

This is misleading in that it greatly overplays the influence of *La Jornada*.... It is true that activists have relied extensively (although rarely exclusively) on *La Jornada* as a regular news source, but even this is less true now than it was several years ago; the *Frente Zapatista [de Liberación Nacional]* (FZLN), *Enlace Civil*, and the *Congreso Nacional Indígena* (among many others) are all 'Internet-savvy' and have been taking an increasing role in rapid electronic distribution of communiques, action alerts, and so on – and each of these has at least as great a role to play in the struggle (and usually a far more proactive one) as *La Jornada*.

As we saw in Chapter 3, the sources mentioned by Hellman do indeed have a central position in the informational infrastructure of the Zapatista solidarity network. On the other hand, and in line with Paulson's observations, this chapter has demonstrated that there are numerous other sources available for people seeking information on the Internet about the EZLN and Chiapas. What is overlooked in Hellman's criticism, and to some extent also in Paulson's response, is the role played by the direct distribution of information from the Zapatista communities to the outside world, despite the fact that this is mediated by the organizations referred to.

The availability of more or less direct information from this first-level actor, the indigenous Zapatista communities, indicates that Hellman's charge concerning the monopolization of information is unfounded. Similarly, it goes some way to refuting those accounts that maintain the Internet is mainly restricted to activists in Europe and the USA (e.g. Ayres 2001b). The second- and third-level actors, for their part, who function as information hubs, may of course rely on some of the same sources for their information – and there is indeed a high degree of informational recycling which can have unfortunate consequences.[15] It must be borne in mind, though, that second-level actors receive their information directly from the first-level, while third-level actors receive theirs from the second-level and from their own human rights observers stationed in Chiapas, as well as from many other sources (e.g. Mexican newspapers and magazines).

Another issue Hellman raises is the illusion of connectedness (Hellman 1999: 179). She argues that the sense of being connected, through the Internet, with other EZLN and Chiapas solidarity activists and the indigenous communities of Chiapas is illusory. This is so because Internet activities are primarily solitary acts that do not bring people together. Stephen (2000: 14) makes a similar point: while the Internet makes people feel 'very connected to the Zapatistas', this feeling of connectedness 'is somewhat individualized'.[16] She admits that Internet activities are important, but warns that they are no substitute for face-to-face interaction and grassroots organization. Hellman's and Stephen's criticisms obviously challenge our definition of the Internet as a social space. What is suggested by Hellman and, less explicitly, by Stephen is that solidarity activities in real (as opposed to virtual) space possess a higher degree of efficiency and legitimacy than Internet-based work. This, however, is a false dichotomy. For, as was argued in Chapter 3, the computer-mediated and physical dimensions of the Zapatista solidarity network are closely related. The Internet has, for example, been vital in arranging meetings in Chiapas, not to mention demonstrations and actions worldwide. Such meetings, it was argued, lead in turn to the creation of computer-mediated information links when people return to their homes and offices.

Althouth most network activists perceive the Internet as central to their activities, very few seem to suffer from the illusion that the Internet substitutes for face-to-face encounters or personal experiences in Chiapas and Mexico. Peter Brown (Brown and Sáenz Ackermann 2000), of the Schools for Chiapas project, points to the limitations of the Internet within transnational solidarity activism. When people go to Chiapas, for example with the Schools for Chiapas project, nothing that they learn has ever been on the Internet, the Internet gives some information to some people about some things, but most of the human reality about what is going on, despite years of work we can't figure out how to put it up on the Internet ... so even though it is cheaper than a postage stamp and faster than the postal system, it doesn't really get across on some of the things that need to be communicated.

This draws attention to an important point, the main concern of this chapter: the potential of the Internet to create resonance between the everyday lives and experiences of senders and recipients in a transnational framing process. If we accept Brown's point, the Internet should be seen as a tool, rather than a social space, where the latter is understood as a social space in which people actually meet. In other words, Brown, like Hellman and Stephen, maintains that some things simply cannot be experienced on the Internet no matter how many messages people receive. At the same time, though, projects like Schools for Chiapas point to a circumstance largely overlooked by Hellman in her criticism of the Internet. As we saw in Chapter 4, most organizations and individuals involved in EZLN solidarity work have visited Chiapas at least once, usually through the civilian peace camp programmes administered by Mexican and Chiapas-based organizations such as Enlace Civil and the Fray Bartolomé de las Casas Human Rights Center or through participation in delegations and short-term projects. To put this differently: in fact, very few organizations and groups rely solely on information obtained through the Internet and other media. Some larger organizations in the network, such as Global Exchange and SIPAZ, even have permanent observers in Chiapas.

Personal accounts of network activists who have travelled to Chiapas are available on the Internet, sometimes in online papers and magazines or via organization websites. This returns us to the close relationship noted between the physical and Internet-based dimensions of the network. As we saw in the case of the denuouncements discussed above, the Internet is not used solely to circulate second-hand information. It is also a circuit for the distribution of first-hand eyewitness accounts by the indigenous communities of Chiapas, as well as by resident network activists. To suggest, as Hellman has done, that solidarity activism takes place either on the physical or on the computer-mediated level is to display a very partial understanding of both the Zapatista solidarity network and the Internet.

The criticisms raised by Hellman and Stephen, and the counter-arguments offered above, prompt us to make a few qualifications to the main argument of this chapter, namely that the Internet has the potential to create resonance between senders and recipients in transnational framing processes. It has been contended that the Internet provides an opportunity for the Zapatista communities of Chiapas to make their everyday lives and experiences available to an audience outside Mexico. This opportunity greatly enhances prospects for the formation of a successful transnational frame. Hellman's and Stephen's scepticism in this regard was in large part repudiated. Nevertheless, we should acknowledge that the potential for creating resonance between the lives of senders and recipients does not rest solely with the Internet. It has therefore been necessary to take a closer look at the relationship between the Internet and the physical dimension of the Zapatista solidarity network. This obviously has direct bearing on the question of resonance. What emerges is an understanding that this resonance is achieved not only through the distribution of denouncements from the Chiapas communities to network activists around the world. It also occurs when these activists visit Chiapas to experience the conditions of the people, experiences which are often relayed via the Internet. The most important insight is that the transnational framing process that has led to the formation of the Zapatista solidarity network has not been a one-way process with activists remaining at their computers reading reports from Chiapas. This latter activity is obviously important, but it rarely stands alone. Instead, activists, whether organizational or individual, rely on a number of different sources and ways of obtaining information, including travelling to Chiapas.

It may be useful in this context to return briefly to the distinction drawn in Chapter 3 between five levels of actors in the informational infrastructure of the network. Excluding the first level, the indigenous communities of Chiapas, we may suggest that the main distribution of information based on physical presence in Chiapas is effected by actors at the second and third levels. Third-level actors (mainly based outside Mexico) often have a presence in Chiapas in the form of observers and volunteers in civilian peace camps. Actors at the fourth and fifth levels, in contrast, derive a comparatively larger degree of information from Internet sources. These sources, on the other hand, will often be provided by actors at the second and third levels.

The most direct way to obtain information about the EZLN and the community is clearly to stay in Chiapas, or alternatively to attend talks given by activists who have been there. As noted in Chapter 4, most network organizations and groups consider this type of informational activity to be the most important aspect of their overall activities. As we have seen, this has not only involved non-Mexicans but also people from organizations such as Enlace Civil, FZLN and CIEPAC, and in some cases even representatives from Zapatista or other indigenous communities of Chiapas. Needless to say, such physical encounters also provide the potential to establish a degree of resonance between the lives of senders and recipients in the framing process. Thus, while the Internet may be central to our understanding of transnational framing, it is important to stress that the process takes place in a number of other spaces. That such activities are often to some extent facilitated by the Internet only underscores our argument about the dialectical nature of the relationship between the physical and computer-mediated dimensions of the transnational Zapatista solidarity network.

Notes

1. As mentioned elsewhere, the terms 'Internet' and 'computer-mediated communication' encompass information distribution via the World Wide Web, as well as via email.
2. This is not to say that other forms of communications media do not have such a potential. Television, for example, has also been instrumental in bridging social and cultural distance through the availability of live images from physically distant places.
3. See Chapter 2 for a brief discussion, with a point of departure in Tilly 1978 of the importance of shared physical space in the formation of social movements.
4. As mentioned in Chapter 2, it should be noted that the distinction between traditional media and the Internet is mainly analytical, as this is becoming increasingly blurred. Newspapers and television thus often find information on the Internet, while Internet-circulated material reflects and distributes what has been reported in newspapers and television.

5. Tendencies towards armchair activism have probably been most visible in regard to the so-called electronic civil disobedience activities described in Chapter 4. In a call for activities of this type, the Chiapas Alert Network (1998) tellingly writes that '[w]ith just a two minute effort, you can help to end the brutal paramilitary violence and intimidation currently directed by the Mexican government and its ruling party against indigenous civilians in Mexico's southern state of Chiapas.'

6. EZLN-related actors are understood here mainly as those indigenous communities in Chiapas that consider themselves to be Zapatista. These are often referred to as Zapatista base communities. The term 'EZLN' is used in this context to refer more strictly to the leadership of the EZLN, the Clandestine Revolutionary Indigenous Committee–General Command of the Zapatista Army of National Liberation (CCRI–CG del EZLN), which issues official EZLN declarations and communiqués. By making this distinction, the term 'EZLN' is used in a narrower manner than hitherto in the book.

7. This view, however, has to be qualified somewhat, considering the EZLN's and Subcomandante Marcos's more direct presence on the Internet during the time around the March for Indigenous Dignity in February/March 2001. This presence was mediated through the Zapatista Information Centre (see Chapter 3).

8. These points build on statements made by the founder of *El Tiempo*, Amado Avendaño, at the 4th International Congress of the Americas, 29 September–2 October 1999, Puebla, Mexico. Avendaño participated in the panel 'The Voice of the Media: The Experiences and Implications of Being One of the EZLN's "Chosen" Publications for the Dissemination of their Messages'.

9. This fact contradicts another point in the quotation from Robberson (1995), namely that communiqués are distributed beyond the borders of Mexico before they are available within Mexico.

10. Mumia Abu-Jamal (a black American) and Leonard Peltier (a native American) have both been convicted of murdering police officers, in 1981 and 1975 respectively. They are viewed by solidarity activists as political prisoners convicted on the basis of race.

11. Ross (2000), commenting on the prolonged silence of the EZLN leadership following the presidential election in July 2000, has worried, though, that the denouncements have a limited impact on non-Mexican activists, as they are local in scope and without the world vision of the communiqués from Subcomandante Marcos. Network activists, however, seem aware of this distinction and tend to value both sources of information.

12. An archive of denouncements is available on the websites of FZLN (2001b) and Enlace Civil (2001).

13. In some cases, however, denouncements are translated into other languages by network activists before they are distributed via, for example, Chiapas95.

14. See also Hellman's (2000) response to Paulson's critique (2000), and Cleaver's (2000) critique of Hellman.

15. In early January 1998, in the tense period following the Acteal massacre in December 1997, messages were circulated on the Internet stating that that the Mexican army had occupied the central Zapatista community of

La Realidad. The rumour was later denied but not before a number of action alerts had been distributed on the Internet. See, for example, messages circulated on Chiapas95 on 3 January 1998 (Chiapas95 1998a; Chiapas95 1998b).

16. The page number refers to a typescript version of the paper sent as an email attachment.

9

Conclusion:
Globalization in Movement(s)?

This book has sought to answer a range of questions regarding the development and functioning of the transnational Zapatista solidarity network. While this network has been the primary object of analysis, the discussion has throughout involved much wider issues. The book has engaged simultaneously with the local and national levels of the EZLN and examined the wider implications of this network for an understanding of contemporary processes of globalization, conflict and social change, as expressed, for example, in the transnational justice and solidarity movement. The relationships between different analytical levels have in themselves been an important objective of the discussion. Understanding the connections between local, national and transnational levels of engagement is imperative if we are to identify the relationship between globalization and critical social action today. The vital question is, how can local and nationally anchored organizations, groups and individuals articulate their concerns in such a way as to connect with distant actors and construct transnational networks and other forms of interaction?

In the course of this study we have examined this process in detail in the specific case of transnational solidarity with the EZLN. We now turn our attention to two related issues that lie outside the analyses conducted so far. These concern, first, the present state and future prospects of the transnational Zapatista solidarity network; and, second, the future of the left and critical social action in a time of globalization and after September 11. Addressing these issues will allow us to reflect more deeply than we have so far on both the Zapatista and the justice and solidarity transnational networks.

The Two Networks and New Challenges

In terms of activity, the transnational Zapatista solidarity network experienced its most intense period between February 1995 and early 1998. This period was characterized by two major events: the Mexican army offensive against the EZLN in February 1995 and the massacre at Acteal, Chiapas, in December 1997. There followed a high level of activity, especially in the months following the Acteal massacre, when a range of new organizations and initiatives were launched. The momentum has been impossible to sustain, and many of these have since dissolved. Nevertheless, the two events were instrumental in drawing new activists and organizations into the network, some of which did remain active after the initial wave of interest had died down. The importance of the events in generating this activity raises an interesting issue. An analytical distinction may be drawn between two networks that are, in reality, intertwined. The first consists of activists and organizations whose activities are closely connected to actual events in Chiapas and Mexico and/or to specific initiatives launched by the EZLN. This network is, to some extent, dormant; it is activated when events in Chiapas and Mexico require attention. The second network is more stable and also more political. Its origins lie mainly in the intercontinental encounter arranged by the EZLN in Chiapas in 1996. The activists involved in this network find important inspiration for their own local and national political activities in the EZLN and its radical democratic critique of neoliberalism. This network is, consequently, less dependent on specific events and initiatives in Chiapas and Mexico than the first network. In terms of the discussion of solidarity in Chapter 5, the first network is more involved in rights solidarity work, while the second is involved in mutual solidarity work.

In April 2001, the EZLN entered into a period of prolonged silence, only interrupted in October 2001 by a communiqué on the assassination of human rights lawyer Digna Ochoa in Mexico City. This led to a decrease in transnational activity, especially on the part of the first of the two networks. The EZLN's silence followed the approval in the Mexican Congress of what was considered to be a mutilated version of the reform on indigenous rights originally presented in late 1996 by a commission of Mexican legislators (COCOPA). During his 2000 presidential campaign, Vicente Fox proclaimed that he would resolve the Chiapas conflict in fifteen minutes. The EZLN tried to take advantage of the new political situation and the apparent willingness of the new government to dialogue with the EZLN by staging the March for Indigenous Dignity in February/March 2001, just a few months after the inauguration of Vicente Fox as president of Mexico. As we saw earlier, the aim of the march was to put back on the agenda the question of constitutional reform of the relationship between the Mexican state and the indigenous population. Despite the public success of the march which ended with EZLN commanders delivering speeches in the Mexican Congress, the momentum was checked when the Fox administration presented a reform proposal that did not live up to the original COCOPA proposal and to the demands of the EZLN and other indigenous groups. For the EZLN, this meant that any basis for serious dialogue with the new government under Vicente Fox was gone. As a result the EZLN decided to withdraw to consider their response. In the meantime, Fox has used their silence to demonstrate to the world that peace exists in Chiapas, when in fact the state is still heavily militarized and paramilitary violence continues amid fear and intimidation.

While these circumstances gave rise to the EZLN silence, it must also be seen in the light of two major events, one national and the other global, which have had significant consequences for the EZLN's analysis of its social and political environment. In 2000, the electoral victory of Vicente Fox and the PAN put an end to seventy-one years of rule by the same party, the PRI, which was formed in the wake of the Mexican Revolution. This central event in Mexican history has been a source of legitimacy for a party which, tellingly, calls itself the Institutional Revolutionary Party. When the EZLN initiated its uprising in 1994, the PRI was seen from the beginning as its major and most direct opponent. The EZLN thus portrayed itself as the defender of the revolutionary and national values betrayed by the PRI in its adherence to neoliberal ideology and an increasingly close relationship with the USA, as reflected in Mexico's NAFTA membership. This critique resonated well within large segments of the Mexican population where the legitimacy of the PRI had been declining for a number of years. In this context, the EZLN's characterization of the PRI as 'sellers of the fatherland' and their complaint regarding the lack of democracy in Mexico found a fertile soil in the 1990s.

With the coming into office of Fox and the PAN, the EZLN has in a way lost its main opponent. This obviously calls for a new analysis of the national political landscape within which the EZLN moves. This change of system in what was widely considered a fair election has taken some of the sting out of the EZLN's democratic critique. Although the thrust of the EZLN's radical democratic critique, as described in Chapter 7, is unchanged, the political context has changed considerably; as such, new analyses and evaluations are needed. Nevertheless, the relevance and strength of the EZLN's critique of neoliberalism remain. For the PAN has in many ways continued the neoliberal policies of free trade and privatization associated with the PRI since the 1980s. The cornerstone of this approach is the Plan Puebla Panamá, a development project that includes southern Mexico and the Central American countries, and that is integral to the ambitious Free Trade Area of the Americas (FTAA) initiative. For critics, the Plan Puebla Panamá is designed to take advantage of cheap labour and natural resources; in consequence the project has attracted considerable resistance, including from the EZLN.

The other major event with obvious consequences for the EZLN is the 11 September 2001 terrorist attacks in the USA. The difficulty of the situation may well be what is behind the prolonged period of silence begun in April 2001. Even though the EZLN has not used armed force since the early days of the uprising, and despite the fact that the US government has not officially labelled the EZLN a terrorist organization, there is no doubt that the social and political climate created by September 11 calls for caution and deliberation on the part of the EZLN. Immediately following September 11, many observers on the left saw the event as an opening, a chance to discuss and reconsider the social, economic and political aspects of the global condition. The outcome, however, seems to have been the opposite, especially in the USA. We have seen a resurgence of national and conservative security values that, in turn, seem to have weakened the legitimacy of radical politics and viewpoints, especially those critical of the USA. In the post-September 11 world, states are tending to act with a greater degree of manoeuvre regarding surveillance and the repression of political dissent. This change has obviously had an indirect impact on the EZLN as well as on the transnational Zapatista solidarity network and activists within it. New political initiatives need to be analysed and proposed with September 11 and this new political climate in mind.

Recalling our earlier distinction between two transnational Zapatista solidarity networks, it is important to note that the EZLN's quiet period does not denote a situation where the network is dormant and waiting to be awakened by new events and initiatives. Throughout the period, the informational infrastructure of the network has continued its circulation of information. The focus of this information has been not so much the EZLN but rather the problems of militarization and paramilitarization that persist in Chiapas. Yet activities have not only taken place in the computer-mediated information circuits of the Internet. For example, in November 2001 Danish high-school students devoted a day of labour to collecting money for a school project in the conflict zone in Chiapas; and in March 2002, the third International Civil Commission for Human Rights Observation visited Chiapas to assess the human rights situation.

Thus, a fairly high level of activity, despite the EZLN's silence, indicates that the network possesses a stable core that works on a continuous basis. As mentioned earlier, network activists often mix rights solidarity and mutual solidarity efforts. It is fair to say, though, that it is the mutual solidarity element that forms the foundations on which the network as a stable social phenomenon rests, even if this is also expressed in rights and material solidarity work. Without this mutual solidarity element, solidarity activities would be both more occasional and ephemeral and connected more narrowly to specific events in Chiapas and Mexico or to EZLN initiatives. This basis also leads one to believe that the network will continue to exist and develop. When speaking about the future development of the transnational Zapatista solidarity network it might be useful to refer to the two networks in terms of core and periphery. It is the core network that we should expect to continue and develop. The periphery network, on the other hand, will be dependent on specific events and initiatives for its involvement in EZLN and Chiapas solidarity activities. Of course, future developments in Chiapas and Mexico may have a partially dissolving effect on even the core of the network. As discussed in Chapter 5, the EZLN and Subcomandante Marcos have suggested that they might take off their masks at some future point and turn the EZLN into a political and unarmed civil society organization, although this is unlikely before a solution is reached in the conflict over indigenous rights. The idea of such a move by the EZLN is not that fanciful, given their ability to present surprising initiatives, and in light of their anti-vanguardist position and continuous emphasis on the larger conflict.

This larger conflict is expressed, to a significant extent, by what has been referred to in the book as the transnational justice and solidarity network. This network barely existed at the time of the EZLN uprising in 1994, when the left was still finding its feet after the end of the Cold War. It began to take shape in the second half of the 1990s, and made its first strong impression in Seattle in November 1999. The EZLN, and especially the intercontinental encounter in Chiapas in 1996, have played an important roles in this development. The prospects for the left have, accordingly, undergone significant change during the 1990s, and the EZLN has seen many of its political ideas and visions echoed in the activities of the transnational justice and solidarity network. Within a larger, global perspective, the EZLN has viewed itself mainly as a catalyst and inspiration for the revitalization of the left. With an apparently vibrant and active transnational justice and solidarity network, the EZLN may in many ways consider this task to be completed and its own presence to be of less importance than was the case in the 1990s. Thus, unless the issue of indigenous rights remains unresolved, there is perhaps good reason to expect a radical change in the EZLN's strategy, and consequently within the Zapatista network.

The EZLN broke its period of silence in autumn 2002 with communications from Subcomandante Marcos on the inauguration of the so-called *aguascalientes* Madrid and the launching of a new political magazine in Mexico, *Revista Rebeldía*. In these interventions, Subcomandante Marcos jokes about rumours attributing the EZLN silence to his death or serious illness, or to internal strife in the movement. This is not the first time the EZLN has disappeared, or that rumours have surfaced about the fate of Subcomandante Marcos. The EZLN apparently uses the periods of silence to deliberate on new developments and prepare responses in consultation with the Zapatista communities.

In this round of communiqués, Subcomandante Marcos took up the conflict between the Spanish government and ETA (Euzkadi Ta Askatasuna); he faults the Spanish government and Judge Baltazar Garzón for their attempts to outlaw Batasuna, the political wing of ETA. In a display of the post-September 11 political climate, both the tone and the content of the message drew much criticism from intellectuals in Spain and Mexico, who accused the EZLN and Subcomandante Marcos for supporting the terrorist methods of the ETA. Among the most vociferous critics was Judge Baltazar Garzón, known for his attempts to have former Chilean dictator Augusto Pinochet tried before a Spanish court. Responding to the criticism, Subcomandante Marcos renounced any support for terrorist methods, stating that the communication had deliberately aimed at provoking a response. Pursuing the logic of his argument, Subcomandante Marcos challenged Garzón, the Spanish government and ETA to meet on the island of Lanzarote in April 2003, with the aim of engaging the parties in dialogue in place of confrontation. However, the initiative was rejected by both sides of the conflict.

Why should the EZLN intervene in this Spanish conflict when its own domestic problems remain unresolved? Perhaps the intervention simply reflects the EZLN's recognition of the current unresponsive national context. By breaking out of this context, the EZLN may hope to generate external pressure on the Mexican government that will further its agenda. Seen from this point of view, the choice of Spain and Europe as the sites for new initiatives is strategic. Spain has one of the largest concentrations of EZLN and Chiapas solidarity activists; Europe is undoubtedly a more receptive environment for the EZLN cause than, for example, the USA, notwithstanding its own numerous activists. While it remains uncertain how the renewed public presence of the EZLN will develop, it does seem to point to a new phase in its transnationalization, and accordingly to increased activity on the part of the solidarity networks. It remains to be seen, though, whether the new post-September 11 political climate has weakened support for the cause, or whether, on the contrary, the narrowing of political space has concentrated the struggle to develop alternatives to anti-democratic fundamentalism and to the supremacy of power and security politics.

In 2003, the EZLN embarked on an ambitious restructuring of the Zapatista communities in Chiapas. The *aguascalientes* that had so far served as the nerve centres of Zapatista territory were renamed *caracoles*. The *caracoles* are to serve as locations for what the EZLN calls good government juntas. The juntas were created in order to strengthen democracy and equality within Zapatista territory and to establish a more direct link with the outside world. This initiative came in the lead-up to the tenth anniversary of the EZLN uprising. This date led to a renewal of solidarity activities in and outside Mexico, but at a more moderate level than was seen only a few years ago. This may suggest two things: first, a dampening of contentious politics, national and transnational, in the wake of September 11; and, second, a deliberate attempt by the EZLN to concentrate on internal and local issues. As mentioned elsewhere, the restructuring process also involved a critique of some elements in the transnational solidarity directed to the EZLN and Chiapas. This perhaps heralds a phase during which the EZLN wishes to strengthen its influence over solidarity activities. This will most certainly push some activists away from the EZLN and Chiapas. What we may expect, therefore, is a situation where the transnational solidarity network will become smaller and concentrated around the core network activists described earlier in this chapter.

Democracy, Globalization and the Left after September 11

We will now briefly consider some of the main ways in which the current phase of transnationalization of the left differs from that in previous phases. Such a discussion obviously involves a degree of simplification, and hence reduction of the diversity of what we term the transnational left.

The current phase of transnationalization of the left lacks an obvious geographical direction. Whereas earlier interactions between leftist actors tended to be directed from the developed to the developing countries, contemporary transnational exchange is often more reciprocal, as was expressed in the notion of mutual solidarity discussed in Chapter 5. This reinforces the basic argument of this book: that the problems of physically, socially and culturally distant actors are increasingly interpreted as aspects of the same processes. This two-way relationship is evident in the case of the Zapatista solidarity network, where the direction of influence has mainly been from a developing country to the developed world. It would not do to paint too rosy a picture of this relationship, however. As we have seen, important social and economic differences persist. Such inequalities will necessarily continue to be reflected in the process of transnationalization of the left. Despite the growing participation of people and organizations from the developing countries, the overwhelming majority of those in the transnational left hail from the USA and Europe. While the Zapatista solidarity network is interesting for the fact that it was inspired by a movement in a developing country, its activists are mostly based in the USA and Europe.

The concerns addressed by the transnational left are of an increasingly global nature. In many ways, the left has always applied a global analysis to the social, economic and political problems it has addressed. This was evident in the 1970s, for example, where the problems of developing countries were perceived to stem from their disadvantaged position in the world economy – hence the distinction between First and Third Worlds. This analysis assumed that the conditions of contention and social change in these 'worlds' were significantly different from each other. Today, this type of analysis is less salient within the transnational left. In the current situation, the left tends to concentrate on issues with implications beyond national and local settings, and it does so in a way that aspires to transcend the First/Third World dichotomy. This is not to suggest that national and local problems are losing their relevance, or that the world today displays less inequality between countries and regions. On the contrary, and as evidenced by the EZLN and the Zapatista solidarity network, the local and national context continues to play an important and often central role. The main difference between then and now, in fact, seems to lie in the way local and national concerns are increasingly analysed as expressions of problems with relevance way beyond that immediacy and locality. Indeed, the main objective of this book has been to demonstrate how the transnational Zapatista solidarity network is to a large extent the product of the EZLN's ability to project a local and national struggle in a way that resonates beyond Chiapas and the borders of Mexico.

The case of the EZLN and the transnational Zapatista solidarity network demonstrates that organizations must interpret and project their particular cause and issues such that it produces transnational resonance. Support and resources often hinge on this ability. For actors operating under repressive local and national conditions, the generation of transnational support may be crucial for their survival. Yet achieving this transnational resonance is no easy task, especially for actors with meagre technological and educational resources. The EZLN has benefited significantly from the communication skills of Subcomandante Marcos, who has a cosmopolitan and well-educated background that makes it easier to connect to a non-Mexican audience than it would have been, for example, for an indigenous peasant leader with little education and experience outside Chiapas. Thus groups and organizations without a skilled communicator run the risk that their messages will fail to reach beyond their locale or, at best, national borders. At the same time, there is growing competition for transnational attention and support, as local and national actors increasingly attempt to give their struggles a global dimension. Whether groups and organizations are able to develop and satisfy their demands is more than ever a question of their ability to 'market' their struggle and project it into the transnational sphere.

The current phase of transnationalization of the left is much more heterogeneous than previous phases. This also implies a movement away from any notion of vanguardism. Earlier phases were marked by the more immediate presence of a leadership, and by well-developed and predefined strategies and objectives. In the present context, the heterogeneity and undefined nature of the left are seen by the majority of its activists as a strength rather than a weakness, as captured in the now common slogan 'One no, many yeses'. The 'no' is anchored mainly in the injustice frame constructed around the concept of neoliberalism, discussed in Chapter 6, while the 'yeses' appear to take their point of departure in different interpretations of the democratic master frame, discussed in Chapter 7. The latter point also indicates that the 'yeses' are not necessarily substantially different, but are often rooted in interpretations of democracy. Accordingly, when we speak of the transnational left as being heterogeneous, this does not imply that it consists of individuals and organizations narrowly pursuing their own goals through a primarily strategic connection to other organizations and individuals. What seems to be emerging, instead, is a transnational left that is not a coalition centred around a leader and with clearly defined goals and strategies, nor an unrelated and disconnected mass of activists, but rather a network of networks that constantly expands, diffuses and contracts in response to specific events and problems. It is generally based within a neoliberal injustice frame and radical democratic action master frame.

We discussed earlier the impact of September 11 on the EZLN and the Zapatista solidarity network. If we extend this discussion also to the transnational justice and solidarity network and to globalization in general, a number of suggestions may be made. As observed, the terrorist attacks have given authorities a new set of discursive tools with which to legitimate their actions and policies. This is evident in the case of policing and surveillance, but also in regard to the defence of neoliberalism and liberal democracy. Several political leaders have used September 11 to express the view that the only way of combating terrorism is through greater liberalization of trade and further expansion of liberal democratic ideas. Rather than putting a brake on these processes, September 11 seems to have provided a rationale for acceleration, and has thus created a potentially difficult situation for those critically disposed towards these elite-led boosts to the globalization process.

The events of 11 September 2001 have not changed the motivations and the conditions underlying the activities of the transnational justice and solidarity network. On the contrary, September 11 and its consequences have only underlined the need for transnational activism and dialogue around questions of inequality and democracy. What has changed, though, is the way these motivations and conditions are perceived by activists themselves, by the public and by authorities. In other words, the premises of debate and activism have altered in a way that needs to be taken into account by activists in the transnational justice and solidarity network. Whether or not activists are able to meet this challenge in a constructive and creative manner will to a large extent determine the future of the network. The apparent success of the network to date is due to its ability to capture the public imagination and media attention in a way that has also forced politicians to take it seriously. If activists fail to formulate a response to September 11 that fosters dialogue rather than confrontation, the network will increasingly come to play a marginal role. The network's ability to mobilize against the US-led war on Iraq is perhaps a sign that a dialogue is beginning which will open up to a range of widely shared concerns in societies across the world. The failure to prevent the war, however, also marks its limits.

The situation after September 11 therefore poses major challenges for the transnational justice and solidarity network. In particular it needs to emphasize how it stands for a critique radically different to that expressed by fundamentalist movements such as al-Qaeda. While such differences may seem obvious to activists themselves, they may not be so in the eyes of the many who only possess limited knowledge based on mainstream media reports. In this regard, it is especially important that the network presents itself as a pro-democracy movement that asks critical questions about how democracy functions but does not challenge its basic values. Furthermore, the network must work to convey itself as a force that does seek social change by the reactionary measures of nationalism and protectionism. It must stress instead the need for an alternative form of globalization based on democratic and human values, one that is distinct from right-wing and fundamentalist projects and elite-led models.

This necessary process of self-reflection may also involve a debate on the apparent heterogeneity of the network, discussed earlier. While the stress on plurality is one of the more promising aspects of the transnational justice and solidarity network, and one which marks a break with earlier instances of leftist transnationalization, it may nevertheless create certain problems and obstacles to progress. This is by no means to recommend the formulation of a manifesto and the creation of a coalition drawing together diverse forces. On the contrary, the rather loose and networked character of the contemporary transnational left should be maintained and seen as a positive value. Yet, rather than just accepting diversity as a value in itself, there must follow a more extensive discussion about what, if anything, binds this diversity together. As argued, this discussion is most likely to take place around the idea of democracy and the way democratic values in their more radical formulation bear also on the social, economic and cultural inequalities and injustice that persist in today's world. Such a globalization of movements and democracy is needed more than ever now, as we seemingly embark on a course where the deadly dance between fundamentalist terrorism and Western power politics is leading only to the globalization of political violence, insecurity and human suffering, and to a reversal of the prospects for global dialogue, human rights and democracy promised by the ending of the Cold War.

APPENDIX

Transnational Zapatista Solidarity Network Organizations

Acción Zapatista, USA (www.utexas.edu/students/nave/about.html).

Building Bridges Human Rights Project in Chiapas, Canada (www.vcn. bc.ca/building).

Café Libertad, Germany (www.free.de/cafe-libertad).

Canadian Solidarity Alliance for the Zapatistas, Canada (www.csazapatistas. homestead.com/home.html).

Casa Bonampak, USA (www.casabonampak.com).

Chiapas Link, UK (www.chiapaslink.ukgateway.net).

Chiapas Media Project, USA/Mexico (www.chiapasmediaproject.org).

Chiapas Support Committee, USA (www.millcityweb.net/myshoshe/ index-start.shtml).

Colectivo de Solidaridad con la Rebelión Zapatista, Spain (www.pangea. org/ellokal/chiapas).

Collectif Ya Basta, France (www.zapata.com/yabasta.php3).

Comitato Chiapas, Italy (www.ipsnet.it/chiapas).

Comité de Solidarité avec les Peuples du Chiapas en Lutte, France (http://cspcl.ouvaton.org).

Community Action on Latin America, USA (www.sit.wisc.edu/~omsuarez/ cala.html).

Denver Peace and Justice Committee, USA (www.djpc.org).

Direkte Solidarität mit Chiapas, Switzerland (www.chiapas.ch).

Food for Chiapas, Canada (www.foodforchiapas.org).

Global Exchange, USA (www.globalexchange.org).

Gruppe B.A.S.T.A., Germany (www.free.de/bankrott/basta.html).

Human Bean Company, USA (www.thehumanbean.com).

Indymedia–Chiapas, Mexico (http://chiapas.indymedia.org).

Internationalt Forum, Denmark (www.cikadenet.dk/if).

Irish Mexico Group, Ireland (http://flag.blackened.net/revolt/mexico. html).

Kristna Fredsrörelsen, Sweden (www.krf.se).

LAG Norge, Norway (www.solidaritetshuset.org/lag).

Mexico Solidarity Network, USA (www.mexicosolidarity.org).

Mexiko-Plattform, Austria (www.oneworld.at/mexiko-plattform).

National Commission for Democracy in Mexico, USA (www.ncdm. net).

Organisationsgruppe Libertad Weiz, Austria (www.chiapas.at).

Pastors for Peace, USA (www.ifconews.org).

Plataforma de Solidaridad con Chiapas de Aragón, Spain (www.pangea. org/spie/chiapas).

Plataforma de Solidaridad con Chiapas de Madrid, Spain (www.nodo50. org/pchiapas).

Pueblo por la Paz, USA (members.tripod.com/~PPLP).

Red de Apoyo Zapatista, Spain (www.nodo50.org/raz).

Schools for Chiapas, USA (www.schoolsforchiapas.org).

SIPAZ, USA (www.sipaz.org).

Strategic Pastoral Action Network (www.spanweb.org).

Tinku, Denmark.

Tonantzin, USA (http://users.rcn.com/laramelt/tonantzin/home.html).

Ya Basta, Italy (www.yabasta.it).

Ya Basta! website, USA (www.ezln.org).

Zapapres, Germany (www.zapapres.de).

Z Magazine/Z Net, USA (www.zmag.org).

References

Albrow, M. (1990) 'Introduction', in M. Albrow and E. King (eds), *Globalization, Knowledge and Society*, London: Sage.

Alvarez, S.E., E. Dagnino and A. Escobar (1998) 'Introduction: The Cultural and the Political in Latin American Social Movements', in S.E. Alvarez, E. Dagnino and A. Escobar (eds), *Cultures of Politics, Politics of Culture: Revisioning Latin American Social Movements*, Boulder, CO: Westview Press.

Anderson, B. (1983) *Imagined Communities: Reflections on the Origins and Spread of Nationalism*, London: Verso.

Anheier, H., M. Glasius and M. Kaldor (2001) 'Introducing Global Civil Society', in H. Anheier, M. Glasius and M. Kaldor (eds), *Global Civil Society Yearbook 2001*, London: London School of Economics, Centre for Civil Society and Centre for the Study of Global Governance.

Appel, K. (2000) The Human Bean Company, Denver, CO. Interview in Denver, CO, October 24.

Archibugi, D., D. Held and M. Köhler (1998) 'Introduction', in D. Archibugi, D. Held and M. Köhler (eds), *Re-imagining Political Community: Studies in Cosmopolitan Democracy*, Stanford, CA: Stanford University Press.

Association for Progressive Communications (2001) Website, online at www.apc.org/english/about/history/index.htm, accessed September 4, 2001.

Ayres, J.M. (2001a) 'Transnational Political Processes and Contention against the Global Economy', *Mobilization,* vol. 6, no. 1.

Ayres, J.M. (2001b) 'Transnational Activism in the Americas: The Internet and Mobilizing against the FTAA', paper prepared for the annual meeting of the American Political Science Association, San Francisco, CA, 29 August–2 September 2001.

Ayres, J.M. (2003) 'Global Civil Society and International Protest: No Swan Song Yet for the State', in G. Laxer and S. Halperin (eds), *Global Civil Society and Its Limits*, Basingstoke: Palgrave.

Baglioni, S. (2001) 'Solidarity Movement Organizations: Toward an Active Global Consciousness?' in M. Giugni and F. Passy (eds), *Political Altruism? Solidarity*

Movements in International Perspective, Lanham, MD: Rowman & Littlefield.

Bangerter, R. (2001/2002) Mexiko-Plattform, Vienna. Email interview received 10 and 31 December and 16 January.

Basáñez, M. (1996) *La lucha por la hegemonía en México 1968–1990*, México DF: Siglo Veintiuno Editores.

Bauman, Z. (1998) *Globalization: The Human Consequences*, Cambridge: Polity Press.

Beck, U. (1999) *World Risk Society*, Cambridge: Polity Press.

Bellinghausen, H. (1997) 'Consulados mexicanos, acosados por actos de respaldo al EZLN', *La Jornada*, 4 March.

Bellinghausen, H. (1998) 'Yo no soy más que un escritor al que le han recomendado no hablar demasiado, expresa', *La Jornada*, 17 March.

Bellinghausen, H. (1999) 'La sociedad civil, protagonista en la búsqueda de un país mejor: Marcos', *La Jornada*, 11 March.

Berger, M.T. (2001) 'Romancing the Zapatistas: International Intellectuals and the Chiapas Rebellion', *Latin American Perspectives*, vol. 28, no. 2.

Blixen, S. and C. Fazio (1995) 'El neoliberalismo: La abolición de la patria y la propiedad. El subcomandante Marcos habló del neoliberalismo al analizar el tema de la tierra en el contexto de las luchas campesinas', *Brecha*, vol. 11, no. 517, 27 October, online at www.brecha.com.uy/numeros/n517/tapa.html, accessed 14 March 2002.

Bob, C. (2001) 'Marketing Rebellion: Insurgent Groups, International Media, and NGO Support', *International Politics*, vol. 38, no. 3.

Boli, J. and G.M. Thomas (1999) 'INGOs and the Organization of World Culture', in John Boli and G.M. Thomas (eds), *Constructing World Culture: International Nongovernmental Organizations Since 1875*, Stanford, CA: Stanford University Press.

Bonfil Batalla, G. (1994) *México profundo: una civilización negada*, México DF: Editorial Grijalbo.

Braudel, F. (1980) *On History*, London: Weidenfeld & Nicolson.

Brecher, J. and T. Costello (1994) *Global Village or Global Pillage: Economic Reconstruction from the Bottom Up*, Boston, MA: South End Press.

Brown, P. and E. Sáenz Ackermann (2000) Schools for Chiapas, San Diego, CA. Interview in San Diego, CA, 4 December.

Bruhn, K. (1999) 'Antonio Gramsci and the *palabra verdadera*: The Political Discourse of Mexico's Guerrilla Forces', *Journal of Interamerican Studies and World Affairs*, vol. 41, no. 2.

Brysk, A. (2000) 'Globalization: The Double-edged Sword', *NACLA*, vol. 34, no. 1.

Buechler, S.M. (2000) *Social Movements in Advanced Capitalism: The Political Economy and Cultural Construction of Social Activism*, Oxford: Oxford University Press.

Burbach, R. (1994) 'Roots of the Postmodern Rebellion in Chiapas', *New Left Review* 205.

Burt, R.S. (1978) 'Cohesion versus Structural Equivalence as a Basis for Network Subgroups', *Sociological Methods and Research*, vol. 7, no. 2.

Callahan, M.I. (2000) Acción Zapatista, Austin, TX. Interview in Austin, TX, 5 October.

Caniglia, B.S. (2002) 'Elite Alliances and Transnational Environmental Movement Organizations', in J. Smith and H. Johnston (eds), *Globalization and Resistance: Transnational Dimensions of Social Movements*, Lanham, MD: Rowman & Littlefield.

Carr, B. (1999) 'Globalization from Below: Labour Internationalism under NAFTA', *International Social Science Journal*, vol. 51, no. 1.

Castañeda, J.G. (1994) *Utopia Unarmed*, New York: Vintage Books.

Castañeda, J.G. (1995) *Sorpresas te da la vida: México, fin de siglo*, México DF: Aguilar.

Castañeda, J.G. (1997) 'Chiapas "War" Ends in a Whimper', *Los Angeles Times*, 15 September.

Castells, M. (1996) *The Rise of the Network Society. The Information Age: Economy, Society and Culture* (I), Oxford: Blackwell.

Castells, M. (1997) *The Power of Identity. The Information Age: Economy, Society and Culture* (II), Oxford: Blackwell.

Castro Soto, G. (2001) CIEPAC, San Cristóbal de las Casas, Chiapas, Mexico. Email interview received 21 September and 11 November.

Ceceña, A.E. (1996) 'Universalidad de la lucha zapatista: Algunas hipótesis', *Chiapas* 2.

Centeno, M. Á. (1994) *Democracy within Reason: Technocratic Revolution in Mexico*, University Park, PA: Pennsylvania State University Press.

Chiapas95 (1998a) 'Mexican army has occupied La Realidad', online at www. eco. utexas.edu/~archive/chiapas95/1998.01/msg00163.html, accessed 12 October 2001.

Chiapas95 (1998b) 'Message from Javier Elorriaga', online at www.eco.utexas. edu/~archive/chiapas95/1998.01/msg00214.html, accessed 12 October 2001.

Chiapas95 (2001) Website, online at www.eco.utexas.edu/Homepages/Faculty/ Cleaver/chiapas95.html, accessed 15 January 2002.

Chiapas Alert Network (1998) 'Help needed for Chiapas world wide Internet campaign', online at www. eco.utexas.edu/~archive/chiapas95/1998.01/msg009 48.html, accessed 19 January 2002.

Chomsky, N. (1999) *Profit Over People: Neoliberalism and Global Order*, New York: Seven Stories Press.

Choucri, N. (2000) 'Introduction: Cyberpolitics in International Relations', *International Political Science Review*, vol. 21, no. 3.

Christian Science Monitor (1995) 'Marcos on the Internet', *Christian Science Monitor*, 27 February.

CIEPAC (2001) Website, online at www.ciepac.org/otras%20temas/Nosotros/htm, accessed 4 September 2001.

Clark, I. (1997) *Globalization and Fragmentation*, Oxford: Oxford University Press.

Cleaver Jr, H.M. (1994) 'Introduction', in *Zapatistas! Documents of the New Mexican Revolution (December 31, 1993–June 12, 1994)*, Brooklyn, NY: Autonomedia.

Cleaver Jr., H.M. (1998a) 'The Zapatista Effect: The Internet and the Rise of an Alternative Political Fabric', *Journal of International Affairs*, vol. 51, no. 2.

Cleaver Jr., H.M. (1998b) 'The Zapatistas and the Electronic Fabric of Struggle', in J. Holloway and E. Peláez (eds), *Zapatista! Reinventing Revolution in Mexico*,

London: Pluto Press.

Cleaver Jr., H.M. (1998c) 'The Zapatistas and the International Circulation of Struggle: Lessons Suggested and Problems Raised', online at www.eco. utexas. edu/Homepages/Faculty/Cleaver/lessons.html, accessed 7 April 2001.

Cleaver Jr., Harry M. (1999) 'Computer-Linked Social Movements and the Global Threat to Capitalism', online at www.antenna.nl/~waterman/cleaver2.html, accessed 14 October 2000.

Cleaver Jr., H.M. (2000) 'The Virtual and Real Chiapas Support Network: A Review and Critique of J.A. Hellman's "Real and Virtual Chiapas: Magic Realism and the Left"', online at www. eco.utexas.edu/Homepages/Faculty/ Cleaver/anti-hellman.html, accessed 28 September 2000.

Cleaver, H. (2000) Interview in Austin, TX, 4 October.

Cohen, J.L. and A. Arato (1992) Civil Society and Political Theory, Cambridge, MA: MIT Press.

Colectivo de Solidaridad con la Rebelión Zapatista (2001a) Website, online at www.pangea.org/ellokal/chiapas/observacion.htm, accessed 24 September 2001.

Colectivo de Solidaridad con la Rebelión Zapatista (2001b) Website, online at www.pangea.org/ellokal/chiapas/cciodh/tercero.htm, accessed 2 October 2001.

Cox, Robert W. (1987) Production, Power, and World Order: Social Forces in the Making of History, New York: Columbia University Press.

Cox, R.W. (1996) 'A Perspective on Globalization', in J.H. Mittelman (ed.), Globalization: Critical Reflections, Boulder, CO: Lynne Rienner.

Dalton, R.J., M. Kuechler and W. Bürklin (1990) 'The Challenge of New Movements', in R.J. Dalton and M. Kuechler (eds), Challenging the Political Order: New Social and Political Movements in Western Democracies, Cambridge: Polity Press.

De Angelis, M. (2000) 'Globalization, New Internationalism and the Zapatistas', Capital and Class 70.

de la Grange, B. and M. Rico (1998) Marcos, la genial impostura, Miami: Nuevo Siglo and Aguilar.

de la Guardia, C. (1999) 'EZLN y la guerra en Internet: entrevista a Justin Paulson (creador del sitio web del EZLN)', Comunicación Educativa 13 (January–March), online at www.cem.itesm.mx/dacs/publicaciones/logos/anteriores/n13/ezln13. html, accessed 15 October 2001.

della Porta, D. and H. Kriesi (1999) 'Social Movements in a Globalizing World: An Introduction', in D. della Porta, H. Kriesi and D. Rucht (eds), Social Movements in a Globalizing World, Houndmills and London: Macmillan.

Diani, M. (1992) 'Analysing Social Movement Networks', in M. Diani and R. Eyerman (eds), Studying Collective Action, London: Sage.

Diani, M. (1996) 'Linking Mobilization Frames and Political Opportunities: Insights from Regional Populism in Italy', American Sociological Review, vol. 61, no. 6.

Diani, M. (2001) 'Social Movement Networks: Virtual and Real', in F. Webster (ed.), Culture and Politics in the Information Age: A New Politics?, London and New York: Routledge.

Díaz Polanco, H. (1997a) *Indigenous Peoples in Latin America: The Quest for Self-Determination*, Boulder, CO: Westview Press.

Díaz Polanco, H. (1997b) *La rebelión zapatista y la autonomía*, México DF: Siglo Veintiuno Editores.

Dominguez, R. (2001) 'Digital Zapatismo', online at www.thing.net/~rdom/ecd/DigZap.html, accessed 22 September 2001.

Dominick, B.: Email received 13 and 20 November 2000.

Donnelly, J. (1993) *International Human Rights*, Boulder, CO: Westview Press.

Dow, J. (2001) Email received 12 September.

Doyle, L. (1995) 'Rebels Try to Advance via Internet', *Independent*, 7 March.

Drainville, A. C. (1998) 'The Fetishism of Global Civil Society: Global Governance, Transnational Urbanism and Sustainable Capitalism in the World Economy', in M.P. Smith and L.E. Guarnizo (eds), *Transnationalism from Below*, New Brunswick, NJ and London: Transaction Publishers.

Durán de Huerta, M. (1999) 'An Interview with Subcomandante Insurgente Marcos, Spokesman and Military Commander of the Zapatista National Liberation Army (EZLN)', *International Affairs*, vol. 75, no. 2.

Economic Commission for Latin America and the Caribbean (2001) 'Panorama social de América Latina 2000–2001 (chapter 1)', online at www.eclac.cl/publicaciones/DesarrolloSocial/8/LCG2138P/Capitulo_I_2001.pdf, accessed 20 January 2002.

Eisinger, P. K. (1973) 'The Conditions of Protest Behavior in American Cities', *American Political Science Review* 67.

Enlace Civil (1998) 'United States Congresspersons Visit Chiapas', online at www.globalexchange.org/campaigns/mexico/news/070698.html, accessed 8 October 2001.

Enlace Civil (2001) Website, online at www.enlacecivil.org.mx/principal.lista.htm, accessed 24 September 2001.

Epstein, B. (2001) 'Anarchism and the Anti-Globalization Movement', *Monthly Review*, vol. 53, no. 4.

Eschle, C. (2001) 'Globalizing Civil Society? Social Movements and the Challenge of Global Politics from Below', in P. Hamel, H. Lustiger-Thaler, J.N. Pieterse and S. Roseneil (eds) *Globalization and Social Movements*, Houndmills and New York: Palgrave, pp. 61–85.

Escobar, A. (2001) 'Culture Sits in Places: Reflections on Globalism and Subaltern Strategies of Localization', *Political Geography*, vol. 20, no. 2.

Espinosa, P. (1996) 'Mi página en Web no es la voz oficial del EZLN: Justin Paulson', *La Jornada*, August 10.

Espinosa-Organista, L. (2000) Denver Peace and Justice Committee, Denver, CO. Interview in Denver, CO, 25 October.

Esteva, G. (1999) 'The Zapatistas and People's Power', *Capital and Class* 68.

Esteva, G. (2001) 'The Meaning and the Scope of the Struggle for Autonomy', *Latin American Perspectives*, vol. 28, no. 2.

Eterovic, I. and J. Smith (2001) 'From Altruism to a New Transnationalism? A Look at Transnational Social Movements', in M. Giugni and F. Passy (eds), *Political Altruism? Solidarity Movements in International Perspective*, Lanham, MD: Rowman & Littlefield.

EZLN (1994a) 'El Despertador Mexicano', online at www.sureste.org.mx/ezln/1994/editorial.htm, accessed 11 February 2002.

EZLN (1994b) 'Declaración de la Selva Lacandona', online at www.ezln.org/documentos/1994/199312xx.es.htm, accessed 7 May 2001.

EZLN (1994c) Communiqué (13 January), online at www.ezln.org/documentos/1994/19940113.en.htm, accessed 14 March 2002.

EZLN (1994d) Communiqué (April 10), online at www.ezln.org/documentos/1994/19940410a.en.htm, accessed 14 March 2002.

EZLN (1994e) 'Segunda Declaración de la Selva Lacandona', online at www.ezln.org/documentos/1994/19940610.es.htm, accessed 7 May 2001.

EZLN (1994f) *Zapatistas! Documents of the New Mexican Revolution (December 31, 1993–June 12, 1994)*, Brooklyn, NY: Autonomedia.

EZLN (1994g) *EZLN: Documentos y comunicados* (I), Mexico DF: Ediciones Era.

EZLN (1995a) 'Tercera Declaración de la Selva Lacandona', online at www.ezln.org/documentos/1995/199501xx.es.htm, accessed 9 March 2001.

EZLN (1995b) 'Convoca el Ejército Zapatista a la sociedad civil a realizar una 'gran consulta nacional',' *La Jornada*, June 8, online at www.ezln.org/documentos/1995/19950608.es.htm, accessed 24 April 2001.

EZLN (1995c) 'Dignity Cannot Be Studied; You Live It or it Dies', in J. Ponce de León (ed.) (2001), *Our Word is Our Weapon: Selected Writings, Subcomandante Marcos*, London: Serpent's Tail.

EZLN (1995d) Communiqué (27 August), online at www.eco.utexas.edu/~archive/chiapas95/1995.09/msg00061.html, accessed 12 October 2001.

EZLN (1995e) Communiqué (29 September), online at www.ezln.org/documentos/1995/19950929.es. htm, accessed 1 September 2001.

EZLN (1996a) 'Cuarta Declaración de la Selva Lacandona', online at www. ezln. org/documentos/1996/19960101.es.htm, accessed 8 September 2001.

EZLN (1996b) 'Primera Declaración de la Realidad', online at www.ezln.org/documentos/1996/19960130.es.htm, accessed 2 March 2001.

EZLN (1996c) Communiqué (January), online at www.ezln.org/documentos/1996/19960130b.es.htm, accessed 30 August 2001.

EZLN (1996d) 'Caminos contra el neoliberalismo, no sólo lamentamos, demanda Marcos', *La Jornada*, 6 April.

EZLN (1996e) 'Segunda Declaración de la Realidad', online at www.ezln.org/documentos/1996/19960803.es.htm, accessed 7 May 2001.

EZLN (1996f) 'Un sueño soñado en los cinco continentes' in *Crónicas Intergalácticas: EZLN*, Planeta Tierra, Montañas del Sureste Mexicano.

EZLN (1996g) Communiqué (30 August), online at www.ezln.org/documentos/1996/19960830.es.htm, accessed 4 October 2001.

EZLN (1997a) Communiqué (June), online at www.ezln.org/documentos/1997/19970614.es.htm, accessed 12 September 2001.

EZLN (1997b) '7 piezas sueltas del rompecabezas mundial', online at www. ezln. org/documentos/1997/199708xx.es.htm, accessed 4 February 2002.

EZLN (1998) 'Quinta Declaración de la Selva Lacandona', online at www. ezln. org/documentos/1998/19980700.es.htm, accessed 10 August 2001.

EZLN (1999a) 'Convocatoria del EZLN a la Consulta Internacional', online at www.ezln.org/documentos/1999/19990117b.es.htm, accessed 7 January 2002.

EZLN (1999b) Communiqué (March 18), online at www.ezln.org/documentos/1999/19990318.es.htm, accessed 28 January 2002.

EZLN (1999c) 'Páginas sueltas sobre el movimiento universitario', online at www.ezln.org/documentos/1999/19990400.es.htm, accessed February 5, 2002.

EZLN (1999d) Communiqué (April), online at www.laneta.apc.org/consulta EZLN/comunicados/mumiaesp.htm, accessed 9 April 2002.

EZLN (1999e) 'Los zapatistas y la manzana de Newton', online at www.ezln.org/documentos/1999/19990510a.es.htm, accessed 20 January 2002.

EZLN (1999f) Communiqué (June), online at www.ezln.org/documentos/1999/19990627.es.htm, accessed 2 March 2002.

EZLN (1999g) Communiqué (June 30), online at www.ezln.org/documentos/1999/19990630.es.htm, accessed 22 October 2001.

EZLN (1999h) 'Clausura del encuentro 'magisterio democrático y sueño zapatista', online at www.ezln.org/documentos/1999/19990801.es.htm, accessed 1 March 2002.

EZLN (1999i) 'Discurso de Marcos en el Encuentro Nacional en Defensa del Patrimonio Cultural', online at www.ezln.org/documentos/1999/19990813es.htm, accessed 16 January 2002.

EZLN (1999j) Communiqué (October), online at www.eco.utexas.edu/~archive/chiapas95/1999.11/msg00086.html, accessed 22 October 2001.

EZLN (2000) Communiqué (June 19), online at www.ezln.org/documentos/2000/20000619.es.htm, accessed 8 January 2002.

EZLN (2001a) Communiqué (January 3), online at www.ezln.org/documentos/2001/20010103.es.htm, accessed 27 January 2002.

EZLN (2001b) 'Palabras del EZLN el 27 de febrero del 2001 en Puebla, Puebla', online at www.ezln.org/marcha/20010227b.es.htm, accessed 28 February 2002.

EZLN (2001c) 'Palabra del comandante David en el IPN', online at www.ezlnaldf.org/comunica/01031604.htm, accessed 28 February 2002.

EZLN (2001d) Communiqué (April 2001), online at www.ezln.org/documentos/2001/ezln010429b.es. htm, accessed 27 February 2002.

EZLN (2001e) 'La cuarta guerra mundial', La Jornada, 23 October.

Falk, R. (1999) Predatory Globalization: A Critique, Cambridge: Polity Press.

Flood, A. (2000) 'The Nature of Economic Globalisation: Where Do We Come From? Where Do We Go To?', online at www.struggle.ws/andrew/prague3.html, accessed 11 October 2001.

Fotopoulos, T. (1997) Towards an Inclusive Democracy, London and New York: Cassell.

Fraser, N. (1995) 'Politics, Culture, and the Public Sphere: Toward a Postmodern Conception', in L. Nicholson and S. Seidman (eds), Social Postmodernism: Beyond Identity Politics, Cambridge: Cambridge University Press.

Freeman, J. (1979) 'Resource Mobilization and Strategy: A Model for Analyzing Social Movement Organization Actions', in M.N. Zald and J.D. McCarthy (eds), The Dynamics of Social Movements: Resource Mobilization, Social Control, and Tactics, Cambridge, MA: Winthrop Publishers.

Fuentes, C. (1994) 'Chiapas: Latin America's first post-communist rebellion', *New Perspectives Quarterly*, vol. 11, no. 2.

Fukuyama, F. (1989) 'The end of history?', *The National Interest* 16.

FZLN (1998) 'Zapatismo en el mundo', online at www.eco.utexas.edu/~archive/chiapas95/1998.12/msg00084.html, accessed 1 April 2002.

FZLN (1999) 'Zapatismo en el mundo', online at www.eco.utexas.edu/~archive/chiapas95/1999.02/msg00075.html, accessed 1 April 2002.

FZLN (2001a) Website, online at http://fzlnguadalajara.tripod.com.mx/FZLN Jalisco/id11.html, accessed 9 April 2001.

FZLN (2001b) Website, online at www.laneta.apc.org/pipermail/fzln-l, accessed September 3, 2001.

Galtung, J. (1980) *The True Worlds: A Transnational Perspective*, New York: The Free Press.

Galván, M. (2001) National Commission for Democracy in Mexico, Sacramento, CA. Email interview received 23 August.

Gamson, W.A. (1975) *The Strategy of Social Protest*, Homewood, IL: The Dorsey Press.

Gamson, W. (1995) 'Constructing Social Protest', in H. Johnston and B. Klandermans (eds), *Social Movements and Culture*, Minneapolis, MN: Regents of the University of Minnesota.

Gamson, W.A., B. Fireman and S. Rytina (1982) *Encounters with Unjust Authority*, Chicago, IL: The Dorsey Press.

Gamson, W. and A. Modigliani (1989) 'Media Discourse and Public Opinion on Nuclear Power: A Constructionist Approach', *American Journal of Sociology*, vol. 95, no. 1.

Gamson, W. and D. Meyer (1996) 'Framing Political Opportunity', in D. McAdam, J.D. McCarthy and M.N. Zald (eds), *Comparative Perspectives on Social Movements: Political Opportunities, Mobilizing Structures, and Cultural Framings*, Cambridge: Cambridge University Press.

Garcia Márquez, G. and R. Pombo (2001) 'Habla Marcos', *Revista Cambio*, 28 March, online at www.cambio.com.co/web/interior.php?idp=21&ids=1&ida=898, accessed 11 January 2002.

Gerhards, J. and D. Rucht (1992) 'Mesomobilization: Organizing and Framing in Two Protest Campaigns in West Germany', *American Journal of Sociology*, vol. 98, no. 3.

Gerlach, L.P. (1987) 'Protest Movements and the Construction of Risk', in B.B. Johnson and V. T. Covello (eds), *The Social and Cultural Construction of Risk*, Dordrecht: D. Reidel.

Giddens, A. (1994a) *Beyond Left and Right: The Future of Radical Politics*, Stanford, CA: Stanford University Press.

Giddens, A. (1994b) 'Living in a Post-traditional Society', in U. Beck, A. Giddens and S. Lash, *Reflexive Modernization: Politics, Tradition, and Aesthetics in the Modern Social Order*, Cambridge: Polity Press.

Gilbreth, C. and G. Otero (2001) 'Democratization in Mexico: The Zapatista Uprising and Civil Society', *Latin American Perspectives*, vol. 28, no. 4.

Gill, S. (1995) 'Globalization, Market Civilization, and Disciplinary Neoliberalism', *Millennium: Journal of International Studies*, vol. 24, no. 3.

Gills, B. and J. Rocamora (1992) 'Low Intensity Democracy', *Third World Quarterly*, vol. 13, no. 3.

Gilly, A. (1971) *La revolución interrumpida*, México DF: Ediciones Era.

Gil Olmos, J. (1994) 'Manifestación de diez mil personas en el Zócalo', *La Jornada*, 8 January.

Gitlin, T. (1980) *The Whole World Is Watching: Mass Media in the Making and Unmaking of the New Left*, Berkeley and Los Angeles, CA: University of California Press.

Giugni, M. (2001) 'Concluding Remarks: Conceptual Distinctions for the Study of Political Altruism', in M. Giugni and F. Passy (eds), *Political Altruism? Solidarity Movements in International Perspective*, Lanham, MD: Rowman & Littlefield.

Gramsci, A. (1971) *Selections from the Prison Notebooks*, edited and translated by Q. Hoare and G.N. Smith, New York: International Publishers.

Granovetter, M. (1973) 'The Strength of Weak Ties', *American Journal of Sociology*, vol. 78, no. 6.

Guidry, J.A., M.D. Kennedy and M.N. Zald (2000) 'Globalizations and Social Movements', in J.A. Guidry, M.D. Kennedy and M.N. Zald (eds), *Globalizations and Social Movements: Culture, Power, and the Transnational Public Sphere*, Ann Arbor, MI: The University of Michigan Press.

Haar, K. (2000) 'EU–Mexico agreement adopted in Denmark: Lots of criticism of Mexico, very few practical measures', online at www.eco.utexas.edu/~archive/chiapas95/2000.03/msg00201.html, accessed 10 October 2001.

Habermas, J. (1987) *The Theory of Communicative Action* (II), Cambridge: Polity.

Habermas, J. (1996) *Between Facts and Norms*, Cambridge: Polity Press.

Halleck, D. (1994) 'Zapatistas Online', *NACLA*, vol. 28, no. 2.

Hamelink, C. (1997) *New Information and Communication Technologies, Social Development and Cultural Change*. Geneva: United Nations Research Institute for Social Development.

Hansen, T. (2000) Mexico Solidarity Network, Chicago, IL. Email interview received 3 and 6 September.

Harasim, L.M. (1993) 'Networlds: Networks as Social Space', in L.M. Harasim (ed.), *Global Networks: Computers and International Communication*, Cambridge, MA: MIT Press.

Harvey, N. (1998a) *The Chiapas Rebellion: The Struggle for Land and Democracy*. Durham, NC and London: Duke University Press.

Harvey, N. (1998b) 'The Zapatistas, Radical Democratic Citizenship, and Women's Struggles', *Social Politics*, vol. 5, no. 2.

Harvey, N. (2000) 'Los zapatistas sí están hablando', *La Jornada*, 20 August.

Held, D. (1995) *Democracy and the Global Order: From the Modern State to Cosmopolitian Governance*, Cambridge: Polity Press.

Held, D. (1998) 'Democracy and Globalization', in D. Archibugi, D. Held and M. Köhler (eds), *Re-imagining Political Community: Studies in Cosmopolitan Democracy*, Stanford, CA: Stanford University Press.

Held, D., A. McGrew, D. Goldblatt and J. Perraton (1999) *Global Transformations: Politics, Economics, and Culture*, Cambridge: Polity Press.

Held, D. and A. McGrew (2002) *Globalization/Anti-Globalization*, Cambridge: Polity Press.

Hellman, J.A. (1999) 'Real and Virtual Chiapas: Magic Realism and the Left', in *Socialist Register 2000*, ed. Leo Panitch and Colin Leys, London: Merlin Press.

Hellman, J.A. (2000) 'Virtual Chiapas: A Reply to Paulson', in *Socialist Register 2001*, ed. Leo Panitch and Colin Leys, London: Merlin Press.

Hernández Navarro, L. (2001) 'Comités, redes y solidaridad del otro lado del océano: Galería de los zapatistas europeos', *La Jornada*, 25 February.

Higgins, N. (2000) 'The Zapatista Uprising and the Poetics of Cultural Resistance', *Alternatives*, vol. 25, no. 3.

Hill, K.A. and J.E. Hughes (1998) *Cyberpolitics: Citizen Activism in the Age of the Internet*. Lanham, MD: Rowman & Littlefield.

Holloway, J. (1996) 'La resonancia del zapatismo', *Chiapas* 3.

Holloway, J. (1998) 'Dignity's Revolt', in J. Holloway and E. Peláez (eds), *Zapatista! Reinventing Revolution in Mexico*, London: Pluto Press.

Holloway, J. and E. Peláez (1998) 'Introduction: Reinventing Revolution', in J. Holloway and E. Peláez (eds), *Zapatista! Reinventing Revolution in Mexico*, London: Pluto Press.

Indymedia–Chiapas (2001) Website, online at http://chiapas.indymedia.org/about. php3#eenlich, accessed 20 March 2002.

Indymedia–Chiapas (2001) San Cristóbal de las Casas, Chiapas, Mexico. Email interview received 1 November.

Institute for Global Communications (2001) Website, online at www.igc.org/igc/gateway/about.html, accessed 6 September 2001.

Jelin, E. (1997) 'Emergent Citizenship or Exclusion? Social Movements and Non-Governmental Organizations in the 1990s', in W.C. Smith and R.P. Korzeniewicz (eds), *Politics, Social Change, and Economic Restructuring in Latin America*, Miami, FL: North–South Center Press at the University of Miami.

Jenkins, J.C. (1983) 'Resource Mobilization Theory and the Study of Social Movements', *Annual Review of Sociology* 9.

Jímenez, M.: Melel Xojobal, San Cristóbal de las Casas, Chiapas, Mexico. Email received 7 and 15 November 2001.

Johnston, J. (2000) 'Pedagogical Guerrillas, Armed Democrats, and Revolutionary Counterpublics: Examining Paradox in the Zapatista Uprising in Chiapas, Mexico', *Theory and Society* 29, September.

Johnston, J. (2003) 'We Are All Marcos? Zapatismo, Solidarity and the Politics of Scale', in G. Laxer and S. Halperin (eds), *Global Civil Society and its Limits*, Houndmills: Palgrave Macmillan.

Johnston, J. and G. Laxer (2003) 'Solidarity in the Age of Globalisation: Lessons from the anti-MAI and Zapatista Struggles', *Theory and Society*, vol. 32, no. 1.

Kampwirth, K. (1996) 'Creating Space in Chiapas: An Analysis of the Strategies of the Zapatista Army and the Rebel Government in Transition', *Bulletin of Latin American Research*, vol. 15, no. 2.

Keane, J. (2001) 'Global Civil Society?', in H. Anheier, M. Glasius and M. Kaldor (eds), *Global Civil Society Yearbook 2001*, London: London School of Economics, Centre for Civil Society and Centre for the Study of Global Governance, pp. 23–47.

Keck, M.E. and K. Sikkink (1998) *Activists Beyond Borders: Advocacy Networks in International Politics*, Ithaca, NY: Cornell University Press.

Keck, M.E. and K. Sikkink (2000) 'Historical Precursors to Modern Transnational Social Movements and Networks', in J.A. Guidry, M.D. Kennedy and M.N. Zald (eds), *Globalizations and Social Movements: Culture, Power, and the Transnational Public Sphere*, Ann Arbor, MI: University of Michigan Press.

Khagram, S., J.V. Riker and K. Sikkink (2002) 'From Santiago to Seattle: Transnational Advocacy Groups Restructuring World Politics', in S. Khagram, J.V. Riker and K. Sikkink (eds), *Restructuring World Politics: Transnational Social Movements, Networks, and Norms*, Minneapolis, MN: University of Minnesota Press.

Klandermans, B. (1989) 'Introduction: Social Movement Organizations and the Study of Social Movements', in B. Klandermans (ed.), 'Organizing for Change: Social Movement Organizations in Europe and the United States', *International Social Movement Research* 2, Greenwich, CT: JAI Press.

Knudson, J. (1998) 'Rebellion in Chiapas: Insurrection by Internet and Public Relations', *Media, Culture, and Society*, vol. 20, no. 3.

Kollock, P. and M.A. Smith (1999) 'Communities in Cyberspace', in P. Kollock and M.A. Smith (eds), *Communities in Cyberspace*, London and New York: Routledge.

Kriesberg, L. (1997) 'Social Movements and Global Transformation', in J. Smith, C. Chatfield and R. Pagnucco (eds), *Transnational Social Movements and Global Politics*, Syracuse, NY: Syracuse University Press.

Köhler, M. (1998) 'From the National to the Cosmopolitan Public Sphere', in D. Archibugi, D. Held and M. Köhler (eds), *Re-imagining Political Community: Studies in Cosmopolitan Democracy*, Stanford, CA: Stanford University Press.

Laclau, E. (1996) *Emancipation(s)*, London: Verso.

Laclau, E. and C. Mouffe (1985) *Hegemony and Socialist Strategy*, London: Verso.

La Jornada (1997a) 'Parlamentarios italianos piden dar cauce a la propuesta de Cocopa', *La Jornada*, 7 February.

La Jornada (1997b) 'Una terrible y anunciada masacre: Cartas de Danielle Mitterrand a gobernantes y parlamentarios europeos', *La Jornada*, 28 December.

La Jornada (2001) 'Zedillo intentó expulsar de México a Saramago en 1998', *La Jornada*, 20 April.

Leahy Resolution (S.Con.Res.76) (1999), online at www.mexicosolidarity.org/legislative/leahy.html, accessed 11 October, 2001.

Le Bot, Y. (1997) *El sueño zapatista*, Barcelona: Plaza y Janés.

Lewis, T.: Global Exchange, San Francisco, CA. Interview in San Francisco, CA, 7 December 2000.

Leyva Solano, X. (1999) 'De Las Cañadas a Europa: Niveles, actores y discursos del nuevo movimiento zapatista (NMZ) (1994–1997)', *Desacatos* (spring).

Lichbach, M.I. and P. Almeida (2002) 'Global Order and Local Resistance: The Neoliberal Institutional Trilemma and the Battle of Seattle', paper online at www.bsos.umd.edu/gvpt/lichbach/GlobalPaper-01b.doc.

Lipschutz, R.D., with Judith Mayer (1996): *Global Civil Society and Global Environmental Governance*, Albany, NY: State University of New York Press.

Lummis, D. (1996) *Radical Democracy*, Ithaca, NY: Cornell University Press.

Löwy, M. (1998) 'Sources and Resources of Zapatism', *Monthly Review*, vol. 49, no. 10.

McAdam, D. (1982) *The Political Process and the Development of Black Insurgency*, Chicago, IL: Chicago University Press.

McAdam, D. (1996) 'Conceptual Origins, Current Problems, Future Directions', in D. McAdam, J.A. McCarthy and M.N. Zald (eds), *Comparative Perspectives on Social Movements: Political Opportunities, Mobilizing Structures, and Cultural Framings*, Cambridge: Cambridge University Press.

McAdam, D., J. McCarthy and M.N. Zald (1996) 'Introduction: Opportunities, Mobilizing Structures, and Framing Processes: Toward a Synthetic, Comparative Perspective on Social Movements', in D. McAdam, J.A. McCarthy and M.N. Zald (eds), *Comparative Perspectives on Social Movements: Political Opportunities, Mobilizing Structures, and Cultural Framings*, Cambridge: Cambridge University Press.

McCarthy, J.D. (1997) 'The Globalization of Social Movement Theory', in J. Smith, C. Chatfield and R. Pagnucco (eds), *Transnational Social Movements and Global Politics: Solidarity beyond the State*, Syracuse, NY: Syracuse University Press.

McCarthy, J.D. (1996) 'Constraints and Opportunities in Adopting, Adapting, and Inventing', in D. McAdam, J.A. McCarthy and M.N. Zald (eds), *Comparative Perspectives on Social Movements: Political Opportunities, Mobilizing Structures, and Cultural Framings*, Cambridge: Cambridge University Press.

McCarthy, J.D. and M.N. Zald (1977) 'Resource Mobilization and Social Movements: A Partial Theory', *American Journal of Sociology*, vol. 82, May.

McConnell, D. (2000/2001) Pastors for Peace, Chicago, IL. Email received 13 November, and 28 and 30 January.

McMichael, P. (2001) 'Can We Interpret the Globalisation Countermovement in Polanyian Terms?', keynote address prepared for the Twenty-five Year Anniversary Celebration and Symposium, 'Globalization and its Discontents: Re-embedding the Economy in the 21st Century', Comparative Development Studies Programme, Trent University, October 12–14.

Maney, G. M. (2002) 'Transnational Structures and Protest: Linking Theories and Assessing Evidence', in J. Smith and H. Johnston (eds), *Globalization and Resistance: Transnational Dimensions of Social Movements*, Lanham, MD: Rowman & Littlefield.

Marín, C. (1998) 'Plan del Ejército en Chiapas: crear bandas paramilitares, desplacar a la población, destruir las bases de apoyo del EZLN', *Proceso*, January 4.

Martin, David: Denver Peace and Justice Committee, Denver, CO. Interview in Denver, 24 October 2000.

Melel Xojobal (2001) Website, online at www.laneta.apc.org/melel, accessed 14 October 2001.

Melucci, A. (1994) 'A Strange Kind of Newness: What's "New" in New Social Movements?', in E. Laraña, H. Johnston and J.R. Gusfield (eds), *New Social Movements: From Ideology to Identitiy*, Philadelphia, PA: Temple University Press.

Melucci, A. (1998) 'Third World or Planetary Conflicts?', in S.E. Alvarez, E. Dagnino and A. Escobar (eds), *Cultures of Politics, Politics of Culture: Revisioning Latin American Social Movements*. Boulder, CO: Westview Press.

Mergier, A. M. (1999) 'Presionan las ONG europeas sobre la Clausula Demo-crática', *Proceso*, 12 December.

Molloy, Molly (2000) Interview in Las Cruces, NM, 16 November.

Monsiváis, C. (1987) *Entrada libre: Crónicas de la sociedad que se organiza*, México DF: Ediciones Era.

Monsiváis, C. and H. Bellinghausen (2001) 'Marcos a Fox: Queremos garantías; no nos tragamos eso de que todo cambió', *La Jornada*, 8 January.

Montes, R. (1995) 'Chiapas is a War of Ink and Internet', online at www.hartford-hwp.com/archives/46/037.html, accessed 7 February 2002.

Morton, A.D. (2000) 'Mexico, Neoliberal Restructuring and the EZLN: A Neo-Gramscian Analysis', in B.K. Gills (ed.), *Globalization and the Politics of Resistance*, Houndmills and London: Macmillan.

Mouffe, C. (1993) *The Return of the Political*, London: Verso.

Municipio Autónomo de San Pedro Polhó (2000). Denouncement (May 26), online at http://laneta.apc.org/pipermail/enlacecivil-l/2000–May/000066. html, accessed 6 September 2001.

Municipio Autónomo en Rebeldía Ricardo Flores Magón (1999) Denouncement (October 17), online at http://laneta.apc.org/pipermail/enlacecivil-l/1999–Oc-tober/000005.html, accessed 6 September 2001.

Municipio Autónomo en Rebeldía Ricardo Flores Magón (2001) Denounce-ment (April 23), online at http://laneta.apc.org/pipermail/enlacecivil-l/2001–April/000236.html, accessed 6 September 2001.

Myers, D. J. (1994) 'Communication Technology and Social Movements: Contri-butions of Computer Networks to Activism', *Social Science Computer Review*, vol. 12, no. 2.

NACLA (1998) 'The wars within: counterinsurgency in Chiapas and Colombia', *NACLA*, vol. 31, no. 5.

Naím, M. (2000) 'The FP interview: Lori's war', *Foreign Policy*, Spring.

Nash, J. (1997) 'The Fiesta of the Word: The Zapatista Uprising and Radical Democracy in Mexico', *American Anthropologist*, vol. 99, no. 2.

Nash, J. and C. Kovic (1996) 'The Reconstitution of Hegemony: The Free Trade Act and the Transformation of Rural Mexico', in J.H. Mittelman (ed.), *Globalization: Critical Reflections*, Boulder, CO: Lynne Rienner.

New York Zapatistas (1998): 'NY Zaps call for protest and electronic CD on April 10', online at www. eco.utexas.edu/~archive/chiapas95/1998.04/msg000 25.html, accessed 22 February 2002.

Nugent, D. (1995) 'Northern Intellectuals and the EZLN', *Monthly Review*, vol. 47, no. 3.

Oberschall, A. (1973) *Social Conflict and Social Movements*, Englewood Cliffs, NJ: Prentice-Hall.

Ocampo, R. (1998) 'Mensaje de los prozapatistas franceses a la selección mexicana: "El EZLN en lucha les desea un buen partido"', *Proceso*, 14 June.

Oppenheimer, A. (1996) *Bordering on Chaos: Guerrillas, Stockbrokers, Politicians, and Mexico's Road to Prosperity*, Boston, MA: Little, Brown.

Otero, G. (1996) 'Neoliberal Reform and Politics in Mexico: An Overview', in Gerardo Otero (ed.), *Neoliberalism Revisited: Economic Restructuring and Mexico's Political Future*, Boulder, CO: Westview Press.

Otero, G. (2001) Email interview received 19 March.

Paez, J. C. (2001) Centro de Derechos Humanos Fray Bartlomé de las Casas, San Cristóbal de las Casas, Chiapas, Mexico. Email interview received 19 December.

Passy, F. (1999) 'Supranational Political Opportunities as a Channel of Globalization of Political Conflicts. The Case of the Rights of Indigenous Peoples', in D. della Porta, H. Kriesi and D. Rucht (eds), *Social Movements in a Globalizing World*, London: Macmillan.

Passy, F. (2001) 'Political Altruism and the Solidarity Movement', in M. Giugni and F. Passy (eds), *Political Altruism? Solidarity Movements in International Perspective*, Lanham, MD: Rowman & Littlefield.

Pastors for Peace (2001) 'The Spring 2000 Caravan for Peace and Reconciliation to Chiapas and Mexico, May 2000', online at www.ifconews.org/chcar.html, accessed 18 September 2001.

Paulson, J. (2001) Ya Basta! Email interview received 1 October.

Paulson, J. (2000) 'Peasant Struggles and International Solidarity: The Case of Chiapas', in *Socialist Register 2001*, ed. Leo Panitch and Colin Leys (with G. Albo and D. Coates), London: Merlin Press.

Paz, O. (1994) 'The Media Spectacle Comes to Mexico', *New Perspectives Quarterly*, vol. 11, no. 2.

Pelosi Resolution (H.Con.Res.238) (1999), online at www.mexicosolidarity. org/legislative/leahy.html, accessed 11 October 2001.

Peoples' Global Action (2001a) Website, online at www.nadir.org/nadir/initiativ/ agp/en/PGAInfos/bulletin.html, accessed 25 January 2002.

Peoples' Global Action (2001b) Website, online at www.nadir.org/nadir/initiativ/ agp/en, accessed 25 January 2002.

Petras, J., with T. Cavaluzzi, M. Morley and S. Vieux (1999) *The Left Strikes Back: Class Conflict in Latin America in the Age of Neoliberalism*, Boulder, CO: Westview Press.

Petrich, B. (1998) 'Parlamento italiano: sin diálogo en Chiapas no se ratificaran convenios con México', *La Jornada*, 28 January.

Petrich, B. (2001) 'Monos blancos, fruto del desempleo en Europa', *La Jornada*, 14 March.

Pieterse, J. N. (2001) 'Globalization and Collective Action', in P. Hamel, H. Lustiger-Thaler, J. N. Pieterse and S. Roseneil (eds), *Globalization and Social Movements*, New York: Palgrave, pp. 21–40.

Podur, J. (2000) Z Magazine/Z Net, Woods Hole, MA. Email interview received 30 August and 5 September.

Polletta, F. (2001) "This is What Democracy Looks Like': A Conversation with Direct Action Network activists David Graeber, Brooke Lehman, Jose Lugo, and Jeremy Varon', *Social Policy*, Summer.

Ponce de León, J. (ed.) (2001) *Our Word is Our Weapon: Selected Writings, Subcomandante Marcos*, London: Serpent's Tail.

Poster, M. (1997) 'Cyberdemocracy: Internet and the Public Sphere', in D. Porter (ed.), *Internet Culture*, London and New York: Routledge.

Rajchenberg, E. and C. Héau-Lambert (1998) 'History and Symbolism in the Zapatista Movement', in J. Holloway and E. Peláez (eds), *Zapatista! Reinventing*

Revolution in Mexico, London: Pluto Press.

Ramonet, I. (1997) 'Disarming the Markets', *Le Monde Diplomatique*, December.

Ramonet, I. (2001) 'Haremos política sin el 'glamour' del pasamontañas', *El País*, 25 February, online at www.elpais.es/articulo.html?anchor=elpepiint&xref=20010225elpepiint_6&type=Tes& date=, accessed 28 February 2002.

Red de Apoyo Zapatista (2001) Madrid, Spain. Email interview received 3 September.

Reuters (1998) 'Chiapas Has Little Weight in EU Trade', *Reuters*, 3 July.

Reuters (2000) 'European Mission Alleges Chiapas Rights Violations', *Reuters*, 6 April.

Ribeiro, G.L. (1998) 'Cybercultural Politics: Political Activism at a Distance in a Transnational World', in S.E. Alvarez, E. Dagnino and A. Escobar (eds), *Culture of Politics, Politics of Culture*, Boulder, CO: Westview Press.

Risse, T. and K. Sikkink (1999) 'The Socialization of International Human Rights Norms into Domestic Practices: Introduction', in T. Risse, S.C. Ropp and K. Sikkink (eds), *The Power of Human Rights: International Norms and Domestic Change*, Cambridge: Cambridge University Press.

Robberson, T. (1995) 'Mexican Rebels Using a High-Tech Weapon; Internet Helps Rally Support', *Washington Post*, 20 February.

Robertson, R. (1992) *Globalization: Social Theory and Global Culture*, London: Sage.

Robertson, R. (1995) 'Globalization: Time–Space and Homogeneity–Heterogeneity', in M. Featherstone, S. Lash and R. Robertson (eds), *Global Modernities*, London: Sage.

Rodriguez, C. (1994) 'Speech to the Native Forest Network', online at http://nativeforest.org/alerts/cecilia.html, accessed 10 February 2002.

Ronfeldt, D. and J. Arquilla (1993) *Cyberwar is Coming*, Santa Monica, CA: RAND.

Ronfeldt, D. and J. Arquilla (1998) *The Zapatista Social Netwar in Mexico*, Santa Monica, CA: RAND.

Rorty, R. (1989) *Contingency, Irony, and Solidarity*, Cambridge: Cambridge University Press.

Rosenau, J.N. (1997) *Along the Domestic–Foreign Frontier*, Cambridge: Cambridge University Press.

Ross, J. (1999) 'UN Gets Chilly Welcome in Mexico', *LA Weekly*, 7 September.

Ross, J. (2000) 'Are the Zapatistas History?', online at www.eco.utexas.edu/~archive/chiapas95/2000. 10/msg00147.html, accessed 1 March 2002.

Ross, J. (2001) Email received 1 September.

Rucht, D. (2000) 'Distant Issue Movements in Germany: Empirical Description and Theoretical Reflections', in J.A. Guidry, M.D. Kennedy and M.N. Zald (eds), *Globalizations and Social Movements: Culture, Power, and the Transnational Public Sphere*. Ann Arbor, MI: University of Michigan Press.

Schmitter, P.C. (1996) 'The Influence of the International Context upon the Choice of National Institutions and Policies in Neo-Democracies', in L. Whitehead (ed.), *The International Dimensions of Democratization: Europe and the Americas*, Oxford: Oxford University Press.

Scholte, J.A. (2000) *Globalization: A Critical Introduction*, Houndmills and London: Macmillan.

Scott, A. (1990) *Ideology and the New Social Movements*, London: Unwin Hyman.

Seidman, G.W. (2000) 'Adjusting the Lens: What Do Globalizations, Transnationalism, and the Anti-apartheid Movement Mean for Social Movement Theory?', in J.A. Guidry, M.D. Kennedy and M.N. Zald (eds), *Globalizations and Social Movements: Culture, Power, and the Transnational Public Sphere*, Ann Arbor, MI: University of Michigan Press.

Shaw, M. (1997) 'The State of Globalisation: Towards a Theory of State Transformation', *Review of International Political Economy*, vol. 4, no. 3.

Shaw, M. (2000) *Theory of the Global State: Globality as an Unfinished Revolution*, Cambridge: Cambridge University Press.

Silverstein, K. and A. Cockburn (1995a) 'Major U.S. Bank Urges Zapatista Wipeout: "A Litmus Test for Mexico's Stability"', *Counterpunch*, vol. 2, no. 3.

Silverstein, K. and A. Cockburn (1995b) 'Chase Memo Tumult: Come Blow Our Horn', *Counterpunch*, vol. 2, no. 4.

SIPAZ (2001a) Website, online at www.sipaz.org/frme.htm, accessed 26 March 2002.

SIPAZ (2001b): 'Chiapas: New Impulse in the Peace Process', SIPAZ Report 6 (2), online at www.sipaz.org/vol6no2/anale.htm, accessed 7 February 2002.

SIPAZ (2001c): 'Indigenous Reform: What is at Stake?', SIPAZ Report 6 (3), online at www.sipaz.org/vol6no3/feate.htm, accessed 7 February 2002.

Sklair, L. (1995) *Sociology of the Global System*, 2nd edition, Baltimore, MD: Johns Hopkins University Press.

Slater, D. (1998) 'Rethinking the Spatialities of Social Movements: Questions of (B)orders, Culture, and Politics in Global Times', in S.E. Alvarez, E. Dagnino and A. Escobar (eds), *Culture of Politics, Politics of Culture*, Boulder, CO: Westview Press.

Slevin, J. (2000) *The Internet and Society*, Cambridge: Polity Press.

Smith, J. (2001) 'Behind the Anti-Globalization Label', *Dissent*, Fall.

Smith, J., C. Chatfield and R. Pagnucco (1997) 'Social Movements and World Politics: A Theoretical Framework', in J. Smith, C. Chatfield and R. Pagnucco (eds), *Transnational Social Movements and Global Politics: Solidarity beyond the State*, Syracuse, NY: Syracuse University Press.

Snow, D.A., E.B. Rochford Jr., S.K. Worden and R.D. Benford (1986) 'Frame Alignment Processes, Micromobilization, and Movement Participation', *American Sociological Review*, vol. 51, no. 4.

Snow, D.A. and R.D. Benford (1988) 'Ideology, Frame Resonance, and Participant Mobilization', in B. Klandermans, H. Kriesi and S. Tarrow (eds), 'From Structure to Action: Comparing Social Movement Research Across Cultures', *International Social Movement Research* 1. Greenwich, CT: JAI Press.

Snow, D.A. and R.D. Benford (1992) 'Master Frames and Cycles of Protest', in A.D. Morris and C. McCluerg Mueller (eds), *Frontiers in Social Movement Theory*. New Haven, CT: Yale University Press.

Stahler-Sholk, R. (2001) 'Globalization and Social Movement Resistance:

The Zapatista Rebellion in Chiapas, Mexico', *New Political Science*, vol. 23, no. 4.

Starr, A. (2000) *Naming the Enemy: Anti-Corporate Movements Confront Globalization*, London: Zed Books.

Stavenhagen, R. (1996) *Ethnic Conflicts and the Nation-State*, London: Macmillan.

Stephen, L. (1995) 'The Zapatista Army of National Liberation and the National Democratic Convention', *Latin American Perspectives*, vol. 22, no. 4.

Stephen, Lynn (2000): 'In the Wake of the Zapatistas: U.S. Solidarity Work Focused on Militarization, Human Rights, and Democratization in Chiapas', in D. Brooks and J. Fox (eds), *Cross-Border Dialogues: U.S.–Mexico Social Movement Networking*, San Diego, CA: Center for US–Mexican Studies, University of California.

Stephen, L. (2001) Email interview received 16 January.

Stephen, L. (2002) *Zapata Lives! Histories and Cultural Politics in Southern Mexico*, Berkeley, CA: University of California Press.

Strauss, A.L. (1987) *Qualitative Analysis for Social Scientists*, Cambridge: Cambridge University Press.

Sørensen, G. (1993) *Democracy and Democratization*, Boulder, CO: Westview Press.

Talalay, M. (2000) 'Technology and Globalization: Assessing Patterns of Interaction', in R.D. Germain (ed.), *Globalization and its Critics: Perspectives from Political Economy*, Houndmills and London: Macmillan.

Tarrow, S. (1988) 'National Politics and Collective Action: Recent Theory and Research in Western Europe and the United States', *Annual Review of Sociology* 14.

Tarrow, S. (1992) 'Mentalities, Political Cultures, and Collective Action Frames: Constructing Meanings through Action', in A.D. Morris and C. McCluerg Mueller (eds), *Frontiers in Social Movement Theory*, New Haven, CT: Yale University Press.

Tarrow, S. (1998) *Power in Movement: Social Movements and Contentious Politics*, 2nd edn, Cambridge: Cambridge University Press.

Tarrow, S. (2001) 'Transnational Politics: Contention and Institutions in International Politics', *Annual Review of Political Science* 4.

Tarrow, S. (2002) 'From Lumping to Splitting: Specifying Globalization and Resistance', in J. Smith and H. Johnston (eds), *Globalization and Resistance: Transnational Dimensions of Social Movements*, Lanham, MD: Rowman & Littlefield.

Ten Dam, J. (1999) 'Solidarity at All Cost? On the Lack of Criticism in the Solidarity Movement with the Zapatistas', online at www.noticias.nl/prensa/zapata/dissolve.htm, accessed 26 February 2002.

Tilly, C. (1978) *From Mobilization to Revolution*, New York: McGraw-Hill.

Tomsin, M. (2001) Comité de Solidarité avec les Peuples du Chiapas en Lutte, Paris, France. Email interview received 8 September.

Touraine, A. (1996) 'Marcos, el demócrata armado', *La Jornada Semanal*, 22 December.

Urrutia, A. (1998) 'Zedillo: que vengan observadores, pero 'sin agenda previa de qué deben decir', *La Jornada*, 9 May.

Urry, J. (2000) *Sociology Beyond Societies: Mobilities for the Twenty-first Century*, London and New York: Routledge.

Veltmeyer, H. (2000) 'The Dynamics of Social Change and Mexico's EZLN', *Latin American Perspectives*, vol. 27, no. 5.

Vilas, C. M. (1996) 'Are there Left Alternatives? A Discussion from Latin America', in *Socialist Register 1996*, ed. Leo Panitch, London: Merlin Press.

Wallerstein, I. (1979) *The Capitalist World-Economy*, Cambridge: Cambridge University Press.

Waterman, P. (1998) *Globalization, Social Movements and the New Internationalisms*, London and Washington: Mansell.

Waterman, P. (1999) 'Of Saints, Sinners, and Compañeras: Internationlist Lives in the Americas Today', Working Paper Series, no. 286, Institute of Social Studies, online at www.antenna.nl/~waterman/saints.html, accessed 8 January 2002.

Waters, M. (1995) *Globalization*, London and New York: Routledge.

Watson, R., J. Barry, C. Dickey and T. Padgett (1995) 'When Words Are the Best Weapons', *Newsweek*, 27 February.

Wellman, B. and S.D. Berkowitz (1988) 'Introduction: Studying Social Structures', in B. Wellman and S.D. Berkowitz (eds), *Social Structures: A Network Approach*, Cambridge: Cambridge University Press.

Wilkinson, T. and J. Darling (1994) 'Thousands in Mexico March to Back Indians', *Los Angeles Times*, 8 January.

Wood, E. Meiskins (1995) *Democracy against Capitalism: Renewing Historical Materialism*, Cambridge: Cambridge University Press.

Woods, N. (1999) 'Order, Globalization, and Inequality in World Politics', in A. Hurrell and N. Woods (eds), *Inequality, Globalization, and World Politics*, Oxford: Oxford University Press.

World Social Forum (2001) Website, online at www.forumsocialmundial.org. br/esp/2cartas.asp, accessed 26 January 2002.

Wray, S. (1998a) 'On Electronic Civil Disobedience', paper presented to the 1998 Socialist Scholars Conference, March 20–22, New York, online at www.nyu. edu/projects/wray/oecd.html, accessed 16 October 2000.

Wray, S. (1998b) 'Brief Report of New York April 10 Demonstrations for Chiapas', online at www. eco.utexas.edu/~archive/chiapas95/1998.04/msg00199.html, accessed 10 September 2001.

Ya Basta (2001) 'The Age of Clandestinity', online at www.contrast.org/borders/ tampere/materials/age-of-clandestinity.html, accessed 13 September 2001.

Yúdice, G. (1998) 'The Globalization of Culture and the New Civil Society', in S.E. Alvarez, E. Dagnino and A. Escobar (eds), *Culture of Politics, Politics of Culture*, Boulder, CO: Westview Press.

Zapatista Bloc (2002) 'Zapatismo Transcends Borders: Join or Form a Zapatista Bloc', online at www. stopftaa.org/zapatistabloc/zapblocflyerE.doc, accessed 14 January 2002.

Zapatista Information Center (2001a) Website, online at www.ezlnaldf.org/ list.php?w_cat=MO&sc= pais&si%5B0%5D=Mexico&orderby=pais&grt =1&enot=1&altpage=mundo.inc&lo=Mu, accessed 28 January 2002.

Zapatista Information Center (2001b) Website, online at www.ezlnaldf.org/ comunica/responde.htm, accessed 28 January 2002.

Index